MOVING UP
THE VALUE CHAIN

MOVING UP
THE VALUE CHAIN

The Road Ahead for Indian IT Exporters

K R KASHYAP

PARTRIDGE
A Penguin Random House Company

To order additional copies of this book, contact
Partridge India
000 800 10062 62
www.partridgepublishing.com/india
orders.india@partridgepublishing.com

CONTENTS

CHAPTER 1

Introduction and Overview

During 2013, Indian Information Technology (IT) and Business Process Management (BPM) exporters experienced a slowdown. Economic growth has been slow and uneven in their primary markets: the US and Western Europe.

If you look back at 2013 on how Indian IT exporters have performed, you get a mixed picture. As per the industry body NASSCOM, IT exports slowed down during 2012-2013. From a growth rate of 17% during 2011-12 (in terms of dollar revenues), it dropped to 10.3% during 2012-13. NASSCOM did not change its initial growth forecast for 2013-2014 of 12% to 14%. The question is: Will the IT industry continue to be a major growth engine and a big job creator for the Indian economy during 2014 and beyond?

This (first) chapter provides an introduction and overview. It also provides readers an answer to an important question—why should I invest my time and energy in reading *this* book?

Indian IT Exports are Slowing Down

Of late, Indian IT exporters are facing some unique challenges. Interestingly, none of them mention the benefits they have derived during 2012 and 2013 from a weak Rupee. In fact, for many of them, dollar revenues have been flat in spite of a weak Rupee. Every quarter, you have mixed results. Few of them are unable to achieve "consistent" revenue growth; few others insist that they would not sacrifice growth for profitability. Many large Indian IT exporters did not achieve a growth rate close to 12% in terms of dollar revenues on an annual basis between April and Dec 2013. Is the glass half full or half empty?

In recent years, economic growth has been slow and uneven in the US and in Europe. Global competition is getting tougher. Technology trends have led to a shift in the pattern of IT investments or IT spending. The priorities of global clients are changing: while IT budgets remain flat, client expectations have risen!

Since Jan 2012 PC shipments across the world have shrunk during every quarter, almost touching 2008 levels by end 2013. This has affected the Windows-Intel-PC based ecosystem of the global IT industry. If you look around you find winners as well as losers.

Technology is reshaping businesses: CEOs as well as consulting companies use the term "digital transformation". Global clients expect IT services providers to deliver "more for less": this means more business value at lower costs.

Each of these trends affect IT vendors and IT service providers across the world. They also affect the revenue and profitability of Indian IT exporters. Typically, they have grown faster than the rest of the Indian economy. Many of them are also big job creators. Industry leaders and policymakers are therefore worried about the impact of an industry slowdown.

The Indian IT industry employs nearly 3 million qualified and well paid professionals. Even if the industry continues to be a major employer, the skill sets required are changing. As per the AICTE*, there are more than 3000 engineering colleges across India. Approximately 1.5 million engineers graduate from these colleges every year.

* All India Council for Technical Education.

＊

In recent years, the Indian IT industry has cut down the recruitment of fresh engineers. As per data released by NASSCOM in Feb 2014, net employment growth in the industry during 2013-14 was only 8.6%. This leads us to some important questions:

1. How does an industry slowdown affect the career prospects of young Indian IT professionals?
2. How does it affect the salaries in the Indian IT industry?

IT professionals reading this book would also be seeking answers to such questions from their own perspective!

During 2012 and 2013, the Indian economy has slowed down. The Rupee experienced sudden changes during several quarters. This was due to multiple reasons: the Euro zone crisis, turmoil in global financial markets, current account deficits, gold imports, policy paralysis in India, policies of Central Banks elsewhere in the world, you name it!

During each quarter of 2013, market analysts have reviewed the business mix of major Indian IT exporters. How is it changing across industry segments and across geographies? So far, a weak Rupee has compensated for slow and uneven economic growth across the US and Europe. However, the fact remains that the European market appears to be more attractive than the US market for many Indian IT exporters.

In Dec 2013, NASSCOM remained optimistic about growth picking up in 2014-2015 thanks to Europe. However, global clients based in the US and in UK remain the primary source of Indian IT exports. Most Indian IT exporters are still "underpenetrated" in continental Europe. In the recent past, their clients from the Banking, Financial Services and Insurance (BFSI) industry have been affected by the Euro zone crisis.

Of course, Europe does offer a window of opportunity. But this will also require Indian IT exporters to change course, sooner than later. Even if major Indian IT exporters are willing to change their business mix, this can't be achieved in one or two quarters. This will take time, effort and the right kind of investments.

Interpreting Business Media Reports

Typically, reports in the business media about Indian IT exporters carry a lot of industry data and industry jargon. These can create a smoke screen by giving confusing signals, especially to young Indian IT professionals. This book intends to provide them a "big picture" on the health of Indian IT exporters.

On the one hand, NASSCOM is optimistic about IT exports growing between 12% and 14% during 2013-14. On the other hand, you hear most CEOs saying "this year we will grow faster than the industry" without quoting a number! Why is this so? If you look beyond the first half of 2013-14 you realize that not many Indian IT exporters would achieve a growth rate of 12% to 14% for the full year in terms of dollar revenues. Let me explain why.

Typically, Indian IT exporters get a bigger share of their revenues in the first half of the financial year: March to September. The Oct to Dec quarter has more holidays in the US and in Europe. Many global clients finalize their annual budgets during the Jan to March quarter.

During 2013, after major IT exporters announced quarterly results, business media reports have compared the top 5 exporters: TCS, Infosys, Wipro, HCL and Cognizant. Typically such comparison is from a stock market perspective. The year 2013 was indeed very good for many large Indian IT exporters in terms of stock market performance. Was the good performance due to a weak Rupee, a stronger economic growth or a sound business model? Will 2014 be much better? These are some important questions to be asked.

One needs to look beyond stock market trends to understand the impact on revenues and profitability. Changes from one quarter to another can be confusing. Revenue growth in dollar denominated terms is one useful indicator. This will compensate for movements in the Indian Rupee from quarter to quarter. Another indicator is the pattern of revenues, growth rates and profitability for successive quarters.

One report quoted NASSCOM data on trailing 12 months dollar denominated revenues for all the five top exporters. Between June 2010 and June 2011, revenue growth was a high 29.6%. Since June 2011, it has been slowing down progressively. During 2013, it had reached levels close to 15%. The quarter on quarter revenue growth in dollar terms has also slowed down since 2011. During 2013, it has even fallen below 5%.

One report by ET Intelligence Group analyzed dollar denominated revenues and net profit over 13 quarters till Sep 2013. For the top 4 IT exporters: TCS, Infosys, Wipro and HCL, the net profit as a percentage of sales fell during the last 4 quarters. Over the past four years, net margins contracted for the top 3: TCS, Infosys and Wipro.

Why are market analysts questioning the top management team of major Indian IT exporters every quarter? They are trying to ascertain whether the company is doing well because of a weak Rupee during this quarter or because of the company's strategy and/or business model.

The Rupee has been weak (showing a falling trend) during 2012 and 2013. Each Indian IT exporter is trying to strike a fine balance while taking advantage of a weak Rupee in different ways. In one quarter, some of them try to boost revenue growth through aggressive pricing. In another quarter, they try to control the reduction in margins. How long can they continue with this balancing act?

Often, the top management team in Indian IT exporters use terms like industry shift, business value, business transformation and innovation. This jargon can also create a smoke screen: is the glass half full or half empty? In this book, I will answer this question by explaining the challenges and opportunities faced by the industry.

What can Readers expect in this book?

The Indian IT and BPM industry employs a significant number of professionals born during the 1980s. I have tried to offer them a professional perspective in this book without being company specific. I have covered many topics from the perspective of their global clients: primarily MNCs and global banks. While doing so, I have explained industry shifts and trends, not topics related to technology per se. I have also avoided jargon typically used by the Indian IT industry. I refer to my ideas as "moving up the value chain".

In my opinion, Industry jargon can be quite "context sensitive". For example, the term industry shift can refer to the industry of the global client, the global IT industry or the industry segment where most Indian IT exporters operate, namely IT services. My suggestion is: don't try to impress your clients using industry jargon out of context; it could backfire!

In each major industry, the global competitive landscape is changing due to multiple reasons:
- Slow and uneven economic growth across the US and Europe.
- Technology trends.
- Global competition from Asia as well as competition within each industry to grow faster in emerging markets across Asia.

As a result, the competitive landscape of the global IT industry is also changing. This industry is made up of companies offering IT products, IT solutions and IT service providers. Of course, Indian IT exporters are associated with this industry. But most of them offer IT services, not IT products. Not many of them offer IT solutions. However, any shift in the global IT industry does have a different impact on each Indian IT exporter.

When a global client refers to the term business value, this can refer to the impact of IT products, IT solutions and IT services on the client's business. If the only value proposition you offer is to provide lower cost IT services, can you relate this to the term business value? Relating business value to IT will require looking at the "big picture": this why it is "context sensitive"!

When a global client uses the term business transformation, it usually refers to business value far beyond cost savings. The word innovation is another term often misunderstood. Typically, a client uses such terms in a very specific context. For example, the term business transformation can be associated with a significant change related to the client's business.

A term like innovation is used when the impact on the organization is significant. This could mean a change in the client's business model, creating a new product, a new service or addressing a new market segment. This is why terms like business transformation and innovation are context sensitive.

In my opinion, Indian IT exporters need to learn two important lessons from the Tata car Nano. Although the car was initially hailed as an example of Indian innovation, its business model did not succeed. In this book, I have incorporated these lessons as applicable to Indian IT exporters.

The two lessons I am referring to are:
1. Avoid focusing only on the "low cost" advantage from India: this can backfire in the current global economic environment, especially if it is also sold as "innovation".
2. Innovate by offering a better value proposition to your global client WITH an alternate business model. This can turn out to be a "win-win" approach.

Organization of this Book

The Indian IT industry currently employs a significant number of professionals born during the 1980s. Each one of them is tech savvy: but they also need to look beyond technology. While serving global clients, they need to understand their clients' business environment.

Today's young Indian professionals work for, work with or even compete with multinational corporations (MNCs). They are quite comfortable working with global teams. Many of them aspire to become global citizens. Some of them could even become successful entrepreneurs in the coming years. A significant part of this book is targeted towards the following segments of young Indian professionals:

1. Those currently employed in the IT and BPM industry—they would find something useful in every Chapter of this book.
2. Those already employed by captive units of MNCs and global banks—they would get a "big picture" of the industry shifts experienced by their parent organization.
3. Those early in their career or those currently pursuing a post graduate degree (for e.g., MBA) would get a better perspective on what lies ahead for this industry.

This book is organized into three parts. Part 1 (chapters 2 to 4) introduces what I refer to as a "multi-speed global economy". Chapters 2 and 3 cover the US and Europe. Chapter 4 provides a business perspective on the global economy.

Although Part 1 covers complex topics about the global economy, I have avoided the jargon used by economists. I have tried to provide a business perspective to young Indian professionals. Topics relevant to the Indian IT industry are covered at a high level with references to Part 2 or Part 3 as required.

The theme of Part 2 (chapters 5, 6 and 7) is *getting closer to your global client*. Chapters 5 and 6 cover topics related to MNCs, global banks and global BFSI. Here, I have provided industry insight by leveraging my experience. This helps readers from the IT and BPM industry to understand the challenges faced by their global clients. Chapter 7 summarizes a wide range of topics from the perspective of Indian IT exporters. It explains the impact of changing priorities of global clients, shifts in the IT industry and global competition.

The theme of Part 3 (Chapters 8 and 9) is *how to move up the value chain*. Across chapters 8 and 9, I have covered the business model of Indian IT exporters. Although they are meant for experienced IT professionals, I have written these chapters in such a way that they can be read and understood by young Indian IT professionals and students of management schools. Apart from leveraging my own experience, I have referred to reports from multiple sources: business media, IT industry media and global consultants.

Industry Insight

Moving up the value chain is not a race for achieving higher revenues while maintaining profitability during every quarter. In this book, when I refer to this term it is primarily about large and medium Indian IT exporters becoming globally competitive. This term can be applied in different contexts:

1. For Indian IT and BPM exporters from a business model perspective.
2. For Indian professionals serving global clients from a professional perspective.

This book is intended to provide industry insight without being company specific. Readers, especially senior IT professionals can use the ideas in this book to understand the current strategy adopted by their own employer or by a major competitor.

Today, there are more than 500,000 Indian professionals working in India based captive units of global IT companies, MNCs and global banks. They serve global clients directly or indirectly through their parent organization. They would find many topics related to industry insight quite useful from a professional perspective.

If you look at large Indian IT exporters like TCS, Infosys, Wipro, HCL and Cognizant, each company has reached a critical size. More than achieving revenue growth in every quarter, they need to be globally competitive. They need to compete more effectively with an IBM, an Accenture or a Cap Gemini especially for business in newer technologies. This is more important than growing in terms of revenues and number of employees.

To grow in the IT services industry means getting a bigger share of the client's IT spending. This can happen only by offering a value proposition to global clients that goes beyond lower costs. One option is by addressing the client's business related challenges through newer technologies. Another option is to align your services business model with top management priorities like growth and competitiveness. In the long term, both of them have to be pursued by Indian IT exporters.

This book will provide an independent perspective on becoming globally competitive at an industry level. My ideas are applicable to Indian IT exporters of all sizes. Currently, each of them is trying to expand its global footprint in different ways. They are acquiring or developing new skill sets. They are also diversifying their business by addressing new markets. This book will provide young Indian IT professionals a "big picture"; hopefully, this industry insight can help each one of them in their profession!

Understand Industry Churn

In every quarter, CEOs of major Indian IT exporters talk about the number of new clients they added and the number of new contracts signed. Does this represent an industry churn or a true change in their portfolio of business?

Often, top executives use jargon like industry churn, industry shift or industry disruption. The semantics can be quite confusing. In the English language, terms like shift, churn or disruption can represent change and transformation in different ways. If the size of the overall industry is not changing significantly, would you call it an industry shift or an industry churn?

Industry analysts are looking beyond quarterly results and stock prices. If some companies are growing faster than the others, how are they achieving this? Has their business mix changed? Are some companies getting into the volume business or the commodity business? Which companies are becoming more competitive?

Of course, global companies in the IT industry have been moving work to India. If you take a closer look, you find an interesting pattern of change in the industry. In this Section, I will highlight this pattern: what I refer to as industry churn affecting Indian IT exporters.

A Mar 2013 report quoting data from Angel Research compared the market share of India's top 5 IT exporters with 8 of their global competitors. This was based only on the volume of IT services revenues of the 13 companies in dollar terms. Together, TCS, Infosys, Wipro, Cognizant and HCL Technologies had almost doubled their share of total services revenues between 2007 and 2012. Does this mean they are becoming globally competitive? I am not sure if such reports give the true picture.

Many global IT service providers have a significant share of their employees based in India. Some of them like IBM don't publish their employee strength in India. The Times of India carried a report on Nov 6, 2013 mentioning that the estimated number of employees across four companies: IBM, Accenture, Cap Gemini and CSC stood at 288,000 across India. The Economic Times carried a report on Dec 4, 2013 on how global software companies were expanding their office space across major Indian cities.

Some global IT service providers are redistributing work across their global centers. Some others are facing tough global competition. In the meanwhile, global software companies are also expanding their presence in India. Each of these can have an impact on the revenues of major Indian IT exporters in the next few years.

What are the reasons behind this industry churn? One reason could be IT outsourcing contracts coming up for rebid and renegotiation. As per one estimate (ISG), the size of this market is $ 114 billion during 2014. A significant number of these would involve some component of cloud computing solutions and services.

Technology is also contributing to industry churn. Across the world, IT spending is shifting from older to newer technologies: especially social media, mobile computing, analytics (or Big Data) and cloud computing. Each Indian IT exporter refers to these four areas by a different jargon like SMAC, SCAM or something else.

Industry churn happens because not all IT service providers are able to succeed in newer technologies. Reasons could be:
1. Not having the necessary skill sets in one or more newer technologies.
2. Having the skill sets but continuing with an outdated business model.

Most global clients are looking at getting better value for money from their IT service providers. In the US, many clients are opting for smaller contracts with a shorter duration, when compared to the past. Instead of 5 to 10 year long term contracts with one supplier, they are looking at contracts lasting for 2 to 3 years with multiple suppliers.

Some global clients use terms like re-shoring and insourcing. The rationale need not be about protecting jobs in their home country or saving costs. In recent years, global clients want business critical work to be done close to their headquarters. Some would like to change the mix of work being outsourced to an external IT service provider. Some others would consider setting up their own captive units to perform this work at a low cost location. If they already have a captive unit, they may redistribute work to take advantage of specialization.

What could be the outcome of industry churn? In the next few years, the mix of work done in India by captive units of MNCs and their external service providers (specifically Indian IT exporters) could change. One can view this as a "trickle down" effect.

From the perspective of Indian IT professionals, this is more important than quarterly results of Indian IT and BPM exporters! In the next few years, this will have an impact on the entire industry. It will determine who is getting into newer technologies and who is slipping into the commodity space of IT services.

Get Closer to Your Global Client

Often experts talk about "understanding your client's business". Indian IT exporters need to get closer to their client's business. One part of it is to relate IT solutions and IT services to business problems. Another part of it is to understand the economics and politics of decision making. This term also applies to Indian IT professionals. In the past, they have been focusing on technology: they need to develop a business perspective. They also need to understand the changing priorities of their global clients.

If Indian IT professionals understand the business environment under which clients operate, they can understand the economics and politics associated. Global clients are experiencing economic uncertainty and global competition. The industry in which they operate is also experiencing a shift. As a result, the priorities on capital investments are changing. For example, global automakers are experiencing a shift in demand. In Chapter 2 and Chapter 5 I have used this example to highlight an industry shift.

What do I mean by "economics and politics"? The term economics refers to the entire business case, looking beyond the cost of effort spent on IT services. The term politics refers to the power shift involving Chief Information Officers (CIOs) and changing priorities of top management. Each of these affects decision making on capital spending.

Indian IT exporters need to relate technology and business value. They need to understand the stakeholders in decision making. For example, how are decisions made on matters related to IT spending? In recent years, the difference between terms like IT investment and IT spending has changed. Chief Financial Officers (CFOs) in client organizations look at two components of the cost associated: fixed costs and variable costs. The business case for IT spending considers both these cost components.

This is where Indian IT professionals need to look at the economics of IT spending. For example, cloud computing offers an opportunity for companies in the global IT industry to rework the business case. Already this is changing the old business model of how companies sell IT infrastructure, IT software and packaged applications.

CEOs across many industries are facing a challenging business environment due to competition from global players as well as local players. More than cost cutting, CEOs and CFOs of global clients consider growth and competitiveness as major priorities. Accordingly, their priorities for IT spending are changing.

Typically, Indian IT exporters have been dealing with CIOs of their client organizations. They need to understand the changing priorities of CEOs and CFOs. They also need to move closer to each business unit where IT spending is happening. More than understanding organization politics, they need to understand the stakeholders involved in decision making.

In the next Section, I will provide an overview of Chapters 2, 3, and 4.

Multi-Speed Global Economy

Chapter 2 takes a deeper look into Europe beyond political debates happening since 2011. If you look at the European continent, the term "multi-speed economy" is quite appropriate. This geography consists of the UK, Euro zone and rest of the EU. The topics covered include shifts relevant to the global IT industry.

Since the end of 2011, business media reports in the US and UK painted scary pictures of Euro zone: about the exit of Greece from the Euro zone; about the future of Euro as a global currency; you name it! On the one hand, Europe looks less scary in 2013 than it was projected earlier. On the other hand the Euro zone crisis has affected the European banking system. Slowly, Europe is coming out of recession. Each European business is trying to become more competitive.

In 2013, business focus has shifted in Europe. European executives are desperate for new growth opportunities. In some countries, IT spending has resumed especially on newer technologies. This is why Europe can offer an interesting "window of opportunity" for Indian IT and BPM exporters. In the past, many of them operating in Europe have focused on UK. During 2012 and 2013, many of them reported higher revenue growth rates in Europe when compared to their biggest market, the US.

Chapter 3 covers a wide range of topics on the US economy. If you take a closer look, a lot has changed since the Nov 2012 Presidential Elections. During 2013, US stock markets reached an all-time high and the S&P 500 gained by 30%. If you look deeper into economic indicators, the picture is mixed. In spite of low interest rates, unemployment remains high and growth is uneven across different states in the US.

How has this affected IT spending? US MNCs are reportedly holding cash reserves worth $ 2 trillion. Yet, business sentiment of Corporate America appears to be weak. In Q3 of 2013, there were some surprises: uncertainty on policies of the US Federal Reserve, a government shutdown and even talk of a debt default by the world's largest economy. As a result, during 2013, capital investments by many global clients based in the US did not take off as forecasted earlier.

In Chapter 3, apart from such topics, I have covered a "hot topic" for the Indian IT industry: immigration reform and changes to visa regulations. Uncertainty in the US has led to currency volatility outside the US. During 2013, a weak Rupee has come to the rescue for many Indian IT and BPM exporters. How long will this party last? What if the Rupee rises or experiences more volatility during 2014? Such questions are answered in Chapter 4.

In addition to currency volatility, Chapter 4 highlights the challenges associated with a multi-speed global economy. They include divergent growth rates, shifts in global demand, capital flows and trade flows. These affect MNCs through global manufacturing and supply chains. They also affect the global BFSI industry landscape.

Chapter 4 also covers the topic of captive units being set up by MNCs and global banks based in the US and in Europe. This will affect the future business prospects of many Indian IT and BPM exporters directly or indirectly.

Impact on Global Clients

Most Indian IT professionals are familiar with technology trends. They need to understand two types of industry shifts in order to get closer to their global clients:

1. A change in the business mix or the business model of global clients.
2. A change in the pattern of IT spending and/or a change in the priorities related to IT spending.

I have explained these across Chapter 5 and Chapter 6. Some industry shifts may not be very obvious. On the one hand, economic growth is slow and uneven across the US, Europe and Japan. On the other hand, growth rates are much higher in China, in India and in many emerging economies. Most MNCs and large banks are trying to grow by expanding their global footprint. This will take time, effort and investments. In the meanwhile, some of them are unable to maintain consistent revenue growth and profitability in every quarter. Even MNCs and large banks already having a global footprint are finding that their old business models may not be suitable in every country.

In short, each global client faces unique challenges while navigating a multi-speed global economy. In some industries, the competitive landscape itself is changing. From a business perspective, these represent an industry shift.

Chapter 5 explains this using an example from the global auto industry. In addition, it covers a wide range of topics related global manufacturing and supply chains. They are relevant to Indian IT and BPM professionals working in areas like supply chain management. They are also relevant to those working on solutions and services for manufacturing and retail industries. Topics related to engineering and R&D services are also covered in brief.

Chapter 6 covers several topics related to Banking, Financial Services and Insurance (BFSI) clients. It covers industry shifts associated with global BFSI. The impact is quite different in the US and in Europe. Chapter 6 highlights these differences by covering three major banking businesses: investment banking, retail banking and Asian trade finance.

Together, Chapter 5 and Chapter 6 provide business insight as well as industry insight to Indian IT and BPM professionals. They are also relevant to readers currently employed in India based captive units of MNCs and global banks.

Moving Up the Value Chain

Chapter 7 explains this term: it refers to a series of steps to be taken by Indian IT exporters to address challenges in the short term. It also refers to changing course and getting prepared to address new opportunities in the long term.

How can Indian IT professionals also move up the value chain? This is more about moving up the professional ladder: not necessarily moving up the organization ladder! To do this, they need to relate technology to their client's business and their client's priorities. This applies to cloud computing, big data, analytics, mobile computing, social media, you name it! This way, they can start getting into the solution space of technology. From a professional perspective this is another part of moving up the value chain.

In Chapter 7, I will introduce topics related to the business model of Indian IT exporters. Many of them have relied on a services delivery model with one or more of the following:

1. Offering IT services at lower costs by leveraging teams located offshore.
2. Using long term outsourcing contracts and/or billing clients for the effort spent.
3. Focusing on the CIO organization to reduce sales and marketing expenses.

This is quite unlike the business model based on intellectual property and software products used by many US based companies.

Earlier in this chapter, I used the term "getting closer to your global clients". This will also require Indian IT exporters to understand the changing roles played by CEOs, CFOs and CIOs. Each of them is a major stakeholder in decision making.

Globally, the IT services business is changing: many services related to IT infrastructure, packaged software and custom application development and maintenance (ADM) are getting "commoditized". Moving up the value chain also means moving away from commodity oriented businesses. If IT exporters are chasing revenue growth by slipping into the commodity space, they are moving down the value chain, not moving up!

Existing clients of most Indian IT exporters include Fortune 500 companies, MNCs and global banks. In these organizations, major stakeholders like CIOs, CEOs, CFOs and business unit heads have different priorities. They relate IT to terms like being globally competitive, improving efficiency or productivity. What do these terms mean? Indian IT professionals need to understand them from a business perspective.

In the past, CEOs asked two typical questions while making IT investments. One, how can IT help us "run" our business? Two, how can IT help us "improve" our business? Recently, they have been asking: How can IT help us transform our business?

In the past, Indian IT exporters have answered the first two questions by focusing on their low cost advantage and IT outsourcing. Going forward, they need to understand the new priorities of CEOs. They need to answer such questions from a business perspective.

Most CEOs view IT as an enabler to business. When they refer to transforming their business, what do they mean? They could be referring to two questions. How can IT make us globally competitive? How can IT help us "grow" our business? For many CEOs, growth and competitiveness are a priority. Transforming a business is much more than a routine improvement that can be achieved through IT outsourcing.

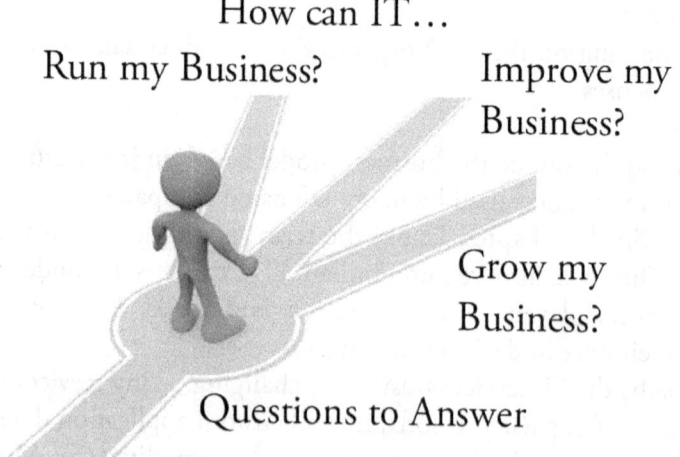

How can IT…

Run my Business?   Improve my Business?

Grow my Business?

Questions to Answer

22

To answer such questions, Indian IT professionals need to understand their client's business and offer an appropriate value proposition. In addition, Indian IT exporters need to make changes in their current business model.

Earlier, IT budgets were pooled and centrally managed by CIOs. In recent years, business unit managers have a bigger role to play in decision making. These decisions could be choosing the appropriate technology and/or choosing the final solution.

As a result of economic uncertainty and industry shifts, the timing of IT spending is also changing. CFOs are controlling and coordinating IT spending across business units. CIOs are still involved in procurement and vendor management. IT service providers need to understand their stakeholders and the role played by other top management executives. All of these are referred to by the term "discretionary spending".

The stakeholders in decision making can be quite different in specific areas like cloud computing, big data, data analytics, mobile computing and social media. The role played by each stakeholder could be different. What applies in the US many not apply in many countries in Europe. This is why Indian IT professionals need to understand decision making by major stakeholders as well as their priorities. Accordingly, they can position technology based solutions more effectively. Even if their client's IT budgets remain flat, they will be able to get a bigger share of it.

Typically, MNCs have businesses spread across the US, Europe and emerging markets like China and India. However, their priorities in each business unit could differ. Indian IT professionals need to understand terms like global competitiveness, efficiency and productivity in a business context. Whenever MNC executives refer to such terms* for each business unit, they convey their priorities.

* The term competitiveness can relate to costs associated and how they compare with competition. The term efficiency can refer to cost optimization, or reduced inputs. The term productivity can refer to getting more "bang for the buck" or getting more output for the same input.

Having understood the cost advantage offered by India and the skills available, MNCs and global banks are improving their competitiveness in a different way. In recent years, many of them have set up captive units in India. A captive unit can be part of a globally distributed function within the MNC organization. This can also leverage newer technologies to offer the necessary environment for collaboration and innovation. Increasingly, India based captive units are offering a wide range of high end services to MNCs. How can the India Inc. move this to the next level?

For this to happen, India needs to position itself as a favored location for a new set of high-end services. These services relate to design, engineering, research and development. This will involve multiple disciplines like R&D, engineering, product design and development. This could also involve addressing complex challenges faced by MNCs across their product life cycles. These challenges could also relate to integration issues across the global manufacturing and supply chains of major MNCs.

In the past, several IT companies in the US have utilized Indian talent in product development. During the last two decades, successful American companies like GE have set up dedicated centers in India focusing on and R&D related services.

Would they move to the next level? If so, how would they affect other Indian IT exporters? Already some of them are looking beyond the software development life cycle. If they can focus on developing the necessary engineering skills, can they find a new window of opportunity? I will answer this question in the forthcoming chapters.

The next two chapters will cover the two primary markets of Indian IT and BPM exporters: the US and Europe. While describing the economic environment in the US and in Europe, I will cover common themes driving capital investments.

This is not the time for Indian IT exporters to remain complacent. Even if the business pipeline in the short term looks good, they need to change course before it is too late. Hopefully, this book can provide fresh ideas, not only for Indian IT professionals, but also for their bosses holding key positions in the industry!

PART 1

A MULTI-SPEED GLOBAL ECONOMY

INTRODUCTION

*I*n Part 1 of this book, I will explain the challenges faced by global clients in what I refer to as a multi-speed Global economy. I will explain the changing priorities of global clients on cost optimization, improving efficiency and effectiveness and achieving a higher productivity in their business.

Chapter 2 is about Europe and Chapter 3 is about the US. They are the primary markets for Indian IT and BPM exporters. In Chapter 4, I will mention how some global clients are navigating a multi-speed global economy by new models of cost arbitrage.

Together, Chapters 2, 3 and 4 (Part 1 of this book) will explain the term I refer to as a "multi-speed global economy". They will provide a new perspective on the global economy to Indian IT and BPM professionals. I hope that Indian readers especially entrepreneurs as well as young Indian professionals will find the topics in this part of the book quite useful from a professional perspective.

In the following three Chapters, I am avoiding terms like business value, business transformation and innovation. Instead I will explain common themes like growth and competitiveness.

Across the three chapters of Part 1, I will also explain trends related to global IT industry, especially those affecting IT companies in the US. I will explain how global clients are leveraging newer technologies to improve global competitiveness and pursue growth opportunities.

CHAPTER 2

Take a Fresh Look at Multi-Speed Europe

UK or Continental Europe?

Currently, Europe accounts for about 20% of Indian IT exports when compared to the 60% share of the US. Most large Indian companies in the IT industry still have a small presence in Euro zone and continental Europe. In the past, their primary focus in Europe has been restricted to the City of London and UK. Why should they take a serious look at Europe still coming out of recession? This Chapter will provide an answer.

In 2005, Thomas Friedman wrote a bestseller titled "The World is flat". This was much before the world experienced what is now referred to as the global financial crisis. When this happened during 2008-2009, the global economy experienced a churn.

During 2011 and 2012 the world faced the Euro zone crisis. In some ways, this led to a second round of churning of the global economy.

This has affected global businesses across the US and Europe. They experienced economic uncertainty, slow and uneven growth across different countries. While they navigated through the Euro zone crisis, they were also affected by technological developments and global competition. For many of them, the world did not become flatter: it became more uneven!

In April 2013, an IMF report classified major economies of the world into three groups using an interesting term: a "three speed" global economy. Indeed, growth rates have been divergent across the US, Europe and rest of the world.

Mixed Signals from Europe

As per the IMF report, the fastest growing economies included China, India and many other emerging economies. Many of the slowest growing economies of the world are in Europe. Some of them experienced a long period of recession since 2008-2009.

Between mid-2011 and the end of 2012, some business media reports from London and New York painted a scary picture of Euro zone: the exit of Greece from the Euro zone, collapse of the Euro currency, you name it! Fortunately, none of these scary events materialized. Euro zone is intact and coming out of recession. However, the crisis did affect the global economy. Its impact has been felt in India directly by many exporters and indirectly by the Rupee.

> *In this Chapter, I will provide a fresh and a balanced perspective about the Euro zone crisis to Indian readers. Looking beyond European politics, I will explain why the world has become uneven for many European businesses. I will also explain why the Euro zone crisis could offer a new window of opportunity for Indian IT and BPM exporters.*

In spite of recession in some European countries, spending on IT doesn't appear to be seriously affected. NASSCOM reported that the growth rate of Indian IT exports in Europe during 2012-2013 was above the industry average. During 2013-2014 many Indian IT exporters reported signing new contracts and/or expanding their revenue share from Europe. Few of them also reported deals involving Mergers and Acquisitions (M&A).

Let us get started. How did a crisis in a small country like Greece affect the entire Euro zone? I have answered this question and explained some terms associated with the Euro zone sovereign debt crisis in a separate box. In terms of its impact, the Euro zone crisis can be compared to the 2008-2009 global financial crisis.

Euro Zone Sovereign Debt Crisis

The term Euro zone refers to 18* countries using Euro as their common currency. Five of them: Ireland, Greece, Portugal, Spain and Italy have been running deficits, especially since 2008. Their economies have not grown in recent years.

* 18 countries include Latvia that joined on Jan 1, 2014.

The term sovereign debt refers to the debt owned by countries. The governments of many Western countries issue debt commonly referred as treasury bonds. They are purchased by global banks, hedge funds or central banks of other countries. These are issued in installments: each called a tranche due for payment on a certain date. Each tranche of debt held by a small country like Greece is still worth a few billion Euros.

A sovereign debt default happens when a country is unable to repay a tranche of its sovereign debt. This can be avoided by what is referred to as a bailout: some form of debt restructuring and rescheduling of the payments. In Euro zone, Ireland was bailed out during 2010. Greece came next. This is what is referred to as the Euro zone crisis.

In mid-2011, it became evident that Greece would require multiple bailouts in the coming years. European policymakers negotiated for months. In the meanwhile, stock markets across the world went up and down. Why did it take so long for European policymakers?

There were multiple stake holders with conflicting priorities. Germany, Euro zone's biggest creditor took a tough stand and insisted on harsh measures. By the end of 2011, a bailout package for Greece was agreed. This affected other stakeholders during 2012.

During 2011, some business media reports in the US and in UK coined the term PIIGS (referring to Portugal, Ireland, Italy, Greece and Spain). Looking back, putting all 5 countries in one basket was inappropriate. The situation in each of the 5 debt ridden countries is quite different. What applies to one country is not even relevant for another.

Why did business media reports talk about scary scenarios like exit of Greece from the Euro zone and collapse of the Euro currency? One major cause of uncertainty was about the impact of the Greek bailout on the other 4 countries. Many experts on both sides of the Atlantic debated on the pros and cons of likely scenarios.

Greece had to implement some harsh austerity measures before receiving its bailout payments. The bailout package for Greece sent a strong signal to other countries in Euro zone during 2012. European politicians realized that Euro zone could not afford any more bailouts. Instead of following a crisis management approach European policymakers began looking at long term implications and how to address the challenges associated.

Even while European policymakers discussed the bailout package for Greece, borrowing costs for other countries went up. This aggravated their deficits, especially in Italy, Spain and Portugal. By 2012, unemployment went up in these three countries, especially in Spain.

In Dec 2013, Ireland announced an "exit" from the 2010 bailout. Is the worst over in Euro zone? Even experts are unable to answer this question. Through linkages in the European banking system, the crisis affected large Euro zone countries like Spain and Italy.

The crisis has affected each Euro zone country in different ways. In the next Section, I will provide a business perspective by looking at Euro zone beyond political debates.

What led to a Multi-Speed Europe?

Since mid-2011, economic indicators have diverged across Euro zone. These include growth rates, debt, deficits, unemployment rates, labor costs and borrowing costs. This is why I am using the term multi-speed Europe.

When compared to Germany, many other Euro zone countries experienced a sharp decline in exports. During 2012 and 2013, some countries like Italy and France have become less competitive due to rising labor costs or higher cost of borrowing for businesses.

The European Union (EU) consists of 28* countries sharing a common market. In addition to Euro zone, the EU includes countries like the UK who have their own currency and are outside the Eurozone. From a business perspective this is quite significant:

- From the perspective of MNCs based in the Eurozone, the UK and the entire EU represent a common market.
- The City of London is a global financial center. Major European banks have a significant presence in UK.

* 28 countries include Croatia that joined EU in July 2013.

This is why Indian professionals need to understand the fallout from the Euro zone crisis from a broader perspective.

The European Central Bank (ECB) is responsible for Euro zone monetary policy. Interest rates and Euro currency matters are decided by the ECB. The ECB was forced to intervene between Dec 2011 and Oct 2012 to avoid a European banking crisis.

This intervention included low-interest loans to European banks and a bond buying program. In spite of ECB's intervention, the crisis has affected large European banks and large European businesses operating in the EU.

On the one hand, the intervention by ECB avoided a major banking crisis. On the other hand, it has led to divergence in the health of banks across Europe. In some countries, banks have accumulated bad loans. In some others, consumers and businesses are facing tougher lending standards by local banks. All these have affected economic growth.

The crisis has also affected global companies (for e.g., S&P 500 or Fortune 500 companies) doing business in Europe. In the next section, I will describe the term "multi-speed" Europe from a business perspective.

Understanding Multi-Speed Europe

European businesses are experiencing two types of divergence. One is about economic indicators between countries, especially between Northern and Southern Europe. As a result, there is a shift in demand for many products and services. Another is a demographic shift across the European continent. This has affected the pattern of immigration into major Euro zone countries like Germany.

Divergent economic indicators can lead to an industry shift. If you take a closer look in each industry, you can identify winners and losers across Europe. Some companies have grown and also become globally competitive. Later, I will provide one interesting example from the European automobile industry.

Large European companies look beyond geographical borders. They view the entire European continent as one market for their products and services. Accordingly, they decide on capital investments, where to locate factories, where to look for supply of skilled labor and professionals, etc. From a business perspective, the term multi-speed economy therefore applies to the entire European continent.

In many Euro zone countries of Northern Europe, the number of older people is quite high. Unemployment is high across many countries in Southern Europe. For e.g., Spain has a relatively younger population: many Spaniards are seeking job opportunities elsewhere in Euro zone and in the European Union (EU). This is one reason driving immigration and demographic changes across Europe.

Many European businesses, especially those based in Germany are striking a balance between skilled workers and immigration across the European continent. Reports in Spiegel International during 2012 explained the changing demographics of Germany.

After German unification, a large number of Germans moved from different parts of former East Germany into various cities across former West Germany during the 1990s. After the Euro zone crisis precipitated in early 2011, immigration into Germany has increased significantly from four countries: Poland, Romania, Bulgaria and Hungary.

During 2011, the net migration into Germany from all over the world was 279,000. Of this number, the share of 6 countries was about 165,000 people. These countries are Poland, Romania, Bulgaria, Hungary, Greece and Spain. Of these 6 countries, the combined share of Euro zone (Greece and Spain) was only 26,000. Far more people are coming into Germany from Central and Eastern Europe than Southern Europe.

During the first nine months of 2012, nearly 500,000 people migrated into Germany from other EU countries*. The share of Poland, Romania, Bulgaria and Hungary was more than 325,000. The share of Southern Europe (Italy, Spain, Greece and Portugal) was about 95,000.

> * The numbers for 2012 mentioned above include seasonal workers and students with degrees in specialized disciplines. Eventually, some of them could move from Germany into other Euro zone countries.

In the next section, I will give an example related to European automakers. I will cover the topic of global automakers again in Chapter 5 from an industry perspective.

Example: European Automakers

The Euro zone crisis is reshaping the competitive landscape for all European automakers. This represents an industry shift affecting global automakers outside Europe like GM and Ford. In Jan 2013, Morgan Stanley published a report on global automakers using a term "clash of the Titans".

The four Titans are GM, Toyota, Volkswagen and Hyundai-Kia. While GM is losing market share in Europe, both Volkswagen and Hyundai-Kia are gaining market share from their European competitors. This is happening due to multiple reasons: the Euro zone crisis is only one of them.

In recent years, demand for automobiles has shifted away from Western Europe towards Central and Eastern Europe. The demand for larger and luxury models is falling. In 2012, car sales in Europe reached their lowest level in two decades. In European cities like Paris and Berlin, car-sharing networks are growing rapidly.

In spite of challenges, German automakers have been firing on all cylinders. They are exporting more cars outside of Europe. They source a significant share of parts and components from Central and Eastern Europe. In recent quarters, German brands like Volkswagen, BMW and Daimler have performed quite well.

More than 80% of high-end cars sold in Germany during 2012 were registered to companies. Of course, many of them were made by Volkswagen, BMW and Daimler! In Chapter 5, I will explain why their European competitors are so concerned about this.

Across Europe, demand for used cars is growing. In 2012, almost 6.9 million vehicles changed hands across Europe. This number was almost twice the number of new car sales. In Germany, since 2011, nearly 183,000 people have signed up for one-way car-sharing systems.

In Oct 2012, a Reuters report compared European sales of major automakers between Jan to Aug 2012 with a similar period in 2010. Three automakers: Volkswagen, Mercedes-Benz and Hyundai-Kia together improved their market share to 35.5% when compared to 30% in 2010.

The combined share of Renault, PSA Peugeot, Fiat and Opel fell to 33.3% in 2012 from 38.6% in 2010. Reduced demand and excess capacity alone can't explain loss of market share suffered by GM Opel, Peugeot, Renault and Fiat. Each one of them operates across the entire European continent with multiple models. Indeed, some European automakers are losing global competitiveness because they have been slow in adapting to an industry shift.

This example is not meant to compare German automakers and their European competitors. This is meant to highlight the industry shift experienced by global automakers. I will explain in Chapter 5 why this is significant from the perspective of global automakers.

What applies to European automakers also applies to manufacturing industries across Europe. This example illustrates how a multi-speed European economy together with global competition can lead to an industry shift. Indian IT and BPM professionals need to look deeper and understand this from a business perspective.

Can Belt Tightening work?

European businesses have realized that the typical solution recommended by Americans: belt tightening or cost optimization won't work in Europe beyond one or two quarters.

Many European automakers suffer from excess plant capacity, lower demand and higher labor costs. This translates into lower productivity and loss of global competitiveness. They are unable to export cars manufactured in one or more countries.

Of course, there will be country specific reasons. What if an automaker has a wrong product mix or an outdated business model? This can't be solved by cutting costs!

In the US, whenever automakers were hit by low demand, they have downsized or resorted to cost cutting in the name of "belt tightening". In Europe, the closure of a factory in one country can affect supply chain partners in another country.

This is why European business leaders are concerned about the long term impact on European manufacturing and supply chains. They are also worried about loss of competitiveness in countries like France and Italy.

Each European business or MNC based in Europe is gradually adapting to industry shifts. They have realized that they can't wait for European politicians to offer them a silver bullet. They need to improve competitiveness without belt tightening.

This can involve changes in the short term as well as transformation in the long term. The first step is to become more competitive within the European continent. The next step is to also become globally competitive.

The term competitiveness can relate to costs associated on the input side. It can also be comparative, in relation to competition. Competitiveness can be improved through cost optimization, improvement in efficiency and higher productivity. Each European client would be focusing on different areas. Indian IT and BPM professionals need to understand these terms from their client's perspective.

Cost optimization and efficiency can be achieved through a reduction in fixed costs. For example, IT outsourcing can reduce fixed costs. Productivity can be improved by getting more "bang for the buck" or getting more output for the same input. Appropriate IT solutions can lead to improvements in efficiency and productivity.

Having covered industry shifts related to European automakers, I will move to topics related to European BFSI.

Impact on European BFSI

The European BFSI landscape experienced a major churn during 2012 and 2013. Initially, the Euro zone crisis, actions by the ECB and European policymakers contributed to this churn. During 2013 Europeans made progress on what is referred to as a Banking Union. In addition, many European banks have undergone significant restructuring. These can have a long term impact on the European Banking system in the next few years.

External factors are also contributing to the industry churn. These include changes in banking regulations* and investigations by regulatory agencies on both sides of the Atlantic. In the following paragraphs, I will explain them briefly.

> * Here is a partial list of banking and insurance related regulations where the clock has begun ticking in Europe: Basel III, European Market Infrastructure Regulation (EMIR) and Markets in Financial Instruments Directive (MiFID) II.

Changes in banking regulations are not new to European banks; the challenge is the timing.

Certain compliance deadlines have to be met while many of them are still recovering from the Euro zone crisis. Some of them are affected by changes introduced by multiple regulatory agencies: in the US, in UK and in Europe.

During 2012, large European banks were investigated in connection with two scandals. One was about LIBOR (London Interbank Offered Rate), a global benchmark for interest rates**. The other was related to money laundering probed by US regulators. In 2013, multiple regulators are investigating a third scandal related to global currency markets.

** Between June 2012 and Nov 2013, US and British regulators had imposed fines totaling $ 3.5 billion on one group of 5 global banks in connection with the LIBOR scandal. In Dec 2013, European authorities levied additional fines totaling $ 2.3 billion on a second group of 8 global banks. The outcome of LIBOR investigations could have a long term impact.

Basel III regulations affect all global banks. They relate to investment banking, risk management and compliance reporting. Global banks based in Europe with US subsidiaries also need to comply with regulations specific to the US.

In the US, banks need to comply with the Dodd-Frank regulations*** and the Foreign Account Tax Compliance Act (FATCA). The former is comparable to Basel III in terms of scope and complexity. The latter affects global bank-to-bank payments involving US banks.

*** The Volcker rule is a subset of the Dodd-Frank regulations. They were finalized in Dec 2013.

Regulations specific to the US also affect European banks with US operations. Some of them are reorganizing their subsidiaries in the US or even scaling down their US operations. Any change in their mix of global businesses could impact their competitors in the US or in Asia.

Even before the Euro zone crisis precipitated, European banks experienced an industry churn in the Asia Pacific region. In June 2012, Thomson Reuters reported how their lending pattern changed between 2007 and 2011. During this period, the share of European banks dropped from 29% to 19%. At the same time, Asian banks improved their share from 61% to 70%.

During late 2011 some experts in the US and UK predicted that global banks based in the US could improve their market share in Asia during 2012. These predictions did not come through. In the next few years, the Asian BFSI landscape could change as a fall out from the Euro zone crisis. Topics related to global BFSI are covered in Chapter 6.

Business media in the UK have been reporting about job cuts, restructuring or reorganization happening in European banks since end 2011. Indian IT and BPM exporters need to look beyond these reports and understand the associated industry shift.

During 2013, business media reports mentioned that global banks operating in London are implementing job cuts, closure of branches and job redistribution. As I will explain in Chapter 6, the BFSI job redistribution in Europe could still be "work in progress".

Having covered general topics about Europe, let us change course in the remaining part of this Chapter. In the following sections, I will cover a wide range of topics relevant to Indian IT and BPM exporters. I will begin by mentioning two reports: one published by the World Economic Forum and another by OECD.

An ICT Perspective on Europe

In this Section, I will mention two reports on Europe from the perspective of Information and Communications Technologies (ICT). One of them is from the World Economic Forum (WEF); the other is from OECD.

The WEF publishes a Global Information Technology Report every year. Apart from trends related to ICT, this report publishes a ranking that WEF refers to as the Networked Readiness Index (NRI tanking).

In its 2013 report, Northern European countries dominate this ranking. Interestingly, the US occupies the 9th position among the top 10, with 7 European countries* ahead of the US. Of course, the NRI ranking varies significantly across major industrialized countries of Europe.

> * The 7 European countries ahead of the US are Finland (1), Sweden (3), Netherlands (4) Norway (5), Switzerland (6), UK (7) and Denmark (8). The numbers in brackets indicate the ranking as per the WEF report.

What is so significant about this report from the perspective of Indian IT exporters? The very fact that so many European countries dominate the global ranking by WEF is important. From the perspective of IT related spending, cloud computing, internet banking and mobile banking, it makes sense to take a fresh look at each of these 7 European countries.

In India, based on data published by NASSCOM and other industry sources, we often hear about India's leading position in global IT services exports. Recently, the OECD published a Science, Technology and Industry Scoreboard on topics related to the knowledge economy. I found one piece of data related to Ireland quite interesting.

The OECD report mentioned that Ireland is close behind India in its share of global ICT services exports. In 2012, India's share was 13.5% at the top of the list; Ireland was close behind at 12.7%. The OECD report mentioned how Ireland's share increased during the last decade, due to its favorable tax environment and ability to attract global IT companies.

Apart from Ireland, Indian IT exporters need to take a closer look at Nordic countries. Google, Microsoft and Facebook already have data centers in countries like Finland and Sweden. Later I will cover topics related to cloud computing in Europe.

In the next section, I will mention four different developments related to UK and the City of London. I will explain why Indian IT and BPM exporters who have a major presence in UK need to keep a watch on them from a long term perspective.

Impact on UK and City of London

The four developments I am referring to are unrelated, but still significant.

1. Tough stand by British politicians on immigration issues.
2. Political debates about a possible exit of UK from the European Union (EU).
3. The role played by London in promoting the Chinese currency (Renminbi) in Europe.
4. The role played by London in the global expansion of Islamic Finance.

Each of the above developments can affect the landscape of European BFSI in the coming years. They can also affect decision making on how global businesses would leverage the City of London in the coming years. Accordingly, Indian IT and BPM exporters need to understand the combined impact on their client's business. I will briefly cover these developments and explain their significance from a business perspective.

In Feb 2014, Swiss voters imposed quotas on immigrants from EU countries. This could encourage some British politicians to adopt a tougher stand on immigration issues with the EU. Already, some of them have been demanding changes to UK's immigration policies. In the past, they were targeting South Asians. During 2013, some of them have begun targeting East Europeans. This has led to some European politicians questioning their counterparts in UK. They are asking: "How can you be so selective on immigration from Europe? After all, British businesses are major players in the European common market"!

During 2013, questions related to UK's future role in the EU have been raised several times by different British politicians. In April 2013, the BBC broadcast an interesting debate on the pros and cons of UK's exit from the EU.

During 2013, several top executives of global companies have expressed strong views on the pros and cons of UK leaving the EU in the near future. The list of such companies is significant: Nissan, Ford, Goldman Sachs, Citigroup, Airbus, Unilever and Nestle. These executives have mentioned the general business impact as well as their own company's preferences to continue their operations in London, if or when UK leaves the EU.

Another variable is the future of Scotland within the UK. In 2014 Scotland is having a crucial vote on its relationship with UK. Business media is now speculating on various "scenarios" that could develop. Any debate about UK's exit from the EU between 2014 and 2017 can no longer be treated as speculative: it can't be ignored from a business perspective.

During 2013, Britain has moved closer to China in many ways. In Nov 2013, The Telegraph reported that during 2012 most people entering UK to live and work came from China. In recent years, China has expanded Renminbi (RMB) settlement with its trading partners. Major European banks: HSBC, Standard Chartered, RBS and Deutsche Bank offer RMB related services in Europe. Next to Hong Kong, London is already a major offshore hub for RMB. I will explain the significance of this development in Chapter 4.

In recent years, Islamic Finance is growing rapidly in Dubai and in Kuala Lumpur. Its size is expected to reach $ 2.6 trillion by 2017. During 2013, British politicians and business leaders are seriously trying to develop London as a hub for Islamic Finance in Europe. London, as a global financial center already has business ties with the Middle East.

Why are British politicians trying to woo China and Middle East on the one side and picking up a fight with their counterparts in Europe on the other side? This discussion is not about geopolitical debates in UK. It is about having a business perspective. For example: What could be the future role played by London as a global financial center? An answer to this question is more relevant for Indian IT and BPM exporters. Many of their clients in Europe belong to global BFSI. I will cover topics related to global BFSI in Chapter 6.

This topic is also relevant for India Inc. This term refers to all Indian exporters, even those outside the IT and BPM industry. In the past, most of them have adopted a "London centric" approach towards their business model in Europe. Even they need to keep a watch on the developments mentioned above from a long term perspective!

IT Spending and IT Outsourcing in Europe

Several surveys have been conducted on IT spending in Europe and changing priorities of top executives towards IT Outsourcing. When European business leaders talk about cost optimization, what does it mean? They are not referring to a cut in IT spending. They are responding to this recession differently. Many of them are focusing on how IT can improve business productivity and reduce unit costs for products and services. Many Indian IT exporters have confirmed that in recent quarters, European executives are more open to consider IT outsourcing.

One survey by European sourcing adviser Alsbridge indicated that a majority of IT leaders in UK, Switzerland, Holland and Nordic countries were feeling to be "stuck in the past" with existing long term contracts. They are likely to consider outsourcing work to external service providers to take advantage of new technologies.

A Gartner report in 2012 indicated that European organizations are likely to focus on enhancing competitiveness rather than cost reduction while making IT investments. Some European banks are "catching up" in mobile banking. Can this offer new opportunities for Indian IT exporters? I will answer this question later.

Going forward, IT outsourcing in Europe is likely to move in a different trajectory when compared to IT outsourcing in the US. Priorities applicable to the US may not apply to Europe: for example, near shoring is preferred by many European executives.

Many European companies are still not comfortable with offshore IT service providers. They are aware of the unemployment situation and are trying to avoid a political backlash. Accordingly, Indian IT and BPM exporters need to tailor their business case and value proposition. Instead of trying to reduce labor costs and employee headcount they need to look at consolidating IT infrastructure and reducing fixed costs.

In Oct 2013, business media reports in India estimated that 4 Indian IT exporters: TCS, Infosys, Wipro and HCL Technologies together had cash reserves of about $ 9 billion. In this financial year (2013-2014) alone, it increased by a billion dollars. With cash reserves in billions of Euros, I am sure that large Indian IT exporters will expand their footprint in Europe. This raises a few questions:

1. Are they willing to make "smart" investments?
2. Are they willing to pursue a different business model in continental Europe when compared to what they have been doing so far in the US and in UK?

As I will explain later, Europe does offer them a "window of opportunity". In the next section, I will cover two sets of political debates in Europe and in the US. The outcome is being closely watched by many US companies, especially those dealing with IT products and IT services. These debates are also relevant to Indian IT exporters.

Is there a divergence across the Atlantic?

Indian IT exporters need to keep a watch on two areas where there could be major differences between policymakers in Europe and in the US:

1. Taxation of internet based businesses.
2. Concerns in Europe about data security and privacy.

In 2012, the European Commission (EC) estimated that EU countries were losing nearly a trillion Euros every year due to tax loopholes and tax avoidance by MNCs.

This led to European policymakers taking a closer look from two perspectives:
1. To identify those companies engaged in tax avoidance.
2. To close tax loopholes and thereby recover additional revenues.

During 2012 and 2013, Google, Starbucks and Amazon were questioned by policymakers in UK and in Europe to check if they avoided paying taxes in some European countries. This led to American politicians also taking a closer look. Some US politicians blamed Ireland for tax avoidance by Apple and Adobe. In Oct 2013, Ireland announced that it was closing a tax loophole made use of earlier by American companies.

In Feb 2014, Bloomberg reported that during recent years, IBM reduced its tax rate to a two decade low, thanks to tax loopholes offered by Netherlands. Taxation debates across the US and Europe could get more complicated due to many reasons.
1. There are multiple tax jurisdictions in UK, in Euro zone, in other EU countries and in Switzerland.
2. Few countries like Ireland, Netherland and Belgium offer tax incentives.

Even if European authorities don't levy additional taxes, they are likely to close tax loopholes currently used by many US based IT companies operating in Europe. This can also affect many Internet Service Providers (ISPs) who have set up their infrastructure in Europe. In recent years, many ISPs serve customers in Africa from their locations in Europe.

In the last two decades, internet traffic has been diverted away from the US to Europe. In 1999, 70% of the internet traffic to Africa passed through the US. By 2012, this dropped to 5% in spite of the huge growth in volume. Clearly, the bandwidth has shifted from the US towards Europe. Any change to taxation policies could lead to ISPs reorganizing their operations across the Europe, Middle East and Africa region.

During 2013, European leaders raised their concerns on data collection by the US National Security Agency (NSA) and its PRISM program. In Aug 2013, the Information Technology and Innovation Foundation (ITIF) and Forrester Research Inc. in the US released reports on its implications on US based and non US based cloud service providers.

European policymakers are "upset" by data collection practices of intelligence agencies in the US and in UK. This is no longer an issue or a concern expressed only by European politicians. It can have an impact on business, especially the IT industry.

What prevents European policymakers or European business leaders to raise new questions during 2014 and beyond? These questions could be on where servers are located, how data is collected and stored or what standards are used for data encryption. This could affect the European business of many companies across the US IT industry. As I will explain in the next Section, one impact could be on the economics or the cost case associated with cloud computing solutions currently offered by companies based in the US.

Cloud Computing in Europe

Before 2013, uncertainty related to Euro zone had contributed to slower adoption of cloud computing in Europe. During 2013 the following reasons have led to slower growth than experts projected earlier:
1. European business leaders were not fully convinced about the economics associated, or the cost case of cloud computing.
2. Large banks and European BFSI were busy with regulatory overhaul or still adapting to industry shifts.
3. European executives were concerned about data security and privacy especially after revelations related to NSA in the US.

What can one expect during 2014? During 2013, European policymakers did make progress on promoting cloud computing. Uncertainty related to Euro zone did not prevent European businesses to make IT investments. In fact, improving competitiveness and addressing growth opportunities are driving higher IT spending in some cases. It is only a matter of time before cloud computing will also pick up in Europe.

As explained earlier, policymakers in Europe and in the US are divided on matters related to taxation, data security and privacy. As a result, the competitive landscape of cloud computing in Europe could change during 2014.

A significant number of US based companies are active in the European market for cloud computing. Typically, they have promoted a cloud computing model based on the economics and the cost case suited to the US.

On topics related to data security and privacy, European executives are likely to remain cautious during 2014. Most likely, US based IT companies need to get ready with typical questions likely to be raised by European business executives. Some of them are:

- Where would servers be located? How are specific concerns related to collection and protection of customer specific data being addressed?
- Would data be encrypted? How would performance issues get addressed?

It is difficult to predict how these questions raised would affect the cost case or the business case for cloud computing in each European country. It is quite likely that a solution already implemented for a similar client based in the US may need some changes to suit a European client under similar business conditions.

As I will explain in Part 3 (Chapter 8), the economics of cloud computing is complex. The country where data is stored is only one of the many variables. The 4 major US based companies: IBM, Microsoft, Google and Amazon have a different "vision" for cloud computing. They also offer a wide choice of server locations across the world.

In Jan 2014, the General Counsel of Microsoft announced in Europe that the company will allow its global customers to have their personal data stored outside the US. Who else would follow: would it be IBM, Google or Amazon?

How does this affect Indian IT exporters addressing cloud computing opportunities in Europe? More than technology, the economics and politics of cloud computing have an impact on decision making. By leveraging cloud computing, European businesses can save costs in many ways. Of course, the politics of data security can also affect US based companies, one way or the other. Some European policymakers and businessmen are also talking about developing a "European cloud". This is why Indian IT exporters need to take a closer look at developments related to cloud computing in Europe.

As I explained earlier, we are talking about a multi-speed European economy. Many Europeans prefer a smaller, cheaper car: they don't mind even if it is from a South Korean brand. Why should Indian IT exporters get worried? Can't they continue to focus on the economics or the cost case related to cloud computing in Europe?

Typically, IT companies are quite knowledgeable about internet usage and spread of e-commerce in the US and in Europe. However, there are many interesting developments happening across multiple industries in Europe. I will explain one of them: how Europeans are leveraging technology for cross border payments.

Payments Ecosystem in Europe

Electronic payments are growing rapidly in Europe. They include all types of payments: between consumers, between consumers and businesses, between multiple banks; between banks and businesses. The sheer number of payment alternatives, the features involved, and options offered are too many. This is why I am using the term payments ecosystem.

The ECB reported that during 2011, the total non-cash payments made in EU crossed $ 90 billion. The ECB report also mentioned that check usage in 17 out of 27 countries within the EU fell to 1%. The next wave could be the widespread usage of mobile payments and mobile commerce in countries across Europe.

Many European businesses are trying to leverage mobile computing and the internet. They can offer convenience, reduced transaction costs, or both to European consumers. Mobile payments can also affect the current business model of many European banks. From the perspective of Indian IT professionals, this represents an industry shift.

Across multiple industries, businesses are promoting mobile payments. This covers the retail industry, European telecom and networking companies and BFSI in Europe. This is also being supported by European policymakers.

Internet penetration and usage of online banking differs across European countries. In some countries, mobile banking is yet to take off.

In Nordic countries and Netherlands, more than 50% of customers do not visit bank branches. In these countries, customers serve themselves through online channels by leveraging the internet.

In UK, Germany, France, Switzerland and Belgium, customers use multiple channels for banking. Although internet penetration is high, the usage of online banking as well as mobile banking in each of these countries differs.

On the one hand, European regulators are promoting the expansion of electronic payments. On the other hand, they are also keeping a watch on the fees charged by European banks, Visa and MasterCard. Given the current state of the European banking system, it will be interesting to watch how these developments influence European customers.

Recently, the European Commission (EC) has backed new limits on fees for card payments: both credit cards and debit cards. Of course, this development is still being watched by large European banks, European retailers and consumers.

Another development is the Single Euro Payment Area (SEPA) by the European Payments Council (EPC). Many European companies as well as global IT companies operating in Europe are watching the payment schemes and frameworks developed by EPC. SEPA comes into full effect by Feb 2014: this could offer new opportunities during 2014 from the perspective of many Indian IT professionals reading this book. They need to become familiar with the publications of EPC like White Papers on mobile payment.

Unlike the US market, credit card penetration across Europe is uneven and not deep enough. This market can be viewed as a business ecosystem comprising of large banks, payment service providers, retail industry, telecom and network operators across Europe.

From the perspective of IT companies, this market is spread across countries, even outside the EU. It involves many areas beyond what is commonly referred to as mobile banking. From the perspective of the Indian IT exporters, this is quite significant.

As in many parts of the world, mobile banking, e-commerce, digital payments and the retail industry are converging together in Europe. If you consider options available for mobile payments in the European BFSI space, this market is complex. If you also include the options available in the European retail industry, the market is also fragmented.

European consumer needs and expectations are growing rapidly. The growing use of mobile phones, especially smart phones is causing an industry disruption in Europe. When each European buys a smart phone, he or she would like to get the best of multiple worlds: convenience in terms of banking, retail purchases as well as reduced transaction costs.

Banks as well as retailers in Europe are getting squeezed from multiple sides. They have to strike a balance on how many options they can offer to customers. They can't support too many technology based payment options.

There are too many stakeholders; the market is fast growing and competition is also intense. New payment service providers don't have a legacy and can offer state of the art solutions. This is why mobile banking could disrupt the business model of many European banks.

Of late, many Asian banks and large banks based in the US are also making an entry into mobile banking. How do they a strike a balance between technology investments, revenues and profits while serving their customers across Europe?

Across Europe, major retailers, large banks and their partners have already invested on specific technologies. Apart from this "legacy", major payment system operators, Visa and MasterCard have their own priorities at a European level. Typically, they cater to large retail businesses, banks and financial institutions. How should Indian IT and BPM exporters approach this market? We are still in the second Chapter of this book: readers need to wait till they complete Chapter 6 for an answer!

In the next few sections I will explain why Europe deserves a closer look. This applies to Indian IT and BPM exporters, India Inc. and even Indian IT professionals.

Can Europe Offer a Window of Opportunity?

In the past, even large Indian IT and BPM exporters are "under penetrated" in Europe. Many of them are still quite "London centric" or focused on those countries where English is widely spoken. In recent quarters, this is changing.

Earlier, I provided an example of an industry shift in Europe. I also mentioned some interesting developments related to the IT industry. These indicate that the priorities of European executives are changing. During 2013, European executives are more open towards IT outsourcing as an option to optimize costs. Information Services Group (ISG), which measures commercial outsourcing contracts reported that this activity grew significantly in the EMEA (Europe Middle East and Africa) region during 3Q 2013.

While bidding for the next generation of outsourcing contracts, Indian IT exporters can't rely on the same business model that has worked for them so far in the US. If they are too focused on cost, they could end up competing with each other. In my opinion, they need to start competing with global companies like IBM, Accenture, Cap Gemini and others. They may also need to look at near shore options within the European continent.

Most European CEOs are trying to figure out how each of their businesses can grow faster than the rest of the European economy. They are also keen to grow faster than their competitors. They are looking for new ideas and new solutions; not a specific technology per se. This is where there could be a gap between needs and expectations of European clients on the one side and the value proposition offered by many Indian IT exporters.

In the past, CEOs in Europe asked two typical questions while making decisions related to IT. One, how can IT help us "run" our business? Two, how can IT help us "improve" our business? Going forward, their top question is: how can IT help us grow our business?

Indian IT exporters need to be prepared with appropriate answers. If their only value proposition is a cost advantage, they may not be able to convince their European clients. Their new value proposition for Europe must look beyond cost optimization. It must relate to improving competitiveness and pursuing growth.

Innovative ideas on how to leverage technology to get more "bang for the buck" and also grow faster would always welcomed by European CEOs. Such ideas can apply to IT solutions, new business processes or new business models. Some ideas may not result in opportunities for IT services immediately. Europe may not always offer a short cut to improving revenues in the short term.

When compared to their counterparts in the Indian BPM industry, Indian IT companies are more "English centric". Is it time for Indian IT professionals to start learning German or French? Indian IT professionals have always been quick to learn a new programming language. However, language skills alone can't help them serve European clients. As I will explain in Part 3, their employers also need to change course, sooner than later!

India Based Captive Units

NASSCOM reported that since mid-2012 over a period of 12 months at least 20 European corporations had set up engineering R&D centers in India. Would more European companies and European banks set up captive units in India during 2014? If they already have a captive unit in India, would these be expanded? How would they distribute work between captive units and external IT and BPM service providers? I will answer such questions in the forthcoming chapters. I will provide some short answers in this Section.

Earlier in this Chapter, I mentioned about job redistribution and near shoring in European BFSI. I also mentioned about the changing mix of investment banking and retail banking. Many European banks are reorganizing their businesses and operations across the UK, Euro zone and rest of the EU. Each of these could involve consolidating certain roles and functions being performed within Europe.

Eventually, European banks could make changes in their operating model to achieve cost optimization in different ways. They could even set up a captive unit, redistribute the work performed in house and work outsourced to external service providers.

It is important to differentiate between the US and Europe when it comes to the role played by India based captive units of MNCs. What applies to global companies based in the US may not apply to their counterparts based in Europe from the same industry. The India based captive units of many European companies have looked beyond IT and BPM related work. These include Unilever, Siemens, Philips and Bosch.

Going forward, many other European companies could set up their captive units in India. Would they follow the pattern comparable to Unilever, Siemens, Philips or Bosch? Would the work performed be in areas such as Engineering R&D, analytics, risk management and regulatory compliance? Can India benefit from this long term trend of captive units being set up by European MNCs? Answers to such questions would be of interest not only to India Inc. but also to Indian policymakers.

It is also important to understand the pattern of job redistribution and reorganization by MNCs in Europe. They are a long term consequence of the Euro zone crisis. Ford did not pull out of Europe, but shifted production from high cost locations in UK and Belgium to Spain. Similarly, Fiat is not pulling out of its home country, Italy. In early 2014 Fiat consolidated its stake in Chrysler and is now transforming into a global automaker. Similarly, most MNCs are reorganizing their European operations in different ways.

In the next few years, MNCs are likely to redistribute their production, business units, business functions as well as jobs across the European continent. From the perspective of IT and BPM services, many European MNCs are likely to look at low cost and "near shore" locations. One of these options could also be setting up captive units within the European continent. They are likely to be in Central and Eastern Europe. Of course, they can also be located elsewhere in the world.

In recent quarters, many Indian IT and BPM exporters have experienced challenges in their biggest market, the US. The next Chapter will cover topics related to the US economy.

CHAPTER 3

Get Used to the New Normal in the US

Between Nov 2012 and Oct 2013, the US economy has undergone a churn. During 2013, there have been mixed signals on the US economy. In this Chapter, I will explain this using a term I refer to as the "new normal" for the US economy. I will also explain how it affects US based companies in the IT industry. This chapter will enable Indian readers to look beyond economic indicators and behind the veil of political debates associated with the US economy. It is based on a detailed study of business media reports, articles by experts and reports from consulting companies.

Let us get started. On multiple occasions after US elections in Nov 2012, business media reports created hype. One was in end 2012: what is referred to as the fiscal cliff. Another was in 2Q 2013 on changes related to the policies of the US Federal Reserve (US Fed). In 3Q it was about the shutdown of the US government for two weeks. On each occasion, after a few days, it was Business as Usual (BAU) for US stock markets.

Is it BAU for Corporate America in terms of capital spending? How did these events affect the growth rate of the US economy? How could they affect decision making by CEOs of US based MNCs and large banks? Sometimes, political debates, economic data and stock market trends can be confusing. For the benefit of readers, I have explained the shocks experienced by the US economy separately (See Box*).

For Indian IT exporters, it is important to understand the US economy from a business perspective. The Indian IT industry needs to separate signal from noise: later in this Chapter I will explain what it means. While serving US based clients, Indian IT professionals need to focus on the real challenges faced. They must not get carried away by political debates and confusing economic indicators.

* Challenges Faced by the US Economy

Since 2009, the debt to GDP ratio for the US economy has gone up due to multiple reasons. In this Section, I will explain its implications. For the benefit of readers, I will avoid the jargon of economists while explaining the topic of US debt.

Readers are aware of the 2008-2009 global financial crisis. In the last decade, most American families accumulated housing loans. Banks packaged them into complex products called mortgage securities. One category of loans referred to as "subprime loans" triggered a shock wave in the US economy. This resulted in high unemployment, slow and uneven growth.

Since 2009, the US Fed followed a low interest rate policy referred to as Quantitative Easing (QE). As a part of QE, economic stimulus packages were offered; US banks were bailed out. The end result is that the US economy has accumulated additional debt relative to its size.

Since 2011, several experts, including economists who are Nobel laureates have offered solutions on how the US can manage its soaring debts. The term debt ceiling refers to an upper limit of public debt targeted by US policymakers. The world's largest economy can't afford to operate without such an upper limit. Ever since Aug 2011, US politicians are unable to agree on how to set this limit going forward.

They have been extending this limit using a piece meal approach. They remain divided on the choice of spending cuts and tax reforms. The debt ceiling debate began in Aug 2011. This was also when the Euro zone crisis precipitated. At that time, crisis management led to Standard & Poor (S&P) downgrading the credit rating of the US.

After President Obama was reelected, the debate resumed during the end of 2012. US politicians debated on the choice of spending cuts and tax increases. They ended up making a temporary deal involving across the board budget cuts. In Oct 2013, this led to a shutdown of the government in Washington for two weeks. In Dec 2013, US policymakers have made another budget deal. The US Fed also announced a change in its QE policy. Corporate America will be watching how these could affect economic growth during 2014.

How do these affect Indian IT and BPM exporters? One indirect consequence of the budget debate is that decisions on immigration reform and changes to US visa regulations were pushed to 2014. Indian IT professionals are aware of this topic. In Dec 2013, Indians were surprised to watch Indo US relations take a sudden twist. During 2014, Indian IT exporters need to be prepared for surprises from a business perspective, one way or the other!

Separate the Signal from Noise

On the one hand, US stock markets reached an all-time high during 2013. On the other hand, the US economy grew by 1.9% during 2013. During the seven quarters from Jan 2012 to Sept 2013, the US GDP grew between 0.1% and 4.1% every quarter, with the average below 2%. It is therefore important to look beyond political debates across America.

Experts are divided whether a GDP growth rate of 2% is "good enough" for the world's largest economy. 69% of the US economy is driven by consumption. Experts like Stephen S. Roach* have pointed out that for 17 quarters ending 2013, annualized growth in real personal consumption expenditure has averaged at a mere 2.2%.

> * Stephen S. Roach is the former head of Morgan Stanley in Asia. He is currently a Professor in the US. He has written several articles about the world's two largest economies: the US and China.

In recent years, Americans have complained about "stubbornly high" unemployment. From nearly 9% in early 2012, unemployment came down to 7% in Nov 2013. Across various states in the US, economic growth and unemployment have been divergent since 2008.

Some industries and some states were affected by a poor housing market. Some states have been affected by reduced government spending. As a result, political opinion has also become divergent. In many ways, the US can be described as a multi-speed economy. According to IHS Global Insight, out of 50 states in the US, only 18 would return to the pre 2008 employment numbers by the end of 2013.

Business media reports in the US and UK on the US economy can be classified into two groups. One set of reports focus on stock market trends, profits and balance sheets. This is what can be referred to as a Wall Street perspective. Another set focuses on the "Main Street": the consumption led US economy. During 2013 there has been a divergence between Wall Street and Main Street!

This divergence is also because US companies are changing their priorities across business units; across market segments; even across products and services. This is why Indian IT and BPM exporters need to separate signal from noise by looking beyond economic indicators and political debates. They need to identify an industry shift and understand its impact from a business perspective. This is also a part of the Indian IT industry "growing up".

Changing Demographics

Across the US, there have been significant demographic shifts during the last three decades. To some extent, the Nov 2012 elections exposed this demographic diversity across America. In this Section, I will briefly explain this from the perspective of Indian IT exporters.

Between 1980 and 2010, the percentage of Asian Americans went up from 1.5% to 4.8%. During this period, the percentage of Latino Americans (Hispanics) went up from 6.4% to 9.4%. As a result of aging, the percentage of population among the Caucasian (White) majority is declining faster than that of African Americans. This is one reason why immigration reform is a topic of intense political debates in the US. This is also significant from a business perspective. Businesses across the US are trying to understand these demographic shifts and also adapt to them.

US unemployment data is skewed by demographic shifts and statewide differences. In recent years, the US labor market has changed. Wages in low skilled jobs have remained flat. Older Americans are moving out of the labor market due to a mismatch of skills. Since 2008-2009, many Americans are accepting temporary jobs or part time jobs. These developments have also affected political debates in Washington. From a business perspective, they also affect the spending habits and shopping behavior of ordinary Americans.

In May 2013, it was reported that only 15% of Americans lived in non-metropolitan counties spread across 72% of the land area. In recent years, this migration of Americans has affected the housing market in many states.

More than 200 of the US Fortune 500* companies have their headquarters based in the top 50 US cities. With small and medium businesses also clustered around them, employment opportunities are better in larger cities. As a result, younger Americans are moving away from rural America.

> * This refers to the Fortune 500 list of companies within the US, not the Global Fortune 500 list mentioned later in this Chapter.

Demographic shifts are more prominent among younger Americans. In recent years, many of them have pursued advanced degrees. They have accumulated student loans. They are also quite technology savvy!

Demographic shifts affect consumer spending. In 2012, Americans aged 55 or older accounted for more than 40% of new car sales. Of course, many younger Americans could be postponing the purchase of a house, purchase of a car or even marriage. At the same time, they have not stopped spending on technology gadgets like smartphones!

The divergence of economic indicators is also regional in nature. Across Midwestern states and the North Eastern part of the US, you find that demographics have changed significantly. Some auto industry experts mention such demographic shifts as one of the reasons for a demand shift in new car sales.

Differences across various states and cities in the US affect consumer demand. They also affect the supply chain from the perspective of the US retail industry. Even US banks are affected by changes in spending habits of ordinary Americans. This is why analytics is becoming more relevant to American businesses across industries!

Even though there is still a shortage of skilled IT professionals in the US, politicians will keep raising the topic of job creation at a State level and at a City level. More than economic indicators, capital spending by Corporate America is affected by demographic shifts, regional and local differences.

How do these discussions matter to Indian IT and BPM exporters? They represent a challenge as well as an opportunity to understand the US economy from a business perspective. Indian IT professionals need to look beyond economic indicators. They need to understand political debates related to job creation, immigration reform and changes to visa regulations from a business perspective. For example, technology like social media and analytics can be leveraged by global clients to understand and adapt to demographic shifts.

Understand a Multi-Speed US Economy

In 2013 experts say that the US housing market has recovered. Even though unemployment is high by historical standards, it has come down in many states. From a business perspective, it is important to understand the pattern of spending and saving by ordinary Americans.

Corporate America is getting used to a multi-speed US economy. A shift in demand or spending pattern affects the US retail industry. It also affects the business model of US banks. Competition for the wallet share of Americans became more intense during Q4 of 2013. Later in this Chapter, I will cover the churn experienced by the US retail industry.

From the perspective of Indian IT exporters, it is more important to look at how conditions in the US economy have affected capital spending by Corporate America. Before the Nov 2012 elections, business media reports in the US analyzed the accumulated profits held in cash by MNCs based in the US. The total pile of cash held was about $ 2 trillion. Interestingly, a significant share of cash was held by US companies in the IT industry.

This led to political debate about jobs, corporate taxes and capital investments. Some experts argued that US companies were holding on to cash reserves due to US elections and uncertainty from Euro zone. Consulting companies offered proposals on how to "unlock" these capital investments, improve US exports and also create jobs. Some of these debates continued during 2013.

During early 2013, political debates focused on profits held by Corporate America outside the US avoiding taxes as per prevailing tax laws. In March 2013, the Wall Street Journal reported that 60 big companies based in the US had "parked" profits worth nearly $ 160 billion outside the US during 2012.

Among them, 26 companies were in technology and health care related industries. Between 2011 and 2012, these profits rose by 15%. Companies like GE responded by pointing out that these profits were being invested to expand the global footprint of US companies. Later I will explain the significance of such political debates. This particular debate was related to tax reform and tax breaks sought by US companies.

During 2013, capital investments did not take off as predicted earlier. Political debates in Washington continued on tax reform, immigration reform and visa regulations. During the second half of 2013, three developments led to some uncertainty:

1. There was some speculation on policies by the US Fed.
2. The US government shutdown for a few weeks.
3. Political debates on the debt ceiling were postponed to 2014.

For Indian IT and BPM exporters, one important question is: Would US companies go ahead making big investments from their trillion dollar kitty in 2014? Later I will try to answer this question by covering topics related to capital investments by US based MNCs. I will also cover topics related to US based companies in the IT industry. Hopefully, these discussions will provide fresh ideas for Indian IT exporters as well as give the "big picture" to Indian IT professionals!

The World is not flat but uneven

In 2005, Thomas Friedman wrote a bestseller titled "The World is flat". Of course, Mr. Friedman wrote this book much before the 2008-2009 global financial crisis. In recent years, especially after the 2011-2012 Euro zone crisis the world did not become flatter for many US based MNCs and global banks: it has become uneven.

For US based MNCs, revenue and profits come from several countries outside the US. They are experiencing slow and uneven growth in their major market segments: in the US, in Europe and in Japan.

They are trying to expand into growth markets elsewhere in the world. To achieve this, many CEOs and CFOs are trying to become globally competitive. During 2013, they are still trying to understand some industry shifts that have a long term impact.

In recent years, the number of US based companies in the Global Fortune 500* list is coming down and their relative ranking is also affected in many ways. The Global Fortune 500 list published in July 2012 contained one interesting metric: what Fortune referred to as winners.

* The Global Fortune 500 list refers to all global companies, not the US Fortune 500 list of companies mentioned earlier in this Chapter.

Winners are those companies which moved up the Fortune 500 ranking between 2010 and 2011. This metric confirmed that many Fortune 500 companies based in Europe were seriously affected by the Euro zone crisis.

However, there was an interesting pattern among winners and losers based outside the US. Of the top 50 winners during 2011, 20 were Asian companies: 15 came from China and 5 from South Korea. This confirmed that the Euro zone crisis indeed caused a churn among the Global Fortune 500 companies.

Fortune referred to 38 companies as losers: they were part of Fortune 500 in earlier years but not in 2011. Of the 38 losers during 2011, 15 companies were from the European continent. Euro zone accounted for 10 and the remaining 5 were from Britain, Switzerland and Denmark.

The Global Fortune 500 list published in 2013 indicated that the number of companies based in the US did not change, but their rankings did change. The real question is: how many of them improved their global competitiveness since 2011?

The 2012-2013 Global Competitiveness Report released by the World Economic Forum covers this topic. This report is based on an exhaustive analysis of competitiveness based on 12 major indicators aggregated into a single index. The changes in ranking of the top 10 countries between 2011 and 2012 are quite significant.

The US slipped in its global ranking from the 5th to the 7th position. Two Euro zone countries, Germany and Netherlands overtook the US in the global race. Finland and Sweden exchanged positions (3 and 4). Germany retained its position (6) in spite of recent developments in the Euro zone.

What are the implications for Indian IT and BPM exporters? Typically, they serve S&P 500 or Fortune 500 companies. Most of their US based clients are trying hard to become globally competitive. They are also keen to address growth opportunities outside the US and thereby improve their global footprint.

Accordingly, Indian IT exporters need to capture a bigger mindshare of CEOs and CFOs in the US. They also need to convert this mindshare into a growing share of IT budgets. To achieve this, they need to offer a different value proposition.

In the past, they have offered low cost services to their US based clients. Their new value proposition needs to match with two new priorities of Corporate America: growth and global competitiveness. Many CEOs in the US are prioritizing their capital spending based on these new priorities going forward.

What Drives Capital Spending?

Earlier I mentioned the trillion dollar kitty held by US companies. Of course, US business media reports have tried to relate this kitty to capital investments by Corporate America during 2013. If you look deeper, the priorities of top management on capital spending have changed. CFOs are prioritizing capital investments, especially those related to IT. This is sometimes referred to as "discretionary investments" in the context of IT spending. In Part 3 of this book, I will cover more topics on the changing priorities of CFOs.

The National Bureau of Economic Research (NBER) in the US studied the pattern of cash holding, tax rules and profitability across US MNCs. The NBER study, released in June 2012 found that US MNCs with high R&D costs held higher cash reserves. It questioned whether US MNCs are holding back investments because of economic uncertainty or tax policies.

The report established a strong correlation between pattern of cash held by US MNCs and R&D expenses. This study suggested that US based MNCs are likely to invest on new products, new services and expansion into emerging markets.

In Nov 2013, the European Commission published a report on industrial R&D by the top 2000 companies across the world. In spite of slow and uneven economic growth in the US and in Europe, these 2000 companies increased R&D investments by 6.2% in 2012.

Of the top 10 companies, 5 were based in the US. Nearly 70% of the total R&D investments made by US based companies were in ICT*, Pharmaceutical and health related industries.

* ICT refers to Information and Communication Technologies.

In the past, US MNCs have grown through M&A, especially when economic growth slows down in the US or in Europe. A survey about M&A by Knowledge@Wharton and KPMG published in 2012 covered decision makers at US corporations, private equity (PE) firms and investment funds. The top reason given by respondents to initiate M&A activity was "to expand geographical reach".

A 2013 study report by PwC and Dealogic provided some insight. When compared to 2008, cross-border M&A between G7 countries (US,

UK, Germany, Japan, Canada, France and Italy) and BRIC countries fell from $ 354 billion in 2008 to $ 334 billion in 2012.

However, the share of buyers from the latter group increased from 14% in 2008 to 35% in 2012. In 2012, the share of divestitures—sale of stake, assets, business unit or subsidiaries represented 30% of US deals.

What do these reports signify? During 2014, Corporate America is likely to prioritize capital spending across different areas: on manufacturing and supply chains, on new products and services, on Mergers and Acquisitions (M&A) and of course on technology. India Inc. as well as Indian IT and BPM exporters need to understand the changing priorities of global clients. Accordingly, they can address the opportunities coming up.

Technology in the US Retail Industry

Earlier, I mentioned two terms: multi-speed US economy and changing demographics. How do they affect consumer behavior, especially spending habits and shopping behavior of Americans? I will answer this question by explaining the impact on the US retail industry. While doing so, I will also highlight an industry shift quite relevant for the US IT industry.

Across the US, old stereotypes of young and old Americans are changing. Chief Marketing Officers (CMOs) in US based MNCs are leveraging technology to understand and adapt to demographic shifts. For example, CMOs are collecting data through social media and smartphones. They are analyzing data across business units to improve effectiveness in sales. This is one reason why consulting companies like McKinsey consider Big Data and Analytics as a "game changer".

One needs to look beyond economic data to understand the impact of technology on the US retail industry. Between 2009 and 2012, total retail sales went up from $ 2.64 trillion to $ 3.1 trillion in revenues. According to Forrester Research, the share of online sales has grown from 5.9 per cent in 2009 to 7.6 per cent in 2012. In many states, the share of online sales is increasing rapidly. In each of the twelve quarters ending Q3 of 2013, there has been a double digit growth in E-commerce in the US. Within E-commerce, the mobile commerce segment is growing at a faster rate in recent quarters.

This represents a shift in the US retail industry. This is already affecting the business model of US businesses, US retailers and US banks in different ways. The popularity of e-commerce has even led to many US politicians pushing for taxation of e-commerce. However, opinion is divided across different states in the US on whether e-commerce needs to be taxed and if so, how. Companies like Amazon are taking advantage of this development.

In the last decade, Wal-Mart disrupted the business model of many US retailers through physical stores. In recent years, Amazon is disrupting their business model by leveraging e-commerce. Later, I will cover topics related to IT companies based in the US. Even they are closely watching the moves made by Amazon Web Services (AWS).

As I will explain later, US executives in the retail industry also need to "worry" about data security and privacy issues. Therefore it will be interesting to watch how they prioritize technology investments and IT spending during 2014 and beyond.

During 2013, many of them were catching up in areas like mobile apps, analytics and social media by setting up labs to test their strategies before the holiday shopping season of Oct to Dec 2013. In the following paragraphs I have summarized what business media reported on the US retail industry during this quarter.

In Oct 2013, the government shutdown raised new concerns for many US retailers. In Nov 2013, many "physical" US retailers broke the American tradition by announcing a Black Thursday instead of a Black* Friday. They also opened their stores for an extended duration.

> * The term Black Friday refers to the Thanksgiving weekend, when most US retailers offer discounts.

In Dec 2013, the impact of unexpected weather during the Christmas shopping season led to some "mixed results" across the US retail industry:

- This affected sales for physical retail businesses. Few smart retailers offered discounts to customers for ordering online; they also set up a "pick-up" counter for such items. This way, customers saved time and retailers avoided shipping charges.
- In some areas, bad weather indirectly benefited internet based retailers. However, UPS and Fedex faced challenges in fulfillment and delivery. Some customers were upset because they received their gift packages after Christmas day!

It will be interesting to watch how US retailers would leverage technology during 2014 while competing with two giants: Amazon and Wal-Mart.

Impact on BFSI in the US

For Indian IT and BPM exporters, a significant share of business comes from clients in the Banking Financial Services and Insurance (BFSI) industry segment. In Chapter 2, I mentioned the impact of Euro zone crisis on European BFSI.

Chapter 6 covers a wide range of topics related to global BFSI. In the following paragraphs, I will briefly explain some shifts related to the BFSI industry in the US. This covers two major banking business segments: investment banking and retail banking. Each is experiencing a shift in different ways.

In recent months, business media in the US carried reports on US banks, especially those having large investment banking businesses. The 6 largest banks in the US now hold 67% of assets in the US financial system. The 5 largest banks in the US provide 42% of all loans outstanding in the US. Clearly, US banks have demonstrated resilience in spite of having suffered the 2008-2009 global financial crisis and the 2011-2012 Euro zone crisis.

Global banks based in the US have a significant share of the investment banking business in Europe and in Asia. Their business model is quite different from that of European and Asian banks. In the last 6 years, they have experienced two major shocks: the 2008-2009 global financial crisis and the 2011-2012 Euro zone crisis.

In April 2013, the Wall Street Journal compared 2012 revenues and profits of top investment banks with 2006 levels. The top 5 based in the US experienced a 13% fall in revenues and a 14% fall in pretax profits. For the top 5 based in Europe the impact was more significant: a 22% fall in revenues and a 61% fall in pretax profits.

There are two sets of regulations affecting US banks: the Dodd-Frank regulations specific to the US and Basel III regulations applicable for all global banks. These regulations mostly relate to investment banking businesses. The impact on specific areas and the time line for regulatory compliance differs. It is also spread over a period of few years.

In recent years, the Consumer Finance Protection Bureau (CFPB) in the US has been playing the role of a watchdog in this segment. It has been associated with enacting and/or enforcement of regulations. These also affect local and regional banks across the US.

CFPB is looking into mortgages, home loans, lending standards, debit card fees, overdraft fees, foreign money transfers, etc. Accordingly, many US banks are experiencing an impact on their fee based services, one way or the other. With interest rates remaining low for long periods of time, this can affect their business model going forward.

In general, BFSI in the US is quite mature in leveraging technology, especially state of the art IT solutions. The current priorities are cost optimization, improved competitiveness and growth. Many US banks are also reorganizing or restructuring to suit the new landscape. Each of these is relevant for Indian IT and BPM exporters.

CIOs and CFOs in large US banks are leveraging analytics to understand the impact of an industry shift. Before taking important decisions, they are doing a risk assessment and a scenario analysis. Accordingly, they would choose options like restructuring, reorganization or change in the current business model. I will cover these topics in Chapter 6.

Earlier in this Chapter, I mentioned that for many IT companies in the US, the world is not flat but uneven. In the next few sections, I will explain why.

Disruption in the US IT industry

Technology trends initially affect the US IT industry. Later, the impact is also felt by the global IT industry. This has been happening in the last few decades. Sometimes convergence of multiple technologies has a big impact on CIOs and the CIO organization across Corporate America. In the past, the Indian IT industry has been quick to respond to such a disruption caused in the US IT industry. As a result, Indian IT exporters have benefited in a big way. Based on my own experience, I will explain this giving a historical perspective.

In the 1990s, proliferation of PCs created the first wave of industry disruption in the US IT industry. During this period, the Indian IT industry was quite small and IT exports were not significant. In my opinion this led to the "birth" of the offshore delivery model from India.

During the late 1980s and early 1990s, the US economy experienced slow economic growth. This was also the period when the term IT outsourcing became prevalent in the US. This was when the US introduced H-1B visas initially (around 1991) and L1 visas (around 1993). Many companies in the US IT industry belonging to the mainframe era convinced CIOs on the economics of outsourcing from a business perspective.

When they experienced an acute shortage of IT professionals with the right skill sets, they looked at India. This was when an offshore delivery model made business sense. I have myself been associated with winning and executing offshore projects from India during the mid-1990s. I am sure my friends in the Indian IT industry will agree with my statement that the offshore delivery model was born in the 1990s!

During the late 1990s, CIOs were focused on what is referred to the Year 2000 (Y2K) problem. They were worried that old programs for mainframe applications might cause a technical disruption when the dates move from the year 1999 to the year 2000. This was also when the internet was still evolving. The "old guard" of the US IT industry was disrupted for a second time. The term "old guard" refers to those IT companies who were slow in adapting to technology convergence caused by the internet.

A few years before and after the year 2000, the global IT industry went through a second wave of disruption. On the one hand, there was a shortage of skill sets among IT professionals. On the other hand, a "technology bubble" burst in the US IT industry. After 9/11, this led to slower growth in the US economy. During the last decade (2000 to 2010), IT outsourcing also went through significant change and transformation. During this period, Indian IT exporters made a big impact on the global IT industry. The Indian IT industry benefited in many ways from the second wave of disruption caused during this decade.

Fast forward to this decade (2011 to 2020) and you can identify technology convergence. If you take a closer look, you can also identify the third wave of an industry disruption. This is also happening because the US is experiencing slow and uneven economic growth.

Readers from the IT industry are already aware of four converging trends:

- Mobile computing and its different manifestations. One of them is the proliferation of tablets and mobile devices. The other is falling PC shipments across the world.
- How social media has already become pervasive across the world.
- How cloud computing is affecting new IT spending by corporate customers.
- How Corporate America is leveraging Big Data and analytics.

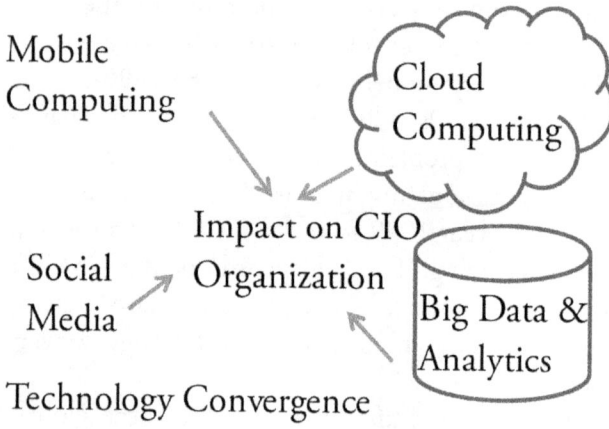

In the US IT industry, a large number of companies have been operating as a part of an ecosystem built around Intel and Microsoft. Apple and Android have created a new ecosystem in mobile computing. All these are having an impact on CIOs and the CIO organization across Corporate America. In this Section, I will mention some areas to watch.

If you look around, already there are interesting signs of an industry disruption in progress. There is intense competition among engineers working on product development and R&D at software labs across the world. CIOs are trying to optimize costs by leveraging technology convergence in different ways in their own organization.

One of the areas to watch is what is referred to as Bring Your Own Device (BYOD). Here, employees are allowed or even encouraged to access corporate IT infrastructure using their own mobile and hand held devices.

As I will explain in Chapter 7, BYOD and cloud computing together have a big impact on CIOs and the CIO organization. The following highlight the pros and cons and the broader impact of BYOD:

- The borders between PCs, tablets, smartphones and hand held devices are getting blurred. Some experts predict that the next wave could be wearable devices!
- Employee preferences like working from home and working from multiple locations are driving BYOD in many companies.
- Many CIOs are looking at leveraging BYOD to avoid investing on hardware. Instead, they are focusing on mobile apps and integrating them with existing applications.

While taking advantage of technology convergence, one company can always step into the stronghold of another, especially in a slow growing US economy. One smart company can disrupt another company's outdated business model. If you look around, this is already happening in software and services. Technology convergence is already beginning to affect the old business models of large US companies like IBM and Oracle.

On the one hand, there is a proliferation of mobile apps built around devices based on Apple's iOS and Android. On the other hand existing software and applications currently used by Corporate America need to be supported. For CIOs, moving applications to a cloud environment are also important. All of these together can lead to a disruption of the current business model of many IT companies based in the US. They could be Independent Software Vendors (ISVs) or IT services providers.

Technology convergence can disrupt the entire US IT industry. This applies to hardware, software or services businesses. Each company in the US IT industry would like to offer products and services faster, cheaper and with better business value. As I mentioned earlier, many of them are cash rich and can afford to be aggressive. Could this lead to a third wave of industry disruption during this decade (2011 to 2020)?

How does this affect Indian IT exporters? They need to quickly adapt to the shift or disruption being caused in the US IT industry. In addition to watching companies in the US IT industry, they also need to watch new players like Amazon and GE.

On the one hand, Amazon is disrupting the US retail industry. On the other hand, Amazon Web Services (AWS) is also challenging IT services companies in the cloud computing market. In Oct 2013, GE announced partnerships with Cisco, AT&T and Intel in the Industrial

Internet market segment. Can Indian IT exporters enter this market? This would require an entirely new skill set and a different business model.

In Part 3 of this book, I will cover more topics on technology convergence from the perspective of IT service providers and the CIO Organization. I will briefly explain this in a few paragraphs.

In the past, replacing desktop PCs with laptops was not so complicated for the CIO organization. This helped US businesses to reduce costs associated with IT infrastructure. Together, BYOD and cloud computing are a different paradigm altogether. They can affect the business model of independent software vendors (ISVs) as well as IT service providers.

The variety of software and apps associated with smartphones and hand held devices are exploding. ISVs based in the US are struggling to strike a balance between new sales and support of older products. Many IT service providers are getting caught in this crossfire! This is why Indian IT exporters need to take a closer look at their old business models. By doing so, they would be better prepared for any industry disruption in the US IT industry.

Many companies in the US IT industry are cash rich. Apart from technology convergence, the US IT industry is also experiencing divergent views of policymakers in the US and in Europe. I will explain two developments that took place during Dec 2013. They are quite significant both from a business perspective and for companies in the US IT industry.

Data Gathering by US Intelligence

Many companies in the US IT industry address opportunities from foreign governments. Their corporate customers outside the US have genuine concerns on data security and privacy. Earlier I used the term separating signal from noise. Indian IT exporters need to understand the broader implications of the revelations related to the US National Security Agency (NSA). As I mentioned in Chapter 2, this has raised some concerns in Europe.

In Dec 2013, a group of US based IT companies* wrote an "Open Letter" to President Obama and Congress raising their concerns on data gathering by government agencies for the purpose of surveillance and intelligence. President Obama responded to their concerns in Jan 2014 by proposing some reforms on data gathering by US intelligence agencies.

* This letter was on behalf of Apple, Google, Facebook, Microsoft, Yahoo, LinkedIn, Twitter and AOL.

In Jan 2014, executives of many companies based in Canada, UK and Northern Europe indicated that they are reviewing ongoing contracts related to cloud computing with American firms. This was both before and after President Obama's speech on NSA reforms. It is therefore difficult to predict the follow up actions that could be taken during 2014.

On the one hand, the US IT industry is concerned about the business impact. On the other hand, they are not in a position to demand changes to government regulations, especially in the US. How does this affect Indian IT exporters? They need to watch how the US IT industry responds to this issue of data collection by the US NSA.

Of course US government agencies have stepped up data collection since 9/11. Companies like IBM, AT&T and Verizon have cooperated with them in making this possible. Going forward, computer security experts in the US are being pulled in two directions: cyber security on the one side and data security and privacy on the other side.

They are feeling pressure from government agencies on the former and consumer groups on the latter. How can they strike a balance? This is why Indian IT exporters need to look beyond political debates in the US from a business perspective. This is part of understanding the "new normal" for the US economy and adapting accordingly. In the next Section, I will explain why data security and privacy is a complex area even for the US IT industry.

Debates about Data Security and Convenience

In recent years, US based internet companies have helped the US retail industry to collect credit card information across the world. In Dec 2013, a security breach reportedly led to information on more than 40 million credit cards and debit cards getting exposed in the US. This involved a major US retailer, Target. During 2014, this could trigger a debate about data security among consumers, retail businesses, MNCs, banks and US authorities. It would be interesting to watch the response from the US IT industry on these debates during 2014.

A typical American has multiple credit cards and debit cards: this is part of their "life style". In recent years and especially during 2013, US retailers as well as large banks based in the US have discovered "weak links" in the long chain of electronic payments involving credit cards, debit cards and smartphones. Let me explain why.

In recent years, spending on technology upgrades by Corporate America is not in sync especially in the US retail industry. Some executives have tried to "pass the buck" when it comes to making IT investments on security solutions. They have chosen to buy insurance for fraud protection instead of spending the same money on a more sophisticated IT solution!

During 2014 and 2015, a number of technology related solutions related to electronic payments are due for replacement. One of them is related to an older generation of cards based on magnetic stripes. Another is related to replacing ATMs based on Windows XP. At the same time, American businesses and banks are also investing on mobile payments. How would they prioritize these conflicting requirements? How can they strike the right balance when the US economy is still recovering?

Of course, social media offers businesses an opportunity to collect a lot of information pertaining to consumers. However, Corporate America needs to strike a balance with their concerns about data security and privacy. Computer security experts are often pulled in different directions by software vendors and IT service providers offering IT solutions where social media and smartphones are used to collect a lot of information.

Both retailers and banks need to educate consumers on the pros and cons of various payment options available. On the one hand, technology is meant to offer more convenience, not introduce new restrictions or barriers to consumers. On the other hand, consumers need to have "trust" while going through the payment transaction. If some of them get worried about an indiscriminate use of their personal information, they would be more careful going forward: they will exercise their own choice. This choice could involve a credit card, a debit card or even a smartphone. In the end, most Americans would always take advantage of the convenience offered by smartphones.

In Jan 2014, the blame game has just begun. Initially, some experts pointed towards an older generation of cards based on magnetic strips.

Few security experts suspected that a certain group of POS (Point of Sale) equipment had been "infected" by a virus. The sheer size and scale of the data breach has raised a number of questions.

1. What share of the fraud losses would be borne by banks? To what extent are retailers liable if or when a data breach happens?
2. What standards of data protection would apply to banks and retailers?

The chain of security in credit card or debit card transactions is quite long and complex. Each transaction passes through retailers, banks, issuers of credit cards and debit cards, payment processors, you name it! Going forward, the US IT industry will need to address a bigger set of issues: on the choice of technology, on the choice of security standards and offer an appropriate security solution. In this long chain, if you are an IT service provider, you can always find a good opportunity to offer something interesting!

As I will explain in Chapter 6, decision making on IT based solutions in retail banking is becoming more complicated in the US as well as in Europe. During 2014 and 2015, the US retail industry, Visa, MasterCard, American Express, US banks of all sizes, Wall-Mart and Amazon would make some key investments. Some of them would be to upgrade older technologies; some others to leverage new technology. However, each of them could move in a different direction or move at a different pace.

This is why Indian IT exporters need to separate signal from noise on topics like data security and privacy. They need to take advantage of this "window of opportunity". On the one hand, companies in the US IT industry hold divergent views on data security and privacy. On the other hand, you can always find innovative companies ahead of the curve.

One can expect some companies based in the US to offer a secure as well as a trusted option for payments using smartphones to a wide range of customers and clients located across the world. One can also expect some aggressive companies to cause an industry disruption, one way or the other. The question is: can Indian IT exporters adopt a sound business model that also enables them to move up the value chain?

Look Beyond US Political Debates

During 2012 and 2013 US policymakers have engaged in several political debates. These relate to jobs, deficits, tax reform, debt ceiling, immigration reform and visas. Each political debate can lead to a smoke screen. This is why Indian IT and BPM exporters need to look beyond political debates from a business perspective.

The US economy is experiencing slow growth and high unemployment since 2009. As a result, wages and salaries in the US have remained flat. Protecting American jobs will remain a priority for many US politicians. This is part of the "new normal" for the US economy.

In recent years, the US trade deficit has widened. US imports have continued to grow in spite of slow and uneven growth in the economy. At the same time, US exports have declined due to multiple reasons: a slowdown in Europe, increased competition from Asian companies and a general decline in US competitiveness, especially in manufacturing.

Several experts and consulting companies have offered proposals on how to improve US exports. They are looking at manufacturing as a new "export engine" for the US economy. They believe that this strategy not only reduces the US trade deficit but also creates jobs. Companies like GE are supporting this view.

Of course, GE is a major exporter. However, most US companies have a long way to go before they can transform themselves into "export engines" in a short period of time. Manufacturing in the US has declined during the last two decades. Many US companies engaged in exports also face competition from Germany and Japan. In addition, their Asian competitors are also trying to expand their global foot print.

So, why is this focus on US manufacturing? Some experts have pointed out that with falling energy costs in the US, inflation and rising wages in China, the cost case for manufacturing within the US is becoming favorable. Some other experts have talked about how 3D printing can transform manufacturing and also create new jobs in the US.

Interestingly, another reason is Boeing. During 2013, across 22 states in America, the billion dollar question being discussed was: Where would the 777X aircraft be manufactured and assembled? The answer became evident in Jan 2014. I will briefly explain its significance.

Most Indian IT professionals are already aware of debates related to US immigration reform and changes proposed on US visa regulations.

Political debates on job creation would be part of the "new normal" of the US economy going forward.

MNCs based in the US are expanding their global manufacturing and supply chains. In the meanwhile, US politicians are trying hard to attract some of this investment into their own states or cities and thereby "create jobs". During 2013, the competition from states and cities across the US to create new jobs took an interesting turn, thanks to Boeing.

Boeing has a healthy order book for its new aircrafts for the next decade. Since early 2013, Boeing has been evaluating options to manufacture its new 777X aircraft. Business media reports mentioned that Boeing received 54 proposals from 22 states offering tax breaks.

In Jan 2014, Boeing confirmed that the manufacturing of its 777X would take place in Washington State. However, jobs in engineering would get redistributed across multiple states to take advantage of tax breaks. This is one example how the politics of creating jobs in manufacturing can influence decisions taken by Corporate America.

Political debates are also affecting companies from the US IT industry. On the one hand, many of them have a global footprint and are cash rich. They have a track record of innovation based on Intellectual Property (IP). Compared to other industries in the US, the IT industry is better equipped to boost US exports.

On the other hand, not all US politicians are on their side. During 2012 and 2013, the IT industry was blamed for tax avoidance, parking profits outside the US, not reinvesting their profits within the US and not creating enough US jobs.

This is why Indian IT exporters need to understand political debates like immigration reform from a business perspective. Some debates on visa regulations are related to issues or concerns raised by the US IT industry. They may not even be related to IT outsourcing or targeted towards Indian companies.

US politicians are pursuing multiple objectives: increase tax revenues, attract investments, boost exports and create jobs. However, all US based companies need to remain globally competitive. Many US businesses are trying to get work done within the global organization at a lower cost location.

During 2013, few large US MNCs like GM and P&G have used terms like re-shoring and insourcing. This refers to previously outsourced work taken back from external service providers. It need not be targeted against Indian companies. It could also mean taking advantage of tax breaks or tax incentives offered within the US, as in case of Boeing.

What if MNCs in the US decide to set up their own captive units in low cost locations? This could mean a net reduction in the scope of work performed by all their external service providers. Indirectly, this could result in some job creation in the US.

This could still have an impact on Indian IT and BPM exporters. This is why they need to look beyond political debates from a business perspective. How can they help their clients navigate a multi-speed US economy? They need to move beyond labor cost arbitrage and outsourcing based business models of the past. I will cover this topic in Part 3 of this book.

Analytics and Business Insight

The power of mobile computing and social media has offered US businesses an opportunity to collect data like never before. Recently, McKinsey published a report on what it called "game changers" for the US economy. Big Data and analytics were one of them.

Many consulting companies talk about "business insight" and the growing importance of analytics. This term business insight refers to the output of analytics. American businesses are trying to leverage analytics to make informed decisions in areas like pricing and marketing. Many CIOs of US based MNCs are trying to adapt to this new paradigm.

In the US, business unit heads as well as Chief Marketing Officers (CMOs) are driving initiatives related to analytics. Earlier, CIOs used to focus on business applications. Now they are focusing on the underlying data to provide data services to managers of Business units. The term business insight is used in this context.

In Chapter 1, I mentioned some typical questions asked by CEOs to their CIOs. One of them is: How can IT transform our business so that our business results can be more consistent and more sustainable quarter after quarter? One of the areas where the top management team is looking for appropriate answers to this question is analytics.

Earlier, MNCs typically analyzed a small pool of business data in a standalone mode independently in each business unit. Now, they are doing this in an interactive mode using analytics to provide sophisticated business insight.

One example is to understand the impact of changing demographics and buyer behavior in consumer facing businesses. Retailers across the US are leveraging analytics to do this in a more organized manner, when compared to the past. They are capturing data through social media and smartphones.

They are applying sophisticated analytics to understand spending habits and shopping behavior of Americans. Using this insight, they are making the necessary changes in their business or in their operations. They are also adapting their business model so that they can grow faster than the rest of the US economy.

Different US businesses view analytics differently. This applies to US based MNCs, US retail industry, US banks and the US health care industry. While there are some common themes, the business priorities in each market segment are quite different.

Even banks across the US are leveraging analytics to understand the changing demographics. They are offering appropriate products and services to suit the changing pattern of spending and saving by ordinary Americans.

This is why Indian IT and BPM exporters need to understand the term business insight. They need to relate this to each US based client. The focus area can be cost optimization, improved efficiency, higher productivity or identifying new growth opportunities.

Why is offering business insight a new paradigm? I will cover this topic in Part 3. Firstly, it requires a different skill set. These skills are related to databases, analytics, knowledge of client's businesses and the industry itself. Secondly, this requires top management contact at the CXO level, beyond the CIO organization. Analytics also involves vast amounts of business specific data, some of which can be business sensitive.

Immigration Reform vs. Outsourcing

Topics related to immigration reform and changes to US visa regulations are of interest to all Indian IT exporters. I will explain why these could affect their outsourcing business models of the past, one way or the other. I am sure many Indian IT professionals are also interested in getting a broader perspective on this topic.

In this Section, I will explain why it is too early to predict changes to US visa regulations. I will explain the likely impact on the old model of IT outsourcing for US based clients. Some developments could directly or indirectly benefit US based IT companies. Some others can introduce a new challenge for Indian IT exporters.

US policymakers have been debating on the topic of immigration reform for quite some time. Interestingly, American politicians as well as executives from major US companies hold divergent views on this topic. During 2013, business media reports in the US and in India have covered a related topic: likely changes to H1-B and L-1 visa regulations.

In Oct 2013, there were two major developments that could affect this debate going forward.

1. Political debates in Washington on the debt ceiling led to postponement of the final decision on immigration reform and changes to visa regulations to 2014.

2. The huge settlement (of $ 34 million) by Infosys with the US Federal Government on a visa issue could still change the course of political debates during 2014.

After the diplomatic standoff between the US and India during Dec 2013, one can't rule out surprises related to US visas during 2014 and beyond. This is why the Indian IT industry can't follow a Business As Usual (BAU) approach on US visas. In the following paragraphs, I will explain why they need to understand the big picture from a business perspective.

Firstly, discussions about changes to H-1B and L-1 visas are part of a larger topic of immigration reform. In recent years, there have been demographic shifts in the US. These affect debates on skilled labor and non-skilled immigrants.

Many American universities are pushing immigration reform from the perspective of job creation in the US. Their rationale is that it would benefit young American professionals with advanced degrees. They are referred to as the STEM (Science, Technology, Engineering and Mathematics) discipline. US based MNCs would like to recruit people with STEM skills. US industry groups hope that changes would also drive capital investments.

Secondly, Republicans themselves hold divergent views on a wide range of topics covering immigration reform and changes to visa regulations. In addition, Republicans and Democrats will remain divided during 2014, a year of mid-term elections. In my opinion, radical changes to immigration reform and visa regulations may not happen during 2014.

Thirdly, the US IT industry in general and Indian IT exporters in particular are more interested in changes to H-1B and L-1 visas. Even if these changes are effective during 2014, they are more likely to benefit US based IT companies. One can also expect few US politicians to push for visa restrictions and increased costs imposed on non US companies. Therefore the impact will differ between large and medium sized Indian IT exporters.

Some of them have begun talking of hiring locally within the US. Some have talked about a rotation policy for employees located on site. This raises some questions on their tactics or strategies. What skill sets are they looking at while hiring in the US? If they hire graduates in STEM discipline, how would the work be distributed across the US and India? These questions need to be answered from a business model perspective.

Fourthly, the industry needs to understand the sensitivity of immigration and visa issues in the US. In the past, several Indian IT exporters and their employees have made use of loopholes in US visa regulations. After the diplomatic standoff during Dec 2013, it could be risky for employees of large Indian IT exporters to take a BAU approach while following US visa restrictions: they need to be more conservative and follow every rulebook. What prevents US authorities to investigate visa fraud by Indian IT exporters in the past?

Is the glass half full or half empty? In my opinion, Indian IT exporters have a window of opportunity during 2014 to start working on alternate business models. Of course, many of them are busy chasing outsourcing contracts coming up for rebid and renegotiation.

Apart from parliamentary elections in India, mid-term elections in the US will take place during 2014. This is the right time for the Indian IT and BPM industry to make some sincere effort in changing course, instead of following a BAU approach in the US market.

US Public Sector and Health Care

So far, Indian IT and BPM exporters have focused on the private sector in the US market. Many consultants have recommended that they need to address opportunities in three market segments where they are underpenetrated.

1. The US public sector in general
2. Cloud computing in the public sector
3. The US health care industry.

In this Section, I will explain the pros and cons associated. Regardless of political debates on government spending and tax reform in the US, one thing is certain. Priorities like efficiency, productivity and competitiveness also apply to public services.

Cloud computing is also gaining importance in these market segments. It is only a matter of time before it would take off. However, Indian IT and BPM exporters need to carefully choose their partners and competitors before getting into these market segments.

As explained earlier, companies in the US IT industry are also experiencing a churn. If Indian IT and BPM exporters are smart, they can take advantage of it to move ahead of global competition. Would large Indian IT exporters compete with Accenture, IBM and other US based IT service providers? If they partner with US based companies, how long would they operate under their shadow? It is time for them to make smart choices!

In the context of US public sector, I will mention a few developments. In 2011, Mr. Vivek Kundra* and his team of IT specialists prepared some reports related to IT spending in the US public sector and the US Federal Government. These reports raised some eyebrows in the US IT industry, especially from IT service providers.

> * The Indian born American, Mr. Vivek Kundra was then a CIO in the White House.

One of these reports reviewed pricing models used by external IT service providers. It highlighted the importance of outcome based pricing. Another report explained how cloud computing helps the US Federal Government save costs. Mr. Kundra even appeared on TV interviews by Indian business media where he explained few of these reports.

However, many IT projects in the US public sector did not take off during 2012 and 2013 as predicted. Many US based IT service providers are facing unique challenges while addressing high visibility opportunities in the US Public Sector and the US healthcare industry.

In recent years, experts and consulting companies have offered many proposals on controlling costs related to health care by leveraging technology. On the one hand, potential is large because the US healthcare industry is undergoing a shift. On the other hand, this market segment has high visibility among US politicians. In Oct 2013, teething troubles faced by healthcare.gov website were widely reported by the business media in the US. Even US based companies are taking a cautious approach!

Earlier, US health care was driven primarily by service providers and insurance companies. Some of them would be forced to change their current business model. They need to shift away from "pay for health services" towards "pay for results" or "pay for outcome". Accordingly, they may demand complex pricing and commercial terms from their IT service providers. This is another reason why even US based IT service providers are cautious.

Going forward, the industry must cut costs, one way or the other. Health care providers, hospitals and insurance companies will be adapting to the new industry landscape. In the long term, the potential is quite significant for both IT and BPM services. Analytics is another area where many US based IT and BPM service providers are focusing on.

Health care providers need to analyze changing trends on patient needs and patterns of spending on various health care services. They need to optimize costs by improving the utilization of their facilities and also improve the "outcome". They also need to improve the quality of service and offer better service levels at the same prices to remain competitive.

Health insurance companies need to collect metrics associated with services rendered by hospitals. They need to understand the demographics and fine tune the health care plans. They can't rely on old data and old patterns of health care spending. They also need to rationalize their pricing and remain competitive.

This is why Indian IT and BPM exporters need to exercise the right choice of partners. This market segment can become crowded and quite competitive. Cost arbitrage alone may not be a good value proposition when compared to their competitors in the US. If they are smart, they can use health care as a stepping stone to eventually address bigger opportunities in the US public sector.

I will conclude this Chapter by explaining the "new normal" of the US economy from the perspective of Indian IT and BPM exporters. I will also explain the pros and cons they need to consider while navigating this new normal.

New Normal for the Indian IT Industry

This new normal comprises of a multiple shifts associated with the US economy:

1. Slow and uneven economic growth will continue for several quarters.
2. CEOs in the US will demand a better value proposition from their IT services providers.
3. Protecting American jobs will remain a priority for some US politicians.
4. Political debates can create a smoke screen: They can delay decision making by clients or lead to divergent approaches taken by companies across the US IT industry.
5. Technology could open new avenues for Indian professionals to offer better business value to their American clients.

Across the US, IT budgets are flat or even falling. In the past, Indian IT exporters have typically operated at the CIO levels. They need to expand their visibility and mindshare with CEOs, CFOs and CMOs. They need to understand the process of decision making by different stakeholders. They need to capture a bigger share of IT spending by respective business units. This will involve time, effort and investments.

Of course, they can pursue outsourcing contracts coming up for rebid or renegotiation. However, US based clients are trying to get more "bang for the buck". While expectations on skills are going up, rates are coming down! Increasingly, US businesses are looking for costs to be more variable, more predictable and more controllable.

This affects most Indian IT exporters. Even if their existing US based clients continue to give them business, they will negotiate on pricing. Even if their revenues continue to grow, profitability can still be affected.

The new normal of the US economy also affects Indian IT professionals. Historically, a role performed in the US has mattered a lot for Indian IT exporters as well as for their employees. Many Indian engineers look forward to working in a US location for personal as well as professional reasons. In the past, many Indian IT exporters have been using an on-site opportunity as a "carrot" to retain talent.

Of course, in recent years, this carrot is losing its credibility and/ or its viability in many Indian IT exporters. This could change further in the next few years due to multiple reasons: visa restrictions, local hiring, changes in the business model, usage of technology options and collaboration tools, you name it!

As I explained in chapter 2, continental Europe offers a window of opportunity. Eventually, Indian IT exporters need to move out of their "comfort zone" in the US and in UK. Eventually, the industry also needs to look beyond software development to expand its US footprint. All this can lead to "churn" in the Indian IT and BPM industry. The mix of revenue, profitability, currency and deployment of people may change across geographies.

If Indian IT exporters are smart, they can get more proactive and try alternate business models in the mature US market. This would be much easier and would also make them more competitive outside the US. This can also be done while competing for outsourcing contracts coming up for rebid or renegotiation. I will cover these topics in Part 3 of this book.

CHAPTER 4

Clients Operate in a Multi-Speed Global Economy

In Chapter 2 and Chapter 3, I explained the economic environment in Europe and in the US using the term multi-speed economy. In the first half of this Chapter, I will expand this term to the global economy. I will highlight the challenges associated from a business perspective. In the second half, I will explain how global companies are leveraging captive units in low cost locations across the world, including countries like India.

The term multi speed global economy refers to divergence of key economic indicators across countries. They include: mismatch of supply and demand; differences in interest rates; changes in global capital flows and currency volatility.

On the one hand, this divergence can offer some unique challenges to MNCs and global banks. It affects decision making by their CEOs and CFOs. On the other hand, it also offers them some interesting opportunities. They can drive down costs by redistributing work to lower cost locations.

MNCs are leveraging their global manufacturing and supply chain to move production and assembly to low cost locations. MNCs and global banks are also redistributing work by setting up captive units at low cost locations. Many of them based in India perform IT and BPM related services to their parent unit. The topics covered in the second half of this Chapter are also of interest to IT professionals employed by these captive units.

Let us get started. I will begin by providing a business perspective on a multi speed global economy. While doing so, I will avoid the jargon of economists.

Divergence in the Global Economy

In 2001, Jim O'Neill of Goldman Sachs introduced a term BRIC referring to four major emerging economies: Brazil, Russia, India and China. What Jim O'Neill then identified was the early stages of a paradigm shift in the global economy: changes in global demand together with divergent growth rates across different countries.

The term BRIC was later expanded to include South Africa (BRICS). Terms like BRIC and BRICS have become standard jargon in business media reports on topics related to the global economy. In the last decade, Jim O'Neill is recognized as an international expert on topics related to the global economy. In 2011, he wrote a book titled "The Growth Map: Economic Opportunity in the BRICs and beyond".

In this book, I have avoided using terms like BRIC or BRICS. In this Chapter, I have provided a balanced perspective as well as an Asian perspective to Indian readers. Apart from covering a wide range of topics affecting exporters, I have also covered few developments related to China. These are usually ignored by business media reports in India.

This divergence in the global economy is not only about growth rates. It is also about capital flows, current account deficits, currencies and interest rates. How do global businesses view this? They don't group diverse countries together as BRIC or BRICS. As I have explained in Chapter 5, many MNCs based in the US and in Europe are already global players.

Increasingly, they are trying to become globally integrated. They are becoming major players in both developed economies and emerging economies. They are adapting their business models to take advantage of such divergence or differences in the countries they operate in.

IMF Calls this a Three Speed World

The IMF report of April 2013 used the term three speed world to describe the global economy. I will mention some highlights of this report from a business perspective. I will also explain why I borrowed this idea while using the term multi-speed economy in this book. The IMF report classified major economies of the world into three groups. The grouping is not only about GDP growth rates.

India, China and many emerging economies fall in the high growth category. The IMF report pointed out some common challenges they face in terms of infrastructure, inflation, financial regulations and economic policies. MNCs and global banks are pursuing growth opportunities in these markets.

The US, Sweden, Switzerland and few others fall in the second category. These economies are large and growing, but not fast enough. The IMF report mentioned specific challenges faced by the US economy. I already covered some of them in Chapter 3.

The third group in IMF's report covers Japan and several European countries. Growth has been slow and uneven in many of these countries.

The divergence across major economies is not only about growth rates, as pointed out by the IMF. It is also about other areas, like interest rates, current account deficits, trade deficits, capital flows and currencies.

From a business perspective, a multi speed global economy comes with challenges as well as opportunities. Either way, MNCs and global banks need to navigate this landscape carefully. They need to get smarter while addressing the challenges associated. At the same time, they can't afford to lose out on opportunities.

In recent years, demand is shifting across countries and also fragmenting within major markets. This causes a mismatch of supply and demand. From a supply chain perspective, this could be a challenge. It could also offer an opportunity for MNCs and global banks to address growth opportunities outside mature markets.

Divergent interest rates across countries affect the costs associated for MNCs. At the same time, they could borrow in a country where interest rates are low. They can proactively invest in another country where interest rates are high!

In recent years, there are significant changes in global capital flows. This affects the business model of global banks. Worldwide, the daily trade in foreign exchange markets is $ 5.3 trillion according to experts. There are many causes for currency volatility: this affects global businesses of all sizes.

What do I mean by navigating a multi speed global economy? I am referring to the above mentioned differences in the global economy. This is not only about economic growth rates in one or two quarters. This affects MNCs and global banks based in the US and in Europe.

In the past, their business models have been closely aligned towards developed economies. They have been operating primarily in the US, in Europe and in Japan. In recent years, each of them is expanding into China, India and other emerging economies. Accordingly, they need to adapt their business models to this new landscape.

While doing so, most of them are leveraging technology, especially IT. As I will explain later they are also taking advantage of labor cost arbitrage. They are moving towards a globally integrated model of shared services. They are setting up captive units across the world to take advantage of lower costs and availability of skilled resources. In short, they are implementing their own "global delivery model"!

Global Shift in Demand

In recent years, global demand is shifting away from the US and Europe towards emerging economies. Demand is also getting fragmented across different market segments. This is also happening due to changing demographics across the world.

A few years back Prof. C. K. Prahalad introduced the term "Bottom of the Pyramid". This term is now part of management jargon associated with the global economy. As a result of shift in demand, CEOs need to prioritize between mature markets and growth markets.

In the former, MNCs face challenges related to overcapacity and increased unit costs. In the latter, they face supply constraints and challenges in meeting the fast growing demand. Demand shifts also affect global banks based in the US and in Europe.

In the past, addressing a shift in demand was not so challenging for MNCs. They could always prioritize between growing market segments in the US, in Europe or in Japan. In recent years, this is not possible because demand is weak across these primary markets. This is why they are looking at growth opportunities in Asia, Africa, Latin America and Middle East. However, while doing so, some MNCs based in the US and in Europe face a dilemma.

On the one hand, they can't ignore mature market segments where they have a big presence. On the other hand, they need to be selective in emerging markets. A business model that works in one country may not even be relevant in another. In China and in India, customers expect the best quality and value for money. MNCs based in the US and in Europe can't simply rely on their brand image. They need to remain globally competitive so that they can take on local competitors. Demand shift also puts pressure on their supply chains.

In the next section, I will cover the topic of diverging interest rates across countries. This affects decision making by CEOs and CFOs of MNCs operating in multiple countries.

Divergent Interest Rates

Low interest rate policies have continued for a long time across much of the developed world: the US, Europe and even Japan. Yet, demand hasn't picked up. In many emerging economies, interest rates are much higher. Yet, this is probably why demand could be lower than expected!

For MNCs, interest rates can affect the business model in different ways. In some cases, they affect the demand for their products. In many cases, they affect the costs associated. Interest rates also have an impact on commodity prices and currencies.

Divergent interest rates can also affect the business model of MNCs. On the one hand, interest rates affect decision making related to pricing. On the other hand, MNCs can take advantage of interest rate differences across countries. They can borrow at lower interest rates in one country to offer credit to suppliers in another country. This topic is related to trade finance: it will be covered in Chapter 6.

For global banks, differences between interest rates across the countries are not new. In the next few years, global banks also need to keep track of multiple interest rate benchmarks across the world. Earlier in this book, I mentioned LIBOR. This refers to London Interbank Offered Rate, a global benchmark for interest rates. One of its equivalents is Euribor (in Europe). After the LIBOR scandal in 2012, regulators across the world are taking a closer look at interest rate benchmarks. This could have an impact on the business model of large banks operating in multiple countries.

Most MNCs address risks associated with interest rates by managing costs at a granular level. They leverage their supply chain partners. They reconfigure global supply chains. By doing so, they address challenges on the supply side as well as on the demand side. I will explain this in Chapter 5.

Across MNCs, CFOs are focusing on management systems. Their business unit heads are cooperating and collaborating with supply chain partners. They are also leveraging IT based solutions to overcome the challenges associated.

Changes in interest rates and policies related to money supply in developed economies affect global capital flows and currencies. In the next two sections, I will cover these two topics. First, I will explain the impact of interest rate policies by avoiding the jargon of economists.

Impact of Interest Rate Policies

In recent years, the US Federal Reserve (US Fed), the European Central Bank (ECB), the Bank of England (BOE) and the Bank of Japan (BOJ) have followed a policy of low interest rates. Each of them has increased money supply through what some economists refer to as an "easy" monetary policy.

The Reserve Bank of India (RBI) Governor has rightly pointed out that interest rate policies by the US Fed and other central banks in the developed world have a spillover effect on the global economy. Any change in interest rate policies can disrupt global capital flows. This can lead to volatility in stock markets and sharp currency movements across the world.

Why is this so? There could be many reasons.
1. There could be a sudden shift in global capital flows into or out of a country, affecting its currency. This is what happened in case of India as explained later.
2. A policy change by one major central bank could trigger a change by another central bank elsewhere in the world.
3. Currency trading in anticipation of a major change in interest rate policies can also lead to currency fluctuations in the short term.

Together, this could have a bigger impact on currencies, on stock markets, or both.

Currencies fluctuate on a daily basis across the world. This movement can also refer to variations in the relative value of major currencies like USD, EUR and JPY against one another. However, a sudden or unexpected movement is referred to as currency volatility. Later I will cover this topic from the perspective of the Indian Rupee.

Shifts in Global Capital Flows

In recent years, the topic of foreign investment has been hotly debated in India. Two interesting acronyms have dominated such debates: FDI (Foreign Direct Investment) and FIIs (Foreign Institutional Investors). I will first explain terms like FDI, FII and global capital flows from a business perspective. Later I will cover this topic from the perspective of India Inc. and the Indian Rupee.

A report by McKinsey published in Mar 2013 highlights the churn experienced in terms of global capital flows in recent years. In the last decade, the share of global capital flows going to emerging countries went up significantly from 5% in the year 2000 to 32% in 2012.

The McKinsey report defines Foreign Direct Investment (FDI) as investment that established at least 10% stake in a foreign entity. Roughly 40% of global capital flows in 2012 came under the FDI category.

Global capital flows can be classified into three types: lending by global banks, FDI (as defined by the McKinsey report) and the remaining types of capital flows predominantly flowing into financial markets (bonds and equity). Investments by FIIs fall into the third category. Most MNCs continue to expand into emerging economies through FDI.

Depending on the country, FDI from MNCs was directed towards development of resources, building supply chains, capturing growing market segments and expanding the local presence. From the perspective of the Indian IT and BPM industry, setting up of captive units in India by MNCs and global banks can also be one form of FDI. However, as explained later India has been unable to attract sufficient FDI in recent years. India continues to rely on FIIs.

After 2011-2012, there has been a shift in global capital flows: in short, the landscape of global BFSI (Banking, Financial Services and Insurance) industry has changed. A shift in global capital flows also affects the business model of global banks based in the US and in Europe. Historically they provided bulk of the lending into Asia.

The investment banking units of global banks are major players in Asian financial markets. They operate directly as Foreign Institutional Investors (FIIs) or indirectly on behalf of other FIIs like pension funds based in the US and in Europe.

In Chapters 2 and 3, I mentioned the churn experienced by global banks based in the US and in Europe. Some large banks based in the US have cut back from Europe and expanded into Asia. Many European banks have been forced to withdraw from markets in Asia. Asian banks have done the opposite: they have continued to invest in Asia, while scaling back their investments in Europe. Some Japanese banks have also purchased assets and businesses from troubled European banks to expand their global footprint.

A significant share of revenues for Indian IT and BPM exporters comes from BFSI clients based in the US and in Europe. In Chapter 6, I will explain how the landscape of global BFSI is changing in recent years. I will cover topics like trade finance and investment banking.

During August 2013, when the Rupee suffered a sudden decline, Indian business media discussed this topic. Some experts questioned why India should be worried. After all, a weak Rupee indirectly helps all exporters! In the next section, I will cover the topic of currency volatility. I will explain why a volatile Rupee can be quite damaging for the Indian economy. It can also be a challenge for many Indian IT and BPM exporters.

Each major country across the world manages currencies differently: some actively manage exchange rates; some allow their currencies to float; some impose additional controls on capital flows and interest rates. For countries like India, current account deficits also play an important part.

Currency volatility first hit Japan in early 2011. After March 2011, the value of Japanese Yen (JPY) relative to other currencies went up significantly. After Oct 2012, JPY moved in the other direction. This is not a challenge specific to Japan. Since then, currency volatility has affected exporters in several other countries almost during every quarter.

Why did JPY rise from March 2011 till the second half of 2012? There could be many reasons: the Euro zone crisis, rising oil and gas imports by Japan after the earthquake, the Fukushima disaster, relative weakness of other global currencies, you name it!

Why did JPY depreciate against the dollar between Oct 2012 and March 2013? Again there could be multiple reasons. The dollar strengthened after the Nov 2012 Presidential elections. The JPY weakened after the new Japanese Prime Minister and the Bank of Japan announced policy changes.

Japanese companies across multiple industries suffered losses since March 2011 due to an unexpected rise in JPY. However, many of them did recover in 2013 partly due to the weakening of the JPY and partly due to changes in their business model. As explained in Chapter 6, currency related challenges faced by MNCs can also offer new opportunities for global banks to offer appropriate financial products and services.

Currency volatility during 2013 is not specific to Japan. The Euro weakened after elections in Italy and unexpected events related to Cyprus. After the debt ceiling debate in the US in Oct 2013, the Euro went up relative to the dollar. Indian readers are already aware of the volatility experienced by the Rupee during 2013 on multiple occasions.

From a business perspective unexpected changes in major currencies affect decision making by MNC operating across countries. When economic growth is already slow and uneven across the developed world, this challenge can be significant for some MNCs.

Currency volatility is also caused by external factors affecting the global banking system: they can be outside the control of MNCs as well as their banks. During 2013, regulators across the US, UK, EU, Switzerland and Japan are investigating the functioning of global currency markets.

With so many external variables, global businesses of all sizes must be well prepared to address the challenges associated with currency volatility. In the past, Indian exporters became used to volatility in international oil prices. In recent months, India Inc. is trying to predict the trajectory of the Rupee during 2014. While India's current account deficit is coming down, inflation is going up. A volatile Rupee can be a challenge to all Indian exporters. At least during 2014, this could be the "new normal" for the Indian economy.

Earlier I mentioned about FDI and the McKinsey report (published in Mar 2013) on foreign capital flows. The report highlights some interesting trends associated with emerging economies. The share of FDI (foreign direct investment) in capital flows into most emerging economies except India is quite high. As mentioned in the following paragraphs, India's inability to attract FDI can also lead to a volatile Rupee.

The McKinsey report reiterates what many Indian business leaders have been saying in recent years. For most emerging economies, FDI is the least volatile type of capital flow. Most MNCs have made use of FDI to expand their global manufacturing and supply chains. Many emerging economies have also benefited from this long term strategy of MNCs. For various reasons, India has been unable to attract enough FDI.

India relies on Foreign Institutional Investors (FIIs) for capital flows into the country. These flows are volatile and also affected by unexpected events and developments in the global economy. The Indian economy has few other weaknesses in this context.

One is that India runs a large current account deficit and also a trade deficit. Another is that India's gold imports and the oil import bill are also affected by currency volatility. As a result, the Rupee can affect exporters and importers, one way or the other.

Why should Indian IT and BPM exporters worry about a weak Rupee? Haven't they benefited from it during 2013? The answer to this question is not so simple. Even if the falling Rupee helps one group of Indian exporters, a weak Rupee is much more harmful for the Indian economy: it has already led to high inflation.

If you look deeper, a weak Rupee is not so good in the long term even for Indian IT exporters! This means that costs will keep rising faster than a falling Rupee. They would be unable to offer their employees a reasonable raise in salaries every year. With visa restrictions, inflation and falling margins what options do they have to retain their key employees?

During 2014, it is also difficult to predict the sentiment of foreign investors. Given that 2014 is an election year, Indian policymakers already responded proactively in Dec 2013 before the announcement came from the US Federal Reserve. During 2014, what if the Rupee swings in both directions?

A volatile Rupee could become the "new normal" from the perspective of Indian IT and BPM exporters. This can also affect decision making by many Indian IT exporters pursuing new outsourcing contracts during 2014 and beyond. I will cover this impact in Chapter 7.

Having covered challenges related to a multi-speed global economy, I will cover one interesting topic related to China. This is not widely reported in the Indian business media. This is an interesting development affecting MNCs operating in the Asia Pacific region. It could also affect Indian exporters directly or indirectly.

RMB Settlement: A Game Changer?

In Chapter 2, I mentioned some developments related to the City of London. Interestingly, London, Frankfurt and Singapore are all competing to become global hubs for Renminbi (RMB) trading. In this Section I will explain why RMB trade settlement could affect Asian trade finance. This topic could also be of interest to many Indian exporters and India Inc. operating in the Asia Pacific region.

Why do I call this development a game changer? In recent years, China has aggressively promoted trade settlement involving its own currency, the RMB. As per HSBC, around 10% of China's external trade was settled in RMB during 2012. As per Deutsche Bank, this share could double by the end of 2014.

Such a rapid growth in a short period could have a significant impact on the business model of many global banks operating in Asia. It could also affect MNCs with global manufacturing and supply chains. According to SWIFT*, RMB was the third most heavily used currency for trade settlement after USD and EUR during the first half of 2013. In Oct 2013, RMB moved to the second place.

> * SWIFT, Society for Worldwide Interbank Financial Telecommunication is an industry body related to global payment systems.

Many businesses in Germany, UK and Australia are joining the RMB bandwagon. In each of these countries, the share of RMB based trade settlement grew significantly during 2013. During 2014 could businesses in Canada also explore this option?

In Jan 2012, the British PM announced that London will be developed as an offshore RMB center. Since then, London has grown to a major offshore hub for RMB trading outside Hong Kong. During 2013, Germany and Australia joined the RMB bandwagon.

During 2012, many European companies began trade settlement involving the RMB, so that they can cut down transaction costs. Leading European banks like RBS, Deutsche Bank, HSBC and Standard Chartered have been offering multiple services related to RMB. Global banks are realizing the importance of RMB. During 2012, Citibank and J P Morgan also announced RMB based products and services.

In Oct 2013, China signed bilateral currency swap agreements with the ECB and with the Bank of England. China also extended its RMB Qualified FII (RQFII) program to large banks based in London and in Singapore.

What does this mean from a business perspective? By using a local currency for settlement, Chinese companies avoid currency risks. A 2013 survey by HSBC confirmed that Chinese suppliers could offer MNCs a discount of 3% or more by using RMB settlement.

RMB trade settlement could upset the business model for many MNCs based in the US and in Europe. So far, they have relied on trade settlement based on USD or EUR. RMB settlement could also affect competition between Asian MNCs and MNCs based in the US. The former are likely to accept RMB payments sooner than the latter.

Trade settlement also affects Asian trade finance. So far, MNCs based in the US assumed that RMB based settlement affects their supply chain partners only in China. Now, they realize that it could also have an impact across South East Asia, South Korea, Australia and New Zealand. In short, the impact can be felt across the Asia Pacific region.

Eventually, MNCs based in the US would be forced to catch up with their competitors based in the Asia Pacific region. I am not sure how many US based IT service providers would support them in joining the Renminbi bandwagon so soon.

This is where Indian IT and BPM exporters need to look for a window of opportunity. They currently serve MNCs and global banks based in the US and in Europe. If they get involved in projects related to Asian trade finance, they can also expand their presence in the Asia Pacific region. In Chapter 6, I will cover topics related to Asian trade finance.

Why Growth and Global Competitiveness Matter

Earlier I mentioned two questions asked by global clients of Indian IT and BPM exporters: How can IT help us "grow" our business? How can IT make us globally competitive? MNCs have two categories of global competitors.

1. Companies from Germany and Japan who are already "export engines".
2. Large Asian companies who are already MNCs or aspire to become MNCs. These include companies in China, South Korea and India.

When executives from MNCs refer to growth, they could be referring to different areas:
- Consistent growth in revenues every quarter (short term focus).
- Growth in terms of market share and expanding their global footprint.
- Profitable and sustainable growth (long term focus).

A recent book by the Boston Consulting Group (BCG) titled "The $10 Trillion Prize" covers the opportunities and challenges faced by MNCs in addressing growing markets, especially across China and India.

Global competition also affects supply chain partners. In Chapter 5, I will explain how MNCs together with their supply chain partners are trying to improve the competitiveness of global manufacturing and supply chains.

In the past, MNCs based in the US and in Europe took advantage of what is referred to as labor cost arbitrage. They have driven down cost of manufacturing and service delivery. In the next few sections, I will cover this topic from the perspective of India based captive units of MNCs and global banks.

Labor Cost Arbitrage and Global Delivery

For the past several decades, global automakers manufacture and assemble cars in those countries where labor costs are lower. Across the world, electronic goods, computers and mobile phones are manufactured and assembled at low cost locations.

What began with global manufacturing in Japan and South East Asia has extended to global services delivery from India. In the IT and BPM industry the term outsourcing is well known. During the last two decades IT services delivery from India has also matured: the term global delivery is now part of the industry jargon in India!

During the last decade, MNCs and global banks have taken global delivery to the next level. Earlier, they engaged external service providers at low cost locations to perform business processes. Having understood this model, they have set up their own captive units.

Today, major MNCs and global banks based in the US and in Europe have nearly 1000 captive units located across India. This is no longer about labor cost arbitrage. Having recognized the value of Indian talent, MNCs are leveraging captive units to deliver better business value to their own customers across the world.

MNCs are building deeper skill sets and addressing more sophisticated or high end services through their captive units. Indian professionals located in their captive units are now getting into areas like Big Data and analytics.

At the same time, external service providers based in India have moved away from BPO (Business Process Outsourcing) to BPM (Business Process Management). This is not merely a change in name by industry leaders or by NASSCOM.

This represents a shift in the mix of services rendered: from an operations focus to address management functions. This way, opportunities lost to captive units of MNCs or global BFSI are made up by offering more sophisticated services to global clients.

In recent years, this model is moving to the next level. MNCs are looking beyond IT and BPM services. The question is: Can the Indian industry use this as a window of opportunity to get into high end services? If so how?

In the next few Sections, I will answer such questions. I will explain the new models of labor arbitrage and global delivery adopted by MNCs and global banks. I will also give an interesting example of shared services in the Airlines industry and explain its significance.

New models of Global Delivery

In the past, terms like labor arbitrage and global delivery were typically associated with IT services providers and IT outsourcing. After the 2008-2009 global financial crisis and the 2011-2012 Euro zone crisis, this has changed. In this Section, I will explain how MNCs and global banks have adopted this model in different ways.

Earlier, key functions in a MNC or a global bank were typically located close to their headquarters within their home country or geography. In recent years, this "hydra shaped" structure is evolving into a more globally distributed organization structure.

In many MNCs and global banks, this is referred to as a shared services or a shared delivery model. As a part of reorganization or restructuring, certain functions could be consolidated across business units. Such consolidation can be at a geography level or at the corporate level. Later, this entire function could be performed by a captive unit.

This new global delivery model is already being implemented in India by captive units of MNCs and global banks. Currently India has nearly 1000 such centers employing between 500,000 to 600,000 professionals. This range of employee numbers is based on 2013 reports from consulting companies, NASSCOM and business media.

A majority of them work on software, IT and BPM services. Among those working on product development and R&D, nearly 50% of work is related to software and telecommunications.

Going forward, one can expect India based captive units moving to the next level:

- Some MNCs and global banks with captive units may offer high-end services, innovation and business insight from India.
- Some others may consider selling off those units offering low end services as a part of a global reorganization.

Technology trends and the role played by analytics are also affecting decision making by MNCs and global banks. Earlier, they did not hesitate to outsource certain areas of software development and IT services. In recent years, top management views areas like analytics as business critical as well as business sensitive.

CEOs are also looking at a different business model and a different operating model for global services delivery. They could distribute work between captive units and external services providers based on a new set of criteria. These criteria could include skill sets, business criticality, cost optimization and specialization.

In the Airlines industry, an interesting model of global services delivery is already prevalent. This is explained separately (see box). In the subsequent sections, I will explain new models of captive units and why they are relevant for India Inc.

Example: Code Sharing in Airlines Industry

Typically, one assumes that two global companies in one industry always compete and seldom cooperate. Even if they do, sharing common facilities is unheard of. However, there is one exception you find in the airline industry. Here, Mergers and Acquisitions (M&A) are quite rare. An alternate model referred to as code sharing* is quite common.

Typically, American and European airlines formed alliances across the Atlantic and across the Pacific. This allowed two airlines focusing on two different parts of the world to offer convenient routes for global travel.

The term code sharing refers to a complex alliance between two airlines whereby they share aircrafts and cabin crew. This model has allowed airlines to offer tickets to even those cities across the world where they did not operate a flight themselves.

Code sharing* allowed one airline to issue tickets for flights operated by another airline. This simplified the booking process for airlines, passengers and their travel agents. Code sharing was later extended to cover sharing of cargo, aircraft maintenance and sales functions.

> * The term code sharing refers to how two airlines shared the same flight by serving two sets of passengers. The code was used in the common ticket. It identified which airline issued the ticket (referred to as the marketing carrier) and which airline operated the flight (referred to as the operating carrier).

The code sharing model can be compared to the shared services model discussed later. In recent years, this model has allowed two airlines to share airport services, check in facilities and support staff at multiple airports.

By sharing services and facilities, airlines can address operational challenges like luggage handling, cargo handling, airport transfers and connecting flights at lower costs. In recent years, airlines have made use of this strategy to reap almost all the benefits of M&A without actually merging together!

In the last decade, this has changed to agreements between multiple airlines spread across the world. This helps them improve utilization of large aircrafts, avoid duplicating their infrastructure and also drive down operating costs. Through this strategy, the airline industry has also overcome seasonal demand and rising fuel prices.

How is code sharing in the Airlines industry relevant to Indian IT and BPM exporters? In my opinion as a management consultant, this is a mature model of shared services delivery. In Part 3 of this book, I will explain new business models applicable for Indian IT exporters. I hope some readers can relate this example to an appropriate business model!

New Models for Captive Units

As per a survey by NASSCOM and McKinsey & Co. during 2012, more than 50% of companies with captive units in India expressed their intention to increase their offshore penetration by 15% to 30% over the next 2 to 3 years. Many of them are moving towards a new model, commonly referred to as a shared services model.

Some captive units of MNCs could move away from a dedicated cost center model to a more sophisticated model of shared services. Work may be distributed across captive units and external service providers. Captive units could take on more responsibilities and also be held accountable for results.

The term shared services model is used in two different contexts. One: how services are delivered by captive units. Two: how the captive unit fits into to the overall organization structure within the MNC or the global bank.

In some of them, key functions are already distributed across the world. These roles cover technical, business and/or management functions. Some functions offer specialized services to multiple business units. Some parts of this model are also based on the code sharing model quite prevalent in the airlines industry (covered separately in this Chapter, see Box).

Consulting organizations use multiple terms while referring to this new structure: a hub and spoke model, globally integrated services, extended global enterprise, etc. Accordingly, captive units delivering high end services follow one of these organization structures.

Such captive units leverage technology to offer the necessary environment for collaboration and innovation. Typically, they work in areas like analytics, risk management, procurement, engineering, R&D, quality control, etc. The captive center itself can be part of a globally distributed function within the MNC organization.

Earlier, captive units performed as another back office dedicated to one business unit of the MNC. In what is referred to the shared services model, resources including people in a captive unit may not be dedicated. They can be shared across multiple business units. This new model helps MNCs to achieve economy of scale as well as specialization.

How can India based captive units also move up the value chain? I will provide some ideas in the following paragraphs. Some of them are already implemented by India based captive units. Some others are likely to be on the drawing board. Some may appear to be too ambitious to be implemented by few captive units in India in the immediate future.

Currently, many India based captive units serve as a dedicated cost center. One option is for them to interact directly with multiple business units of their parent organization. While serving them, they can also meet stringent service level agreements (SLAs) and performance metrics on delivery and quality of service.

Over a period of time, they can perform like any other global external services provider. If they can achieve this maturity, what prevents them to be treated as an independent profit center? This is why I mentioned that many of the topics I cover in Part 3 are also relevant to captive units of MNCs and global banks.

In Chapter 3, I mentioned about technology convergence. In this era of mobile apps some MNCs and global banks are looking at setting up an internal "software marketplace" through one of their captive units. Here, business units leverage a "software store": they buy and sell mobile apps to each other. They also share business related ideas to develop new mobile apps instead of "reinventing the wheel".

Here, the captive unit can even function like a software business unit driving innovation across the parent organization. It could even commercialize the mobile apps by selling them to other companies in the same industry. India Inc. needs to pursue such "out of the box" ideas for the industry to move up the value chain.

The question is: can India be the preferred location for such ideas to materialize? More than skill sets, what policy environment in India would MNCs and global banks expect? Could captive units already based in India move towards such a model in the near future? If so, what is required to make this happen? In Part 3 of this book, I will cover more topics related to India based captive units of MNCs and global banks.

In the next two Chapters I will identify some priority areas for MNCs and global banks. Chapter 5 explains a wide range of topics related to global manufacturing and supply chains. Chapter 6 covers topics related to global BFSI.

PART 2

GET CLOSER TO YOUR GLOBAL CLIENT

INTRODUCTION

In Part 1 of this book, I explained the challenges faced by global clients in a multi-speed Global economy. In Part 2 of this book, I will cover specific challenges faced by MNCs and global banks. I will also explain why Indian IT exporters need to change course sooner than later. Otherwise, it will take a long time before they can move up the value chain.

In the following three Chapters, I will avoid using terms like business value, business transformation and innovation. Instead I will offer my own ideas, both directly and indirectly on how Indian IT professionals can get closer to their client's business. Readers can associate my ideas and opinions with the appropriate jargon used in their own organization.

I am confident that Chapter 5 and Chapter 6 will provide industry insight to readers in the Indian IT and BPM industry. The topics covered in these two chapters are also relevant for readers employed in India based captive units of MNCs and global banks.

If readers pursue some ideas, they can also move up the value chain from a professional perspective. Some ideas can be pursued within your current organization; some others can be pursued from outside! Some ideas can also be pursued by becoming an entrepreneur!

CHAPTER 5

Industry Trends—Global Supply Chains

Indian IT and BPM exporters typically serve S&P 500 or Fortune 500 companies. These multinational corporations (MNCs) based in the US and in Europe operate global manufacturing and supply chains. Their businesses are also global in nature.

In Chapter 4, I explained the challenges faced by MNCs and global banks while navigating a multi-speed global economy. This chapter covers topics related to global manufacturing and supply chains. By using an example from global automakers I will highlight an industry shift. I will make use of examples to explain common challenges faced by MNCs based in the US and in Europe. Thereby, I will provide industry insight and enable young Indian IT professionals understand what business value is all about.

In Chapter 4, I covered some topics related to captive units of MNCs located in India. Topics covered in this Chapter are quite useful to Indian professionals already working in captive units of MNCs or seeking a career with MNCs. I will begin by taking a close look at the changing market share of global automakers based in the US, in Europe and in Japan.

Industry Shift: Global Automakers

In Chapter 2, I briefly mentioned the industry churn experienced by European automakers. Only 5 to 10 years back, automakers from 6 countries dominated the world: US, Japan, Germany, France, Italy and Sweden. In the last 5 years, the global footprint of automakers from each of these 6 countries has changed!

The following factors have contributed to the industry churn:

- Global automakers based in the US, in Europe and in Japan have a complex web of cross shareholding and joint ventures spread across countries. In recent years most of them have experienced a fall in demand in their home country.
- Car sales across India, Brazil and Russia crossed 2.5 million during 2012. However demand growth across these three countries slowed down during 2013.
- Global automakers share common suppliers across countries. Their alliances cover purchase of parts, engines and contract assembly. They are trying to rebalance their global manufacturing and supply chains.

In recent years, automakers from India and China have tied up with and invested in European automakers.

1. In 2008, Tata Motors of India acquired Jaguar Land Rover of UK.
2. In 2010, Geely from China purchased Sweden's Volvo Cars.
3. Dongfeng Motor of China operates a joint venture with Renault. In Feb 2014 it purchased a stake in Peugeot.

In recent years, this competitive landscape has changed at various levels for all major automakers: at a country level, in Europe and at a global level. In Jan 2013, Morgan Stanley published a report on global automakers, where it mentioned the race for global leadership as "the clash of the Titans". Morgan Stanley used the term Titans referring to 4 automakers: GM, Toyota, Volkswagen and Hyundai-Kia.

Together, they had 40% share of worldwide sales during 2012. In 2012, Volkswagen came close to challenging GM in terms of volumes: GM sold 9.29 million cars worldwide and Volkswagen 9.07 million. In 2013, Toyota came close to the 10 million mark of worldwide sales (9.98 million). Volkswagen overtook GM: it sold 9.73 million cars against 9.71 million cars sold by GM. In China, VW sold more cars than GM for the first time. This explains the intense global competition among the top three automakers!

During the last few years, global automakers are changing their global footprint and their geographic focus. The Renault-Nissan alliance will be taking joint control of the Russian automaker OAO AvtoVAZ in 2014. Renault already has close ties with Nissan: it is now looking towards China. In Jan 2014, Fiat took full control of Chrysler. The combined company will have a primary listing on the NYSE, be incorporated in the Netherlands and have a tax domicile in the UK.

GM and Ford are gradually pulling back or pulling out of Europe, depending on how you look at it. During 2013, GM made some major announcements. They included:

- The withdrawal of its Chevrolet brand from Europe.
- A shift in its Asia focus with a new headquarters organization in Singapore.
- A decision to stop production in Australia by 2017.

During 2012, Ford announced the closure of two of its plants in UK and one plant in Belgium. In 2013, Ford expanded in Spain and also announced that it will be closing two of its factories in Australia by 2016. In short, Ford is reorganizing its global footprint.

This example is not about specific automakers: this is about global competitiveness and its impact on the global supply chain of major automakers. On the one side, there is a geographical shift in demand. On the other side few automakers are stuck with a wrong product mix and/or a mismatch between plant capacities. They are rebalancing their focus across the US, Europe and emerging markets, especially in Asia.

MNCs in the US and in Europe need to have the ability to withstand shocks in the global economy. The latter is also referred to by the term supply chain resilience. Later I will cover these two topics.

Can Car Sharing Services be a game changer?

Slow economic growth and changing demographics are affecting customer preferences in the US and Europe towards purchase of cars. Recently KPMG published a survey report on the changing face of the global auto industry: Global Automotive Executive Survey 2013.

An overwhelming majority of respondents (72%) mentioned that going forward they anticipate alternatives to car ownership, such as car sharing or pay-on-use to become popular. In this Section, I will explain why this is interesting from an auto industry perspective.

In major European cities, the balance is tipping away from car ownership towards other alternatives. Such a shift in demand can cause a major churn in the European auto industry. It also affects the supply chain of automakers and auto dealerships.

Like car sharing services, many public services related to transportation are gaining acceptance in the developed world. These offer city dwellers new options to move around the city and also reduce the costs associated for public utilities. Many reasons contribute to this shift: economic environment, government policies, smart grid initiatives, traffic and road conditions, energy and environmental concerns. These offer new opportunities for the IT industry to leverage social media, analytics and mobile computing.

In the US, driving cars is the most preferred option. Car ownership, like house ownership is part of the American psyche. However, many younger Americans are using options like car sharing services and public transportation.

In the past, US automakers have relied on consumer credit to improve their sales. If car sharing services become popular, it can still make an impact in some states and some cities across the US. Why did Avis purchase ZipCar for $ 500 million? Nearly 60% of ZipCar's customers are younger than 40.

In Chapter 2, I mentioned that German automakers are pursuing new business models like selling used cars and launching car sharing services. In Europe, Daimler's Car2Go service and BMW's car sharing venture DriveNow are the major options. This could have an impact on the current business models of other European automakers.

How is this example relevant and useful to Indian IT professionals? Experts refer to the growth of car sharing services using an interesting term: a subscription economy. Here, you pay for usage of transportation services instead of an ownership based model.

Across Europe, if car sharing services become popular, it could also disrupt conventional taxi services in major cities. While taxis charge you based on distance, car sharing is charged by the hour (by ZipCar) or by the minute (by Car2Go and DriveNow). Both Daimler and BMW are ramping up this city based service across Europe.

Across many cities in the US, two new business models are gaining acceptance:

1. Car sharing services like ZipCar, Enterprise CarShare and Car2Go.
2. Ride sharing apps and services like Uber and Lyft.

Industry experts anticipate that new businesses would leverage smart phones, GPS, call centers, social media and mobile apps to expand this market significantly in the next few years. This is why Indian IT professionals need to take a closer look.

A pay per use business model of car sharing is quite different from purchasing or car leasing. In addition to basic car sharing services, new businesses can offer a wide range of sophisticated services to young, tech savvy customers. These include insurance, gas cards and incentives. Given the high prices of electric cars, this business model could expand in many different ways in the next few years. I am sure some readers can also compare the business model of car sharing to that of cloud computing in the IT industry!

Retail Industry and Consumer Goods

In Chapter 3, I mentioned shifts in the US retail industry. In this Section, I will cover challenges faced by the retail industry and supply chains of MNCs offering consumer products. The challenges faced are quite different from those faced by global automakers. They relate to the fulfillment side: exploding variety of products, volatile demand, shorter product life cycles, etc.

In recent years, MNCs are rapidly expanding into China, India, Africa and other emerging markets. They need to address typical challenges like fulfillment of volatile customer demand, adapting to shifts in demand, global competition etc. They also need to address supply chain bottlenecks.

Experts in the retail industry and MNCs offering consumer products talk about agile supply chains. This term refers to their ability to change direction and respond to a change in market conditions. For example: sudden changes in demand and seasonality.

In Chapter 3, I mentioned the challenges faced by UPS and Fedex in the US during the Christmas shopping season. Similar challenges can be faced by MNCs. If they can't respond quickly to a spurt in demand, they will lose an opportunity to sell their products. They could even incur big losses in fulfillment.

MNCs can't quickly change their supply chain partners. However, they can always quickly reconfigure the supply chain to address changes in demand. They can change the mix of products across the supply chain "on the fly" based on changes in the demand side. The change could be in terms of product brands, packaging, product models or variants.

Reconfiguring the supply chain means making changes at the appropriate stage without causing a disruption. In global supply chains, decisions have to be taken on the right mix of product brands, product models or variants. Typically, such decisions have to be taken on the fly while ordering for parts, while manufacturing and while shipping.

Here, managers keep looking at the way forward. They also make decisions together with their supply chain partners based on up to the minute information. This way, they avoid causing a disruption in the supply chain.

MNCs based in the US and in Europe are expanding in large emerging markets like China and India. As a result, product variety is increasing in terms of features, price points and product-service combinations. For many Fast Moving Consumer Goods (FMCGs) the demand is seasonal in nature with a large number of sales outlets. Some products have a short shelf life. Demand is volatile for many consumer durables and electronic items.

As a result, MNCs face some unique challenges. The number of supply chain partners, distributors, sales outlets and SKUs (stock keeping units) are multiplying. This exploding product variety increases the costs associated and puts a lot of pressure on their supply chains. MNCs are addressing these challenges through automation and reducing costs per transaction. In recent years, the internet, digital technologies, use of barcodes, RFID and GPS have become widespread.

These avoid paper based transactions and manual intervention where there could be chances of errors creeping in. They have also helped MNCs reduce cost per transaction at each stage of global supply chain. Cloud computing could be another option.

As I explained in Chapter 2 and Chapter 3, demand is shifting in the US and in Europe. This is happening due to multiple reasons: slow and uneven economic growth, demographic shifts, changing customer needs and preferences, changing patterns of saving and spending, you name it! This also puts additional pressure on the global supply chains of MNCs.

Short Product Life Cycles, Product Mix Challenges

In consumer durables and electronic goods, in addition to growing variety, MNCs face multiple challenges associated with shorter product life cycles. In many of these products, MNCs have a short time window for sales. In this Section, I will provide some examples related to major Japanese companies.

In consumer electronics, challenges associated with product life cycles are quite complex. Since 2008, the big three Japanese companies, Sony, Panasonic and Sharp have experienced different types of challenges. As a result, each of them had to change course.

In the past, they had invested in LCD displays and high end TVs where demand has been shrinking. Each of them suffered due to a product mismatch and increased competition from Samsung and LG in major markets. As per one estimate, their combined losses in 5 years ending March 2013 amounted to $ 38 billion.

In 2012, Sony's top management announced that they would shift the product focus away from TVs and display technologies towards mobile devices, imaging technology and gaming. In Feb 2014, after suffering huge losses during 2013, Sony took some tough decisions. One was to sell off its PC division. Another was to hive off its TV business into a separate business unit. However, Sony's top management mentioned that its "three pronged strategy" would still be pursued.

For many MNCs, product life cycles (PLCs) are getting squeezed. The time associated with developing a new product and the time to market must be drastically reduced. The costs associated across the PLC need to be optimized in spite of increased variety.

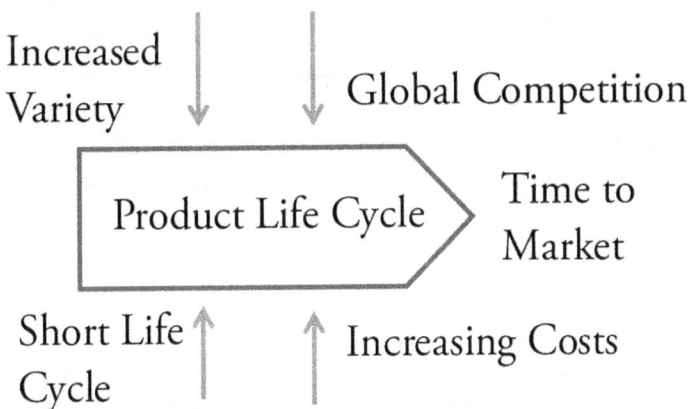

For many MNCs, managing the product portfolio in a multi-speed global economy can be quite challenging. This implies that engineering functions are also undergoing a major transformation across many MNCs. Topics related to engineering and R&D services are covered separately (see Box).

For high value consumer products and industrial goods, MNCs need to manage product life cycles (PLCs) across different countries. Sometimes, mature products in one country can't be "recycled" to another country. However, MNCs can still achieve economy of scale by managing their global product portfolio more effectively.

Many MNCs are looking at new strategies based on product platforms. As mentioned in the earlier example, automakers are designing cars for multiple countries. They are building multiple models based on the same platform.

Increasingly, MNCs need to manage the PLC together with their supply chain partners. This adds another level of complexity from an engineering and management perspective. Later I will explain how MNCs are collaborating with their supply chain partners in addressing common challenges.

So far, I explained an industry shift and challenges faced by MNCs. In the next Section, I will explain why competitiveness matters a lot for MNCs operating a global manufacturing and supply chain.

Growth and Global Competitiveness

Earlier I mentioned that growth and global competitiveness are both important. What does this mean? While MNCs are expanding their global manufacturing and supply chains, they take a global view. Of course, politicians in the US as well as in Europe will try to influence some decisions. Ultimately, MNCs need to take the tough decisions.

After March 2011, Japanese automakers faced a series of multiple shocks: an earthquake, the Fukushima disaster (that led to electricity shortages), flooding in South East Asia, a rising Yen, slow growth across the US and Europe, you name it!

However, by early 2013, the three major Japanese automakers: Toyota, Honda and Nissan recovered and also took advantage of a falling Yen. During 2012, Honda increased its global sales by 19% reaching 3.82 million cars. The global sales of Nissan grew by 5.8% to 4.94 million cars. During 2013, Honda became a net exporter from the US.

During 2013, business media reports have compared VW and other German automakers with their European competitors. Long before the Euro zone crisis, VW had expanded into Central and Eastern Europe. With multiple plants across Europe, VW is able to offer the right models at the right prices in many countries across the European continent.

This helped VW to consolidate its position across Europe in spite of the Euro zone crisis and setbacks in Western Europe. By crossing a major landmark of 9 million cars sold worldwide in 2012, VW also demonstrated that it remains resilient at a global level.

Like Volkswagen in Germany, Toyota in Japan has withstood multiple challenges associated with the global economy. In the US, Toyota faced quality problems and product recalls. Toyota also lost market share to GM in China. In Feb 2014, Toyota announced that it would stop manufacturing in Australia by 2017.

Yet, Toyota increased its share of the US market to 14.4% in 2012 from 12.9% in 2011. Toyota also retained its lead over GM in worldwide sales during 2013. In the years ahead, one needs to watch the global race between Toyota, GM and Volkswagen.

The examples mentioned earlier in the context of global automakers are also relevant for other MNCs engaged in manufacturing. This is why Indian IT and BPM exporters need to move beyond cost optimization towards making their MNC clients globally competitive.

Recently a report in The Economic Times referred to what it called as "one car wonder stories" of Renault, Ford, Nissan and Honda in the Indian market. It doesn't matter if global automakers have a few successful models in China and in India: they need to build volumes. This is possible only if they remain globally competitive.

In the past, automobile industry experts emphasized economy of scale, cost optimization and efficiency. Automakers have now realized that they can't become globally competitive by cutting costs in one country and expanding the supply chain in another country. Growth in volumes and global competitiveness go together. To manage this effectively, they need to integrate the demand side (sales, fulfillment and marketing) and supply side from end to end.

Automakers are looking at different ways to leverage their manufacturing and supply chains to become globally competitive. They are also adapting their business model and taking advantage of technology in different ways. They are learning from global leaders in every industry and applying best practices.

Today, MNCs are analyzing patterns of demand and sales at a "local" level. They are trying to understand customer preferences, buyer behavior and local competition. They are applying this knowledge to quickly respond from a supply chain perspective. They are making necessary changes to their existing supply chains "on the fly". In every country and in every market segment, they are trying to remain globally competitive.

In the previous sections, I mentioned some common challenges faced by MNCs.

1. A mismatch between production capacity in one country or region with demand.
2. The need for MNCs to reconfigure their supply chain to balance supply and demand.
3. The need for them to review and manage their product mix.

Each of these have to be done proactively: this requires business insight, especially customer insight. Later I will cover these two topics.

Earlier, automakers typically designed an entire car for one of the three major market segments: US, Europe or Japan. Now, they are designing a car that suits China, India and a few other countries with minor modifications.

Through modular designs, they can utilize excess capacity and also reconfigure their supply chain if and when required. Another strategy is about a common product or a common platform. Global players like Volkswagen and Hyundai-Kia have been quite successful in using this strategy.

German automakers like BMW, Daimler and Mercedes Benz are exporting cars originally designed for China to markets in the Middle East and Latin America. Each of them is taking advantage of their superior quality and reliability by selling used cars across Europe. This is why some of their European competitors are so worried.

Earlier, automakers followed a model of "global manufacturing" spread across different countries. They are now extending this model to engineering, product design and product development. These jobs are also distributed at multiple locations across the world.

There are many more examples of how successful European companies are expanding their global footprint in spite of challenges in their home countries. To name a few: Unilever, Nestle, Siemens, Philips, the list can go on. Indian IT and BPM professionals need to borrow ideas on how to improve global competitiveness from some of their own clients.

In 2012 and 2013, global consulting organizations have published reports on changing priorities in the area of manufacturing and supply chain management. They highlight one common theme: a shift from cost optimization to areas like supply chain resilience, agile supply chains and risk management. In the next two sections, I will cover these topics.

Supply Chain Resilience and Agility

In the past, MNCs aggressively pursued cost optimization and Just in Time manufacturing to drive down costs. In the last 5 years, their global supply chains experienced multiple shocks. As a result, most MNCs have realized the risks associated with putting "too many eggs in one basket". They priorities have changed.

In this Section, I will explain terms like supply chain resilience and supply chain agility. A resilient supply chain is capable of withstanding shocks or disruptions. An agile supply chain can be reconfigured by MNCs and its supply chain partners. Both these terms highlight the changing priorities of MNCs.

The term resilience refers to quickly bouncing back from unexpected shocks. If an MNC's supply chain is not resilient, a part of it could break down or not be able to function properly. This is why MNCs are leveraging technology to improve supply chain resilience.

Earlier I mentioned the term agility in the context of the retail industry. This term applies to the supply chain of MNCs. Agility is the ability to quickly reconfigure supply chains in response to shifts in the demand side as well as in the supply side.

An agile supply chain offers more options for MNCs and their supply chain partners to respond. The response time required would be lower if the supply chain is more agile. Agility will require robust processes at the MNC level as well as at the supplier level. Resilience and agility can be an important competitive advantage for MNCs in addressing growth markets. Technology plays a key role in both these areas.

Successful MNCs demonstrate both resilience and agility. They are leveraging analytics in both these areas. Using analytics, they can evaluate "what if" scenarios in their supply chains before they can be reconfigured. They can make use of advanced mathematical models and statistical techniques to predict what could happen. Accordingly, they work with their supply partners to make necessary improvements or changes, as applicable.

The supply chain partners of MNCs also need to respond quickly with a sense of urgency. They must meet the necessary criteria in terms of product quality. If quality is not consistent, reconfiguring a supply chain will not be satisfactory. MNCs could face problems at a later stage in terms of product quality, customer satisfaction or both.

During natural disasters, MNCs can reroute supplies, make use of alternate warehouses or storage locations. If one or more suppliers are unable to perform during a disruption, an MNC could deploy another supplier. All these can be part of reconfiguring a supply chain. By doing so, a supply chain can continue to function in spite of external shocks.

Production may be shifted from one factory that has been disrupted to another factory not affected by the disruption. The two factories could even be located in two different countries. Supply chain reconfiguration can also apply to transportation, warehousing and logistics. While reconfiguring supply chains, MNCs need to integrate them with the underlying processes. For example, ordering, fulfillment and delivery must happen in the same manner so that customers don't face any challenges.

A supply chain can't be modified or reconfigured without prior planning and performance assessment. In order to successfully reconfigure a supply chain, MNCs need to build both resilience and agility over a period of time. Each supply chain partner needs to be adequately prepared. Each supply chain partner needs to understand and follow the MNC's processes.

Improving supply chain resilience and agility will require significant investments. These investments can be in terms of tools, techniques as well as processes. Each of them can be addressed through appropriate technology based solutions.

In the past, MNCs have resorted to outsourcing functions related to supply chains. While they continue to do so, they are retaining control at an appropriate level. This is to ensure that their global supply chain performs satisfactorily from an end to end perspective. This is why vendors of supply chain solutions talk about end-to-end capabilities.

In recent years, Airbus and Boeing have experienced delays and quality related problems while launching new aircraft models. The reasons could be related to poor collaboration or inadequate supplier integration across their global supply chain.

Collaboration is therefore very important when MNCs launch a new product or a new initiative. They will need the cooperation and participation of all their major supply chain partners. For a global company like Caterpillar, one can imagine the number of suppliers and the complexity involved in supplier integration!

By working in a collaboration mode, the supply chain partners play an important role in ensuring the success of a new product or a new initiative. This is where joint planning and working in a partnership mode are important for all MNCs.

Decision Making in Global Supply Chains

In recent quarters, many MNCs operating in emerging markets were affected by currency volatility. They include prominent names like Wal-Mart, Unilever and Coca Cola. Typically, such companies with a global footprint have been managing currency risks for several years. As I explained in Chapter 4, this time, it is different!

As mentioned earlier management priorities of MNCs are also changing. As a result of these, decision making in global manufacturing and supply chains is becoming more complex. In this section, I will explain its implications.

MNCs need to be well prepared to address volatile demand. They may also be required to respond to shocks affecting the global supply chains. They need to quickly respond if or when required. Their executives therefore realize the importance of "need for speed" in decision making related to global supply chains.

Technology deployment can help MNCs to reconfigure their existing supply chains in two ways:
1. It enables MNC executives to make more data driven decisions.
2. It also helps them make faster and more informed decisions.

Managers of global supply chains use terms like efficiency, effectiveness and productivity. Each of these areas can be improved by appropriate technology based solutions. Indian IT and BPM professionals need to understand these terms from a business perspective.

Apart from reducing inventories, MNCs are focusing on more effective utilization of cash and working capital. For example, before placing orders, MNCs would like to make an independent assessment on their supplier's ability to deliver. This could involve making an assessment of the supplier's cash position or requirements for additional working capital.

They would also like to optimize working capital across multiple suppliers and negotiate a better deal. They may offer better credit terms if required. I will cover this topic later from the perspective of supply chain financing. Increasingly, MNCs are avoiding a "one size fits all" approach on supplier credit: they are tailoring them to each supply chain partner. Such decision making will require a lot of collaboration.

The challenges and trends mentioned earlier affect many MNCs. This is not only about managing costs, improving capacity utilization and productivity. What applies to one country may not even be relevant in another. Today, MNCs need to look beyond national and geographical borders.

They need to manage their product mix in every market segment they operate in. They are building agile supply chains and also improving supply chain resilience. They are leveraging global resources across the world through better product and platform strategies.

From the perspective of supply chains, MNCs based in the US and Europe need to address multiple and conflicting goals. They need to strike the right balance between their global aspirations. How can they remain competitive in mature markets and also pursue growth opportunities elsewhere in the world?

There is also an opportunity cost in addressing growth markets. MNCs can't afford to be a junior player in key market segments. This could affect their brand image and positioning.

In mature markets like the US, Europe and Japan, MNCs need to prioritize between the market segments they are currently addressing. They may even be forced to withdraw from slow growing market segments. Does this explain why Ford and GM seem to be gradually pulling out of Europe?

Today, supply chain management is not about cost optimization alone. It is about optimally utilizing factory capacity, supply chain capacity and fulfillment on time. Accordingly, MNCs and supply chain partners are addressing problems from an end to end perspective. Their needs and expectations of supply chain solutions have also changed.

In recent years, MNCs with global supply chains are also struggling to strike a balance between old fashioned retailers with physical outlets and emerging retailers leveraging the internet infrastructure. Both groups fiercely compete with each other. Some MNCs can get caught on the wrong foot in meeting challenges associated with fulfillment.

In many countries, customer preferences are changing: ordering on the internet is becoming more acceptable for high value consumer durables and electronic goods. In Chapter 3, I mentioned some developments during the Oct to Dec 2013 holiday shopping season in the US. Many US retailers are adapting to this "new normal" of the industry.

Some consumers may visit a retail outlet for "window shopping" or a "demonstration" while actually making their purchase on the internet. This way, they can get "more bang for the buck". Some others who are technology savvy may do the opposite. They would complete their "window shopping" on their mobiles. This way, they not only manage to get the best deals from physical stores, but also save time and effort. In short, customers are able to leverage the best of both worlds: malls and internet retailers.

Some MNCs are trying to look at the "big picture" across their physical retail outlets and internet based outlets. They are trying to optimize cost of fulfillment while reducing the overall inventories across their supply chain. Their decision making is based on leveraging technology: it is also data driven.

MNCs are trying to improve metrics like sales per employee across their physical retail outlets as well as internet based outlets. They are also focusing on collaboration with retailers to maximize sales, while avoiding conflicts.

As I explained earlier in this book, Amazon is disrupting the current business model of the retail industry in the US and in Europe. Amazon is forcing the retail industry to embrace technology. All other retail and fulfillment businesses have to stay competitive. They are now moving to the next level in terms of cost optimization, efficiency and productivity.

Some of them are trying to reduce the cost per transaction (or focus on cost optimization). Some others are trying to increase revenue per employee (focus on improving sales). Few of them are leveraging external service providers to handle fulfillment and delivery.

This competition between different types of retailers can affect the supply chain infrastructure of MNCs. Their sales and marketing functions need to adapt accordingly. They need to strike a balance across their supply chain and avoid unnecessary conflicts.

In this balancing act, Chief Marketing Officers (CMOs) of MNCs are leveraging appropriate technologies. These could be Big Data, analytics, social media, mobile devices, you name it. Accordingly, supply chain solutions are becoming more sophisticated. Topics related to Big Data and analytics are covered separately (see box).

Big Data, Analytics and Business Insight

In Chapter 3, I explained the importance of analytics in the context of US businesses. I also mentioned convergence of multiple technologies. In this section, I will explain the terms Big Data and Business Insight from the perspective of MNCs.

MNCs are collecting data in real time from multiple sources. Part of this data is structured while much of it is still unstructured. The term Big Data encompasses all of these. This term is also gaining importance with global banks and global BFSI.

The term "Big Data" refers to three V's associated with data: volume, velocity and variety. In recent years, the volume and variety of business related data generated by MNCs is exploding. The market for large and specialized databases has grown. Software vendors like SAP are positioning their HANA database in a wide range of industries and client environments.

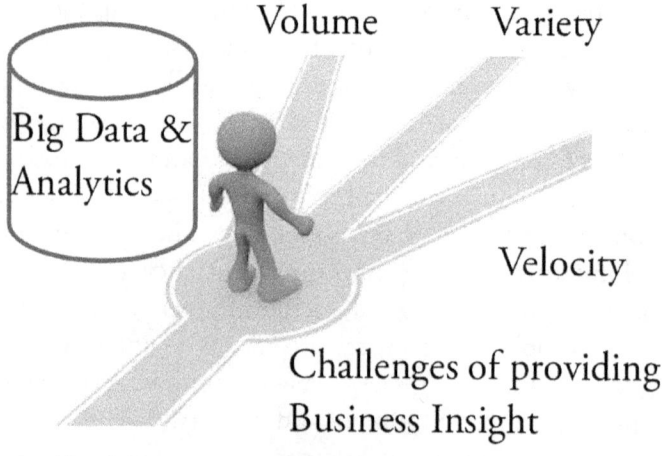

In a supply chain scenario, the term business insight refers to supply chain insight as well as customer insight. Such insight helps supply chain executives make informed decisions. Considering its importance, many MNCs are setting up captive units to focus on analytics.

In the past, concepts like Just in Time were used to optimize inventories across the supply chain. MNCs are moving to the next level by leveraging analytics. They use terms like smarter fulfillment: this goes beyond optimizing inventories.

For example, analytics can help MNCs avoid operational challenges in the supply chain. They can simulate scenarios and be prepared to address challenges related to storage space and logistics. They can collaborate with their supply chain partners to avoid bottlenecks during a peak season. They can address typical challenges experienced during a holiday shopping season.

Analytics is also an area where MNCs are looking at the appropriate model for captive units as a part of their strategy for global services delivery. Most MNCs conduct business in multiple countries. They also operate global manufacturing and supply chains. Analytics can help them identify and address new opportunities across countries.

Captive units specializing in analytics can help the MNC optimize costs associated and get more "bang for the buck". This can include "what if" scenarios, simulation, use of statistical techniques and mathematical models.

The skill sets required for analytics are complex: they may not be available from external service providers. This is why MNCs are looking at setting up a dedicated captive unit for analytics. Through specialization, these captive units can serve multiple business units. MNCs can also leverage them to develop sophisticated analytical models over a period of time for their major businesses.

Can Indian BPM exporters expand into analytics? Some of them are already doing this. However, skill sets required for analytics are quite different from BPM or ADM services. Analytics is more about problem definition and problem solving. As I will explain in Part 3, skill sets alone can't help them to be successful in this new business.

In some situations, the problem associated with a supply chain may not be well defined even in MNC organizations. Business managers may be looking at symptoms instead of the real causes of a problem. Analytics can help them arrive at the right problem definition. It can also help managers evaluate alternate solutions in terms of pros and cons.

A solution applied in one part of the supply chain can affect other parts of the business of the MNC. Analytics can therefore enable managers and executives make informed decisions like reconfiguring the supply chain. While collaborating with supply chain partners, MNCs are also leveraging analytics. They can evaluate responses or alternative solutions to complex problems. They can use simulation to choose the best options available.

Leveraging Technology in Supply Chain Solutions

For MNCs, technology has always played an important role in managing global supply chains. In recent years, their priorities are shifting. In this Section, I will cover these shifts from the perspective of technology based supply chain solutions. In the next Section, I will explain its implications from the perspective of Indian IT and BPM exporters.

During the last two decades, MNCs based in the US and in Europe have made use of packages from Oracle and SAP to manage their supply chains. Earlier, MNCs focused on two areas: optimizing costs and improving efficiencies. In recent years, productivity improvement across the entire supply chain is a priority area.

MNCs have realized the importance of leveraging technology to enable them quickly expand their global footprint. They need not have a large supply chain when compared to their competitors in each growth market. As long as the supply chain remains resilient and agile, they can still be effective. If they face supply chain disruptions or volatile demand, they can mitigate the risks associated by reconfiguring their supply chains.

In recent years, MNCs with global supply chains have reconfigured their supply chains from a cost perspective as well as to improve their global competitiveness. They have improved their processes to increase the output, reduce cycle time and thereby get more "bang for the buck". This means better outcomes for the same inputs.

In recent years, the focus has also shifted from the physical supply chain to the financial supply chain. The former covers better utilization of physical assets, optimizing costs and reducing inventories. The latter relates to the flow of money and covers optimization related to financial assets like working capital. MNCs are offering extended credit facilities to their global suppliers directly or through banks.

Typically, MNCs operating global manufacturing and supply chains have relied on global banks based in the US and Europe as well as regional banks in Asia. Global banks help MNCs manage risks associated with currencies and interest rates. Regional banks also offer products and services to the supply chain partners of MNCs.

MNCs are leveraging the power of internet and digitization to move away from paper based transactions to electronic transactions with their supply chain partners. One example is e-invoicing. The terms trade finance and Supply Chain Financing (SCF) are used in this business. In recent years, both MNCs as well as global banks are developing sophisticated SCF solutions. I will cover these topics in Chapter 6.

Both MNCs and their supply chain partners must have sufficient visibility on each other's side. In the past, MNCs have been sharing information with their supply chain partners as and when required. There are many areas where leveraging technology can improve supplier insight. One area is supply chain visibility (SCV). The term visibility applies to orders, payments, forecasts etc. for better planning and readiness.

In recent years, MNCs are leveraging the power of internet to extend their information systems beyond organization borders and beyond geographical borders. Today MNCs as well as their supply chain partners use collaboration software and sophisticated tools. Supply chain partners routinely access and update the information systems of MNCs.

A significant number of employees in MNCs as well as their supply chain partners are always "on the move". Mobile computing can therefore make a significant impact in global supply chains. In earlier applications, MNCs as well as their supply chain partners typically provided status updates to each other.

Thanks to smartphones and internet, they have moved to the next level to offer better visibility to each other. Areas include ordering, shipping, fulfillment, warehousing, logistics, you name it! In the next few years, with wearable devices, they can move to a higher level of supply chain collaboration.

This is where supply chain visibility, collaboration and analytics together play an important role going forward. Analytics can help MNCs to develop alternate scenarios and identify bottlenecks so that they can be addressed proactively. Collaboration can help them and their supply chain partners to jointly address common challenges.

Implications for Indian IT and BPM Exporters

Indian IT and BPM exporters serve MNCs with global supply chains. What opportunities can they pursue going forward, especially in a multi speed global economy? In this Section, I will provide some answers.

Typically, MNCs and their supply chain partners make use of packages in their global manufacturing supply chains. They are in areas like customer relationship management (CRM), enterprise resource planning (ERP) and supply chain management (SCM).

In recent years, cloud computing solutions and services are gaining importance in this market segment. Cloud computing allows MNCs to share data, share applications and provide better supplier insight. It also reduces costs associated, avoids duplication and associated errors. At the same time, there are challenges because some packages have been customized in the past. MNCs are looking at deriving benefits in the following ways:

1. To operate their supply chain beyond organization boundaries together with their supply chain partners.
2. To address challenges in fulfillment on the demand side by offering appropriate solutions to cover distributors and sales outlets.
3. To build in resilience and agility in their supply chains.

In this market, Oracle, SAP and Salesforce.com are the major players. The Software as a Service (SaaS) option in cloud computing is changing this landscape. Increasingly, MNCs are looking at converting fixed costs into variable costs by taking advantage of usage based pricing. As a result, the economics of cloud computing is becoming more important than technology based features in this market segment. More topics related to cloud computing will be covered in Part 3 of this book.

Earlier in this book, I mentioned an important question asked by CEOs of MNCs: How can we leverage IT to grow our business? Many CEOs are looking at new ideas to "scale up" their supply chains. They are not looking at a specific technology. They are also looking for a solution provider; not a service provider offering lower rates.

If Indian IT and BPM exporters can leverage their business and domain knowledge, they can also to provide answers to the questions mentioned above. It is important for them to move away from a primary focus on offering services at lower costs to delivering real business value. You can call this business transformation, innovation or whatever industry jargon you like. I would consider this a part of moving up the value chain.

Why are European competitors of German automakers getting worried?
1. Is it because they have been less successful than Volkswagen (VW), BMW and Daimler in exporting cars?
2. Is it because these three automakers are disrupting their business models by selling used cars and offering car sharing services?

Technology has a role to play in pursuing new business models. Of course, German automakers are ahead in this game. However, what prevents their global competitors to leverage technology and pursue a different business model?

This is why Indian IT and BPM exporters need to identify an industry shift. By doing so, they can offer innovative solutions to their MNC clients to try new business models. To do this, they need to first understand their client's business. In the past, they have partnered with package software vendors. They need to take such partnerships to the next level. If they are willing to change their old business models, they can move away from support services that are getting commoditized.

There are many options to serve their clients better. They can leverage their technology skills to offer custom solutions. They can address integration issues. Small and Medium Indian IT exporters can also offer specialized solutions in niche market segments.

Today, MNCs are expanding rapidly into new growth markets. Many of them are making huge investments to improve their global supply chains. In the past, Indian IT exporters focused on a services model primarily in the US and in UK. Going forward, they can play a bigger role not only across Europe but also across the world.

MNCs will continue to leverage the power of analytics and move to the next level in decision making. They would combine the power of supply chain insight together with customer insight. They would also reap the benefits of end-to end intelligence across their entire supply chain. However, their expectations from service providers would also go up!

Technology can be leveraged to improve transparency and avoid manual intervention across the global supply chain. Both MNCs and their supply chain partners routinely track the status of shipments on their own. They provide regular updates to each other on the progress being made. Many such solutions are customized for MNCs and their supply chain partners.

Which Industry Vertical?

Typically, global IT services companies adopt a complex matrix organization based on industry verticals. However, this can lead to a situation where they may be trying to offer a "one size fits all" solution to diverse companies in one industry segment. Instead, they can look at group of companies in multiple industries with close business relationships. This is sometimes referred to as a cross industry approach. In this Section, I will give some examples to explain where this approach can be used.

In Chapter 2, I gave an example of mobile payments. Here, a cross industry payment solution can be explored. One part of it addresses the retail business; the other part of it addresses the banking side. A similar approach can be used for a global supply chain. This extends beyond the borders of an MNC organization to include supply chain partners.

During 2013, many large Indian IT and BPM exporters have been talking about an organization structure based on industry verticals. While competing with global players, a better approach would be *not* to follow a similar industry vertical based organization structure. Sometimes, one needs to look beyond artificial borders created by an industry vertical structure. I will explain why in Chapter 6 and Chapter 10.

It is better to adopt an organization structure best equipped to address the business opportunities. It is more important to align this based on the portfolio of your global clients. If you are trying to address an industry shift, an old industry vertical based structure may not always be the best approach.

Here is my suggestion for my friends working with large Indian IT exporters. Instead of disrupting your own organization structure, why can't you disrupt the current business model of your global competitors like IBM? Can you leverage startups and SMEs based in India and develop an alternate business model?

In my opinion, changing the organization structure alone may not give a head start for large and medium IT exporters in India to move up the value chain. Instead, they need to focus on an appropriate business model. One example could be a sound cross industry strategy addressing multiple industry segments.

If you take a closer look at global software vendors like SAP, you can appreciate this better. SAP is positioning its HANA database in multiple industry segments. By taking advantage of technology convergence, SAP wants to grow faster than its competitors.

Global banks as well as the global IT industry on both sides of the Atlantic are watching SAP AG. In recent years, SAP is building an ecosystem around its HANA database to address a wide range of opportunities in Big Data and cloud computing.

Having signed up more than 2100 corporate customers for HANA, SAP can generate downstream opportunities for many customized solutions and services. In Dec 2013, SAP announced a new initiative in India for supply chain solutions. In Chapter 6, I will mention some interesting announcements from SAP in the global BFSI space.

Engineering and R&D Services

Earlier I explained the industry shift in the global automotive industry. The challenge is to optimize costs in each phase of the entire product life cycle. This involves multiple disciplines like R&D, engineering, product design and development. In recent years, MNCs are leveraging technology and global services delivery to manage their product life cycle.

Today, MNC executives would like to reduce product development costs, while demanding higher throughput and better quality. They would like to create a stream of new products and product variants to serve different market segments across the world with smaller budgets.

In 2012, Carlos Ghosn of Renault Nissan coined the term "frugal engineering". Since then, some business leaders in India have also used this term in the context of offering a better value proposition from India in the area of engineering services.

India has a large pool of engineering talent. In recent years, R&D outsourcing from India is growing. Can Indian IT exporters move up the value chain from product support services into high-end services related to engineering and R&D?

NASSCOM is quite optimistic. As per one of its estimates, Engineering and R&D Services exports from India could reach a size of $ 40 billion by 2020. As per NASSCOM, India now has a 23% of the global engineering and R&D outsourcing market. Currently almost 50% of India based captive units engaged in this market segment offer services in two major industry segments: software and telecom.

Of course, Indian engineers routinely work on different phases of the software life cycle with their counterparts in the US and Europe. However, not many of them have the necessary experience working across the entire product life cycle involving other engineering products.

So far, Indian engineering teams have looked towards their parent units or "headquarters" to award work to India based captive units. When will they be able to say "this is what the market segment needs, and here is a specific product idea or a product proposal on how the need can be met by the India team"? For this you need product management expertise, architects and technical experts. Many captive units in India have a long way to go before they can reach this stage.

In the past GE has leveraged Indian talent for product development and R&D related services. Boeing and Airbus have also utilized engineering talent from India. In recent years, many jobs in engineering and R&D in global companies are distributed across the world. As per one expert, only 35% of the Boeing 787 Dreamliner parts are made in America. Another 35% comes from Japan's "Heavy Industries": Mitsubishi, Kawasaki and Fuji Heavy Industries respectively. What would it take for Boeing or Airbus to consider India as an important location for engineers working on their new generation of aircrafts?

Each MNC has different needs and expectations about Indian talent before they can even consider deploying them on global design teams. In this market segment, engineers need to address complex challenges across the entire product life cycle with global teams. It could also involve integration across the global manufacturing and supply chains. Building the necessary skill sets would take time, effort and investments.

To address this growing market, Indian IT exporters need to move away from a service delivery mindset to demonstrating a problem solving approach. They need to become trusted and reliable business partners to their MNC clients before getting into this space. This may even require a new business model altogether. However, it is time for India Inc. to make a beginning, sooner than later. These topics will be covered in Part 3 of this book.

CHAPTER 6

Industry Trends—Global BFSI

Many Indian IT and BPM exporters depend on global Banking, Financial Services and Insurance (BFSI) clients for a significant part of their revenues. In this Chapter, I will cover a wide range of topics related to global BFSI. I will also consolidate BFSI related topics covered in Chapters 2, 3 and 4 to highlight the industry shift in some of the major banking businesses.

In Chapter 5 I covered topics related to global manufacturing and supply chains. Global banks are associated with MNCs in two ways.
1. They offer a wide range of financial products and services to MNCs based in the US and in Europe.
2. Global banks are closely associated with trade finance and global capital flows. The challenges faced by MNCs also affect their business models.

In this Chapter, I will extend the topics covered in Chapter 5 to explain trade finance and Supply Chain Financing (SCF).

Topics covered in this Chapter are relevant for Indian professionals associated with the IT industry as well as the BPM industry. They are also useful to readers employed by India based captive units of global banks. I will begin by highlighting the industry churn in global BFSI. I will expand specific topics later.

The Post Financial Crises BFSI

In recent years, economists, banking experts and consultants have offered some interesting opinions on the impact of the 2008-2009 global financial crisis and the 2011-2012 Euro zone crisis on global BFSI. In this Section, I will mention some of them: I hope they would give readers a "big picture".

In the US and in Europe, slow and uneven economic growth has affected the demand for banking products and services. In addition, interest rates have remained low over an extended period of time during the last five years. In Chapter 4, I mentioned the global shift in capital flows. All of these affect the business model of large banks.

On the one hand, large banks are trying to expand their global footprint. On the other hand, each bank in the US or in Europe is facing a different set of challenges. Few banks face a shortage of capital; few others are carrying risky assets and are trying to repair their balance sheets; few are even restructuring. All of them highlight an industry churn.

Several consultants have mentioned that offering financial services now involves operating two diverse businesses: the "business of money" as in the past and the "business of information" going forward. This is one reason why there is an industry shift.

In the last few years, central banks across the world have followed policies to maintain low interest rates. This implies that the "cost of money" is lower than what it was before 2008. This has a significant impact on the business model of global BFSI. At the same time, the "cost of information" has gone up. In this Chapter, I will explain why this is significant from the perspective of the IT industry.

Across the world, like the retail industry, the banking industry is discovering the "value of information". On the one hand, the retail industry is looking at spending habits of consumers and patterns of spending. On the other hand, the banking industry is looking at both spending and saving habits of retail customers. With low interest rates, banks of all sizes are facing revenue and/or profitability challenges. Slow and uneven economic growth is affecting their corporate clients in almost every country.

Another area affecting large banks across the US, Europe and Asia are changes in regulations. They have been introduced by multiple regulating agencies. In Chapter 2 and Chapter 3, I mentioned about changes in regulations across the US, UK and Europe. Many of them pertain to investment banking businesses. Changes pertaining to capital requirements such as Basel III affect all banking businesses directly or indirectly.

With global competition, bank executives at various levels talk about "customer centricity" and customer insight. This applies to all banking businesses, especially retail banking and corporate banking. All these have caused an industry shift or an industry churn in global BFSI.

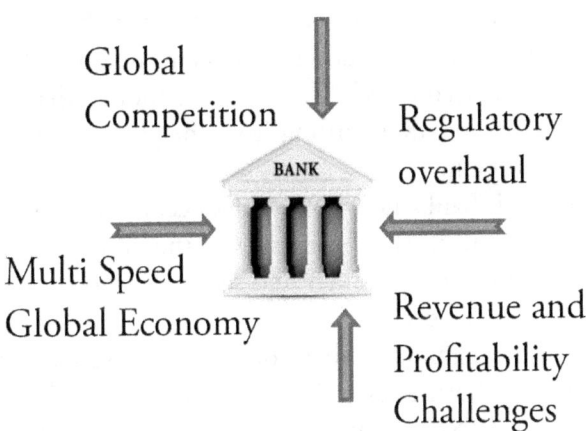

Understanding Industry Churn

In recent years, the landscape of retail banking is changing rapidly. In some retail banking businesses, the borders between old fashioned banks, retailers and non-finance companies is disappearing. Instead of physical branches and personal relationships, technology is becoming a key differentiator in this business. As a result, technology is causing an industry churn, leading to winners and losers.

Some global banks are ahead of the curve: they have avoided the financial crisis and/or made timely investments in technology. Many have successfully leveraged the internet; some have also introduced mobile banking. These technologies have enabled them to cut costs, improve efficiency and also improve productivity. They are now moving to the next level: growing the banking business and making use of social media and analytics.

In recent years, banks are also being challenged by IT companies and new players offering mobile payment solutions. Some smaller banks are challenging their bigger competitors. Thanks to smartphones, customers find mobile payments more convenient and cost effective compared to credit cards and debit cards.

Economic uncertainty and changes in regulations have led to increased focus on risk management. Its importance is being realized by banking executives at various levels. Earlier, the focus was more oriented towards risk reporting and regulatory compliance. Now, risk management is becoming more proactive and tied to each banking business. Large banks are also leveraging the power of Big Data and analytics in this area.

In Chapter 5, I explained developments related to global supply chains and challenges faced by MNCs. I also mentioned that the focus of many supply chain executives is shifting from the physical supply chain to the financial supply chain.

On the one hand, banks need to leverage technology based solutions themselves to stay ahead in this business. On the other hand, they have an opportunity to offer new products and services to both MNCs as well as their supply chain partners.

In recent years, a significant share of banking revenues comes from transaction banking businesses. However, not all banks have been successful in serving MNCs. Many banks are trying to reduce the "cost per transaction" from the perspective of MNCs in different ways. They are offering new products and new services to help MNCs as well as their supply chain partners manage their global supply chains.

Several global banks are expanding their trade finance business. In this business, old paper based transactions like use of check payments and LCs (letters of credit) are being replaced by e-invoicing and electronic payments. Thereby, banks can reduce transaction costs and also get a bigger share of business from MNCs and their supply chain partners. As I will explain later, companies like SAP are offering new solutions in this market segment.

In the following sections, I will expand each of these trends and developments. I will explain the pros and cons from the perspective of Indian IT and BPM exporters.

Understand Industry Reports and Surveys

During 2012, several industry reports and surveys have been published on trends related to global BFSI. Business media in the US and in UK have also carried reports on global banks. In this section, I will mention some of these findings at a high level.

The global investment banking business is dominated by large banks based in the US and in Europe. In April 2013, business media reports in the US, Europe and UK covered FY 2012 results of major global banks. Revenues and profits from investment banking differed widely across major global banks based in the US, UK and Europe.

One report in the Wall Street Journal compared 2012 revenues and profits of investment banks with 2006 levels. In recent years, US banks have experienced a dip in revenues, but have been able to maintain profitability.

The top 5 investment banks in the US (excluding Lehman) experienced a 13% fall in revenues during this period. The corresponding drop in pretax profits was 14%. Between 2006 and 2012, the top 5 European banks suffered a 22% fall in investment banking revenues. The corresponding drop in pretax profits was more significant, at 61%. Indeed, the business of investment banking is experiencing a churn in many ways.

Why did investment banks in Europe experience a significant drop in profitability? European banks have been experiencing a churn almost every year since 2008. After the 2008-2009 global financial crisis, the Euro zone sovereign debt crisis affected Ireland. After Ireland was bailed out in 2010, Greece came next. The Euro zone crisis has led to a significant industry shift for BFSI in the European continent.

A May 2013 report by Morgan Stanley and Oliver Wyman mentions a geographical shift in the global investment banking business. I will explain this in simple words avoiding industry jargon. One part of the industry shift is a change in the geographic focus by global banks. Some US based banks are reducing their footprint across Europe. Some European banks are pulling back from their US based subsidiaries and US operations. Many large banks are changing their business mix across different geographies.

In Chapter 5, I gave an example from the global auto industry to highlight the changing landscape of global automakers. The geographical shift is also leading to winners and losers among global banks based in the US, in Europe and in Asia.

Contrary to predictions in early 2011, many Asian banks have grown faster during 2012 and 2013. Many of them did not suffer a major hit from the Euro zone crisis. They are filling in the vacuum created by large banks based in the US and in Europe. In recent years, some European banks have expanded significantly into Asia and Africa. It was reported that Standard Chartered Bank has 64% of revenues from the developing world.

As a result, few European banks have grown during 2012 and 2013 in spite of the Euro zone crisis. In the next few years, how will large banks based in the US and in Europe expand into Asia? How will Asian banks expand their global footprint? These are interesting trends to watch.

In Chapter 4, I mentioned that large banks have begun offering Renminbi based trade settlement. Technology is also playing a big role in supply chain financing. Later I will relate these two topics while covering the business of trade finance in Asia.

Regulatory Overhaul

In the past, haven't global banks faced changes in regulations? How is it different this time? Regulatory overhaul is happening at a time when global banks are still recovering after the 2008-2009 global financial crisis and 2011-2012 events related to the Euro zone. Multiple regulatory agencies in the US, UK and Europe are driving these changes. The time line for regulatory compliance is also quite different in the US, Europe and rest of the world.

This time, the number of changes involved and the scope of changes is quite large. Common changes across the US and Europe such as Basel III relate to investment banking and risk management. In areas like anti-money laundering and trading of derivatives, global banks need to comply with regulations from multiple agencies. Projects related to regulatory overhaul are likely to be large in size, complex and extending for a longer duration.

With London being a global financial center, the impact of regulatory overhaul is more complex for banks located in UK. They need to strike a balance between financial markets of US and Europe*.

> * Here is a partial list of banking and insurance related regulations where the clock has begun ticking in Europe: Basel III, European Market Infrastructure Regulation (EMIR) and Markets in Financial Instruments Directive (MiFID) II.

> * Here is a partial list of US regulatory requirements: the Foreign Account Tax Compliance Act (FATCA), the Dodd-Frank Act and the Volcker rule.

As I mentioned in Chapter 2, there are many other developments affecting the City of London. What applies to a European bank based in London may not apply to another European bank based in Eurozone or elsewhere in the EU.

Many global banks were affected by banking scandals either directly or indirectly. In the last few years they relate to the following areas:
1. Manipulation of the London Interbank Offered Rate (LIBOR), a global benchmark for interest rates.
2. Anti-money laundering.
3. Allegations of rigging the global currency market.

How do these developments affect IT service providers? They need to understand the long term implications of regulatory overhaul and banking scandals:
1. The outcome of investigations on some banking scandals could lead to more changes in banking regulations across the world.
2. Regulatory overhaul and regulatory compliance could remain "work in progress" for the next few years.
3. More than job cuts in global BFSI, a slow process of job redistribution has been triggered by regulatory overhaul across many banks.

Accordingly, Indian IT exporters operating in global BFSI need understand this from their client's perspective. In the past, bank executives viewed IT in terms of its role in regulatory compliance and reporting. In recent years, IT is playing a bigger role in risk management. Later I will cover topics related to risk management and analytics. I will also explain the significance of job cuts and job redistribution in global BFSI.

In the next two sections, I will cover topics related to investment banking and retail banking. I will explain how the industry shift affects each of these two businesses.

Impact on Investment Banking

In recent years, many global banks have experienced a fall in what is referred to as FICC revenues (Fixed Income, Currencies and

Commodities). For the top 5 US based banks, the 2013 FICC revenues were 9.4% lower when compared to corresponding FICC revenues during 2012. The impact on revenues can be due to many reasons:

1. In recent years, the Euro zone crisis forced many investment banks to reduce their holding of what is referred to as "risky assets".
2. Many global banks have undergone a process referred to as deleveraging. In simple words, this means repairing both sides of their balance sheets.
3. Regulatory overhaul, especially Basel III requirements forces banks to seek additional capital. The Volcker rule in the US imposes additional restrictions on certain types of trading. As explained earlier, the impact and timeline for compliance may differ.
4. In anticipation of regulatory overhaul or in response to changes in regulations, some banks have begun a process of reorganization.

Each of the above affects revenues and profitability in different ways. As a result, many global banks are reviewing different aspects of their investment banking business. They have prioritized them based on a detailed assessment of risks. Some have accumulated additional capital; some have downsized or even sold off entire businesses. As a result, many of them appear to be "leaner" than what they were a few years back.

In recent years many European banks have undergone restructuring, implemented job cuts and even pulled back from few businesses in the US and in Asia. Since 2011, European banks have revamped their balance sheets: they have reduced their risky assets on the one side and increased their capital on the other side.

Historically, global banks have maintained a certain mix of investment banking and retail banking businesses. Typically, the two sides (investment banking and retail banking) follow a different organization structure. In the next few years, this could be modified to meet regulatory requirements in specific countries or specific regions. In recent years, regulatory agencies in the US, UK and Europe are proposing changes that could affect this business mix or force European banks to restructure. The process of reorganization and restructuring in many European banks is still work in progress.

Some banks have leveraged technology to reduce transaction costs and improve profitability in their FICC revenues. In Jan 2014, the Swiss

Bank UBS struck two deals to outsource most of its fixed income trading platform. Large banks like Goldman Sachs, J P Morgan, Deutsche Bank and Morgan Stanley have restructured their commodities businesses.

Indian IT and BPM exporters need to understand these developments from a business perspective. Investment banks are optimizing the costs associated with trading platforms, expanding the use of analytics and consolidating their IT and networking infrastructure. They are also focusing on risk management.

Impact on Retail Banking

In recent years, slow and uneven economic growth has affected the retail banking business. The demand for many retail banking products and services has changed in the US and in Europe. In the past, retail banks expanded through branches and physical infrastructure. In many countries, rising costs and banking regulations impose constraints on this option.

Across the US and in Europe, large banks are cutting back or even consolidating their branch infrastructure. They are making use of sophisticated ATMs, internet banking and mobile banking. In short, retail banking has become technology intensive.

Customers are demanding more facilities and more options from their banks. I mentioned in Chapter 3 that banks in the US need to upgrade older technologies like Windows XP based ATMs and replace magnetic stripe based cards with chip based credit cards and debit cards.

In the retail banking business, CEOs and CFOs are asking some interesting questions while making IT investments. How can IT help our bank reduce transaction costs? How can IT help us retain customers and also offer them a wide range of banking services?

Banking executives understand that they need to strike the right balance. Too many options will increase the cost per transaction and render the retail banking business unprofitable. Offering too few options could upset existing customers.

After offering a new technology based option, banks are also evaluating the customer experience and transaction costs. They are making necessary changes as required. Many banks in the US and in Europe are not trying to offer all services to all types of customers. They would like to remain competitive by offering a better customer experience.

On the one hand, they would understand customer preferences by leveraging technologies like social media and analytics. On the other hand, they would reduce transaction costs through mobile banking and internet banking. Some banks are also specializing in retail banking services and banking channels. In short, banks are leveraging technology in smart ways so that they can grow their business faster in a multi speed global economy.

Banks can leverage social media and mobile banking to collect valuable data pertaining to customers. They can also make use of analytics for decision making on banking services. However, as I explained in Chapter 3, customers are also worried about data security and privacy. On the one hand, banks can't afford to upset customers by being intrusive. On the other hand, they don't like to lose an opportunity to offer a new product or a new service to existing customers. How do banks strike a balance?

While encouraging customers to leverage internet banking or mobile banking, banks are also addressing concerns related to data security and privacy. They realize that a bad experience could affect customer satisfaction and customer retention. I will cover the topic of mobile banking in the next Section.

Beyond Borders: Mobile Payments

Across the world, and especially in Europe, mobile banking, e-commerce, digital payments and the retail industry are converging together. In this Section I will explain this marketplace from the perspective of Indian IT exporters. I mentioned in Chapter 2 that payment systems in Europe extend beyond borders: to cover multiple countries.

In the past two decades, IT has played a key role in how money flows between banks across the world and how banks process these payments. The system has evolved from checks, clearing systems, credit cards, debit cards, Automated Teller Machines (ATMs), Point of Sale (POS) devices and the list continues.

In recent years, extensive use of mobile phones, especially smartphones has changed this landscape. The convergence of mobile payments with social media, Big Data and analytics also offers new interesting opportunities for IT products, IT solutions and IT services.

The borders between banks, retailers, mobile network operators and payment system providers are changing. From a business perspective, mobile transactions are much richer in terms of data delivered. At the same time, a mobile payment option offers more convenience to customers. In the past, large banks in the US and in Europe have issued credit cards and debit cards. These business models are challenged by mobile payments where the fees payable to banks can be lower!

It has become quite common during 2013 to find two diverse companies from two different industries coming together to offer a solution involving mobile payments. The same mobile payment solution can be viewed differently by the banking industry and by the retail industry. This is why one needs to take a fresh look at old ways of industry segmentation. This is what I refer to as looking beyond borders.

For many large banks, choosing and implementing a mobile payment solution can be quite complicated. They can't afford to upset their customers by not offering convenient and less costly options. New mobile payment methods need to coexist with older systems, especially credit cards and debit cards in the US. In addition, data security and privacy concerns need to be addressed. Any solution therefore can be quite complex.

On the one hand, banking solutions need to be country specific in Europe. On the other hand, payment systems also extend outside the European continent. Mobile payments are also becoming popular across Central and Eastern Europe. In many of these countries, internet penetration is not as widespread as that in Western Europe. In addition, there could be country specific issues to be addressed like taxation.

European banks also operate outside the European continent. They cover Middle East and Africa. This is sometimes referred to by global banks as EMEA region. A wide range of mobile payment options, including mobile wallets are offered across the EMEA region. However, when European banks offer mobile payments outside the EU, there may be specific taxation and regulatory issues to be addressed.

In many countries across Asia and Africa, mobile payment is addressing a majority of customers who haven't used any form of electronic banking in the past. This could be a new paradigm for many banks based in the US and in Europe.

Given the geographic diversity, each European bank looks at mobile payment solutions from its own perspective. This can be quite challenging for IT companies. All these imply that external IT service providers need to take a closer look before jumping into offering a solution.

What are the implications of these trends from the perspective of IT companies? They need to offer appropriate solutions while addressing complex issues related to technology, data security, cost of transactions and convenience. For many global IT vendors, striking a balance between these divergent criteria could be a challenge. This is why Indian IT and BPM exporters need to play multiple roles like a consultant or a solution provider.

Here is a question for managers in large Indian IT and BPM exporters who talk about an organization structure based on industry verticals. If you have a mobile payment solution, does it belong to the banking industry or the retail industry? As I mentioned in Chapter 5, sometimes it is better *not* to create artificial borders by an industry vertical structure. It is more important for you to become a solution provider than demonstrate an industry vertical based organization structure of a global competitor!

Industry Shift: Mix of Banking Businesses

As I mentioned earlier, the industry shift also relates to the change in business mix. This term can be used in different contexts:
1. The mix between two major segments, investment banking and retail banking.
2. The geographic mix of banking businesses pursued by large banks.
3. Customer focus in terms of banking products and services.

In terms of geography, large banks are prioritizing their businesses across the US, Europe and Asia. In terms of customer focus, they are offering MNC clients a different mix of banking products and services. For example, trade finance is a major focus area for MNCs in Asia.

Going forward, global banks could follow a different mix of investment banking and retail banking in the US, in UK, in Europe and in different parts of Asia. Accordingly, they would be leveraging technology based solutions quite differently. This has a direct and indirect impact on Indian IT and BPM exporters.

Typically, many IT companies have followed an industry centric approach to solutions associated with BFSI. They offer a solution common across multiple countries, and sometimes global in nature. This "one size fits all" approach needs to change in many countries, going forward.

How many IT companies will be able to offer a "comprehensive" banking solution? Even if they offer one, would it be cost effective for every global bank? Later I will cover the topic of technology deployment in global BFSI. I will also explain new market segments where a cross industry focus can be more effective.

Across the US, Europe and Asia consulting companies and banking experts are looking at "next generation" banking models. Under these models, each bank would offer specialized banking channels catering to different market segments. Each channel offers a set of services based on one or more models of customer relationship.

In the next few years, global banks in the US, in Europe and in Asia would pursue different "next generation" banking models. However, each global bank could leverage technology in a different way.

What do these trends and developments imply? IT companies across the world can no longer use a one-size-fits-all approach to banking solutions. The economics of technology deployment would differ across global banks. Their business mix and business model could be quite different in the US, in Europe and in Asia.

This is why Indian IT exporters of all sizes need to identify the right opportunities. They can't afford to remain general purpose service providers. They need to become solution providers. It makes sense for each of them to understand customer preferences among their BFSI clients. They need to identify which segment they would specialize on. In some cases, they need to adopt a country or a region specific strategy instead of one across global BFSI.

Typically, business media reports in the US and UK have covered industry trends related to banking in two areas: investment banking and retail banking. Large banks based in the US and in Europe are also focusing on another business: trade finance.

This business covers areas like supply chain financing and transaction banking. It is typically associated with global manufacturing and supply chain of MNCs. In the next two sections, I will cover the industry shift related to trade finance in Asia and Supply Chain Financing.

Asian Trade Finance

Rising exports from Asia, especially China, South Korea and South East Asia has led to rapid growth in the trade finance business across Asia. This business is closely associated with global manufacturing and supply chains of major MNCs. Many European banks are now targeting Asian businesses aspiring to become MNCs. Instead of loans and deposits, they are focusing on sophisticated banking services related to trade finance.

During 2011-2012, business media reports in the US and in UK highlighted the challenges faced by European banks. One area where they lost market share was in Asian trade finance. Interestingly, large banks based in the US did not fill the vacuum created: Asian banks made significant gains as a result of this industry churn.

The 2008-2009 global financial crisis and the 2011-2012 Euro zone crisis have affected the competitive landscape of global BFSI especially in Asia. In June 2012, Thomson Reuters reported how the lending pattern in the Asia Pacific region changed between 2007 and 2011. During this period, the share of European banks dropped from 29% to 19%. At the same time, Asian banks improved their share from 61% to 70%.

The trade finance business is related to global trade and global supply chains. In May 2012, reports from Morgan Stanley and Dealogic covered trade finance in Asia. In end 2010, Euro zone banks excluding German banks had a 43% share of this market.

By 1Q 2012, two Japanese banks, Mitsubishi UFJ and Sumitomo Mitsui improved their combined share to 26%, making substantial gains. American banks are trying to "catch up" in this fast growing market.

A May 2012 report from Morgan Stanley and Dealogic highlighted gains made by Japanese banks in this market segment. In end 2010, Euro zone banks excluding German banks had a 43% share of this market. By 1Q 2012, two Japanese banks, Mitsubishi UFJ and Sumitomo Mitsui improved their share to 26%, making substantial gains. So far, large banks based in the US have made marginal gains in this rapidly growing market segment.

In the next few years, Asian trade finance is likely to be affected by few major developments.

1. RMB trade settlement mentioned in Chapter 4 is already expanding beyond South East Asia and South Korea. In April 2013, China and Australia made a currency deal whereby this could also expand in the Asia Pacific region.

2. Supply Chain Financing (SCF) mentioned in Chapter 5 is gaining importance. In the next section, I will cover topics related to SCF.

3. Many IT vendors are leveraging analytics, mobile computing and cloud computing to offer sophisticated solutions. These technologies are likely to be deployed in banking solutions and services related to trade finance.

Supply Chain Financing (SCF)

In Chapter 4, I mentioned that interest rates are divergent across different countries. I also mentioned a shift in global capital flows. In recent years, these two developments have affected global supply chains and the business of trade finance.

In Chapter 5, I explained the challenges faced by MNCs in managing their global manufacturing and supply chains. Interestingly, these challenges offer an interesting business opportunity for large banks.

In recent years, MNCs are taking advantage of low interest rates and access to credit. They are offering additional benefits to their supply chain partners. This is evolving into what MNCs and global banks refer to as supply chain financing (SCF).

This could be driven by multiple objectives.

1. Supply chain partners, especially SMEs across Asia are facing challenges related to high interest rates in their home country.

2. Apart from liquidity, SMEs require hand holding by MNCs so that they have access to credit facilities and can quickly respond to changes in the supply chain.

3. By offering SCF, MNCs can optimize their working capital and also negotiate lower pricing, driving down costs associated in their supply chain.

4. By offering this "carrot", some MNCs based in the US and in Europe can get a competitive advantage when compared to their competitors in Asia.

This can be a win-win combination for both MNCs and their supply chain partners. Global banks are also seeking growth opportunities through this stream of business. Indeed, this is evolving into entire business ecosystem across global banks, few local and regional banks in Asia, MNCs and their supply chain partners.

However, there are still some operational challenges for MNCs in implementing SCF across countries. Any payments across borders will need to comply with regulations and address taxation issues. These can be country specific or at a global level.

While assessing the credit risk for suppliers and managing working capital, especially cash, MNC executives will need additional support. This is where large banks come in.

Typically, MNC executives have the necessary knowledge and expertise to manage the physical supply chain: covering the flow of goods. They are good at optimizing inventories and reducing costs. However, while managing the financial supply chain involving the flow of money, they still need expert advice.

Banks have better knowledge of the financial supply chain (FSC). They are conversant with regulatory requirements and taxation issues. They are good at addressing risks associated with currencies and interest rates.

In this business, global banks based in the US and in Europe are likely to offer sophisticated solutions to their MNC clients. Different banks use terms like transaction banking, SCF and financial supply chain management (FSCM) in this stream of banking business. They offer a wide range of products and services. Many services also extend beyond the MNC organization to supply chain partners.

For European and Asian banks, this business can extend across the Middle East, South East Asia, Australia and New Zealand. It would also involve multiple currencies other than USD, EUR and JPY.

Why do I refer to this as a business ecosystem? This involves a complex web of transactions: business to business, corporate to bank and interbank transactions. There are many opportunities for MNCs as well as global banks to leverage technology, optimize costs and offer value added services to supply chain partners.

The term SCF covers a wide range of functions and services related to supply chain partners. These functions may be spread across the MNC organization as well as a global bank which is supporting the MNC.

Typically services like E-invoicing offered to supply chain partners reduces transaction costs and optimizes working capital for MNCs. In recent years, global banks also share risks and responsibilities with their MNC clients. They offer multiple options for payment such as payment hubs. They handle bank to bank transactions at a country level by partnering with local banks. In some situations, the global bank would even authorize payments to supply chain partners on behalf of their MNC clients.

This new business ecosystem is quite different from traditional systems like ERP and treasury management used in the past. Global banks are working with IT product vendors and external IT services providers to offer advanced payment hubs. Global banks are also trying to expand their footprint across Asia through this business.

Job Redistribution in Global BFSI

In Chapter 4, I mentioned two terms: labor cost arbitrage and a shared services model. Indian IT and BPM exporters need to understand the process of job redistribution happening with their major BFSI clients.

A Dec 2012 report in Financial Times estimated that three global investment banks: Bank of America, JPMorgan and Deutsche Bank were planning to move 3000 jobs from the City of London to other locations in UK. Another report in late 2012 mentioned that UBS was cutting 10,000 jobs. By early 2013 it was clear that UBS was moving out of investment banking and expanding its wealth management business. In the US, it was reported in July 2012 that since 2008, Credit Suisse cut 500 jobs in the New York area and also added 450 jobs in North Carolina.

At the surface, it may appear that large banks are downsizing or cutting jobs related to investment banking. You need to look deeper at the pattern of job redistribution.
1. Global banks are moving out of high cost locations in New York and London. They are also consolidating and restructuring their banking business.
2. Many European banks are expanding into the Middle East, in North Africa, in Central and Eastern Europe.
3. Few European banks are changing their business mix. For example, Swiss banks are focusing on wealth management while they scale down some other investment banking businesses.

Large global banks based in Europe are following different patterns in job redistribution. Some of them are reorganizing their US operations due to two reasons. One, of course is cost optimization. Another is related to impact of US regulations. Likewise, few US banks are prioritizing their businesses across Europe. If or when European banks redistribute their businesses and operations inside or outside of Europe, how does it affect US banks directly or indirectly?

All European banks have a significant presence in London. Typically, investment banking in Europe has been London centric. If European banks are moving away from London to locations elsewhere in the European continent, what are the underlying reasons? Some European banks could be taking a long term view on the role likely to be played by London as a global financial center. In Chapter 2 and Chapter 4, I explained how the Euro zone crisis is affecting the City of London and UK.

Indian IT and BPM exporters need to assess the long term impact of these geographic shifts. Accordingly, they need to identify new opportunities to expand their share of the global BFSI industry segment.

Job redistribution in global BFSI is not about cost cutting: it is a process of business transformation. Accordingly, Indian IT and BPM exporters need to leverage their banking knowledge as well as technology skills. They need to look beyond old models of IT outsourcing. In Part 3 of this book, I will cover these topics.

Risk Management, Big Data and Analytics

How do trends and developments associated with risk management in BFSI affect Indian IT and BPM exporters? These have to be viewed from multiple perspectives.

1. What are the time lines for compliance as mandated by regulatory agencies? What internal deadlines are being set by CEOs or CFOs to their CIOs?
2. How can IT reduce the cost of regulatory compliance?
3. How can IT offer better support to the function of risk management?
4. What role can be played by technology, especially Big Data and analytics?

In addition, they need to leverage their industry knowledge to understand the "big picture". How are global banks addressing regulatory compliance and risk management in the long term? They need to look at the organization structure being adopted by each global bank in addressing this function. Here are a few specific areas to look at:

1. Does the organization structure involve some form of a shared services model? If so, would this eventually lead to a global bank setting up captive units in low cost locations?

2. How could this affect external IT and BPM service providers going forward?

I explained risk management earlier in the context of regulations. Together, the 2011-2012 Euro zone crisis, regulatory overhaul and outcome of investigations into scandals highlight the need for better risk management practices.

In recent years, the function of risk management has undergone a major shift. From an earlier focus on regulatory compliance and risk reporting, this function is moving closer to the banking business. This applies to investment banking, banking services to corporate clients and retail banking. The focus of risk management differs in each of these businesses.

Faced with economic uncertainty across the US and Europe, this has become a priority for CEOs and CFOs of global banks. Increasingly, banks are leveraging technology, especially Big Data and analytics in assessing and managing risks. This way, they can reduce costs associated and also maintain profitability in spite of the uncertainty.

Earlier, banks analyzed multiple silos of data from a limited perspective. Using Big Data, they are now able to leverage analytics to perform risk assessment in real time while processing loan applications.

This is also being done before important decisions are taken in multiple banking businesses. Bank executives also use risk dashboards for assessment and reporting of risk at multiple levels. Regulations like Basel III also focus on risk management.

The role of analytics in credit risk management is also gaining importance. Credit risk has to be assessed by banks periodically for corporate clients. On behalf of MNCs, banks need to assess risk for supply chain partners in global manufacturing and supply chains. Typically, MNCs as well as their banks have additional controls in areas like anti-money laundering.

Analytics is also becoming important from the perspective of security and preventing fraud. As banks deploy sophisticated solutions across the world, they are also facing challenges associated with data security, privacy and fraudulent transactions. This affects their reputation and is therefore a priority area from a management perspective.

Priorities for Technology Deployment

In global BFSI, technology is an enabler to the business and also a differentiator from a competitiveness perspective. Earlier I mentioned that banks operate two businesses: one pertaining to money and the other pertaining to customer information. Increasingly, bank executives are leveraging technology in both these areas.

In recent years, economic uncertainty, changing demographics and multi-speed growth are driving technology adoption in different ways. Banks are relying less on physical infrastructure of branches. They are also leveraging technology to understand customer preferences and build relationships.

In the past, technology investments were focused on reducing transaction costs. In addition to cost optimization, CEOs and CFOs of global BFSI clients are now trying to grow their business while optimizing the capital required.

A technology based banking solution must address the changing priorities of bank executives. In the past, each banking business leveraged technology to improve efficiency. Going forward, they need to support more clients and more number of transactions so that banks can drive down costs per transaction.

In recent years, banks engaged external IT and BPM service providers in different ways. They scaled up the business without additional investments on infrastructure and without hiring more people. Process improvements and automation were used together with BPO (Business Process Outsourcing). In recent years, this is changing.

Large banks based in the US and in Europe are operating in a multi-speed global economy. They have a wide choice of technologies related to banking. However, deploying each of them would also require major investments. For some banks, this is a challenge.

Going forward, global banks based in the US, Europe and Asia will follow a different strategy towards technology related investments. In addition to IT outsourcing, banks will look at multiple options for global services delivery.

Many large banks are looking at avoiding capital costs and conserving the capital to be made available to expand new businesses. In such a scenario, they are likely to avoid investing on IT infrastructure and communication infrastructure. Accordingly, they would structure IT outsourcing deals with external services providers.

Large banks are evaluating various options for cloud computing from the perspective of data security and privacy. Once these areas are addressed, investments would follow. Eventually, they will choose an appropriate cloud computing model to convert fixed costs into variable costs. This way, they can balance their revenues and profitability.

Banks would achieve cost optimization in different ways. They are likely to pool their capital investments on critical functions like analytics and risk management. Such investments will include state of the art technologies and software. This will allow banks to get the best out of technology deployment.

Going forward, each global bank based in the US or in Europe could adopt a different strategy for technology deployment. In Part 3 of this book, I will explain how Indian IT exporters can play a bigger role in helping their clients choose and deploy new technologies.

In Chapter 4, I mentioned about captive units being set up by MNCs and global banks. In the next Section, I will cover this from the perspective of global BFSI.

Captive Units in Global BFSI

Like many MNCs, large banks would consider setting up a captive unit in low cost locations where infrastructure and skills will be shared by multiple business units. For the current India based captive units of global BFSI, this needs to be viewed from multiple perspectives:

1. Would the industry shift encourage large banks based in the US and in Europe to set up their own captive units or expand existing ones?
2. What work would they outsource to external service providers going forward?
3. How would a large bank choose between near shore and offshore options?

While engaging external service providers, banks would look beyond cost optimization. They will distribute work across captive units and external service providers. By leveraging multiple skill sets, they will get the best of both worlds to achieve specialization.

In business critical and sensitive areas, they are likely to leverage captive units. In analytics, they could choose service providers on a selective basis. In short, the old model of IT and BPM outsourcing could change going forward.

Each global bank is addressing risk management and analytics at multiple levels: in each business unit; at a country level, a geography level and at a corporate level. Accordingly, the choice of a captive unit or an external service provider can differ at each level.

In recent years, a number of India based captive units in the BFSI space have been either set up or expanded their operations. These include captive units of Citibank, Deutsche Bank, Standard Chartered Bank, Fidelity, Franklin Templeton and Goldman Sachs.

Each global bank is also likely to make a clear choice on what type of work will be performed by captive units and what would be outsourced. Indian IT and BPM exporters need to get used to this "new normal" in global BFSI, sooner than later.

Many large banks based in the US and in Europe already operate captive units offering BPM services. Multiple business units can leverage some of them using a shared delivery model, as I explained in Chapter 4. This could be a part of the bank's strategy to apply a global delivery model, optimize the costs associated and also drive specialization.

In Big Data and analytics, banks are exploring the development of sophisticated models. Typically, this work is closely tied to their banking business. In such areas, banks typically avoid engaging external service providers. However, all the skills required for analytics can't be developed by a captive unit. In such cases, external service providers could be used on a selective basis to provide the necessary skill sets.

In Chapter 7 and Part 3 of this book, I will cover more topics on captive units by MNCs and global BFSI from the perspective of Indian IT and BPM exporters. They need to understand this "new normal" in global BFSI and adapt accordingly.

New Market Segments beyond BFSI

I will conclude this Chapter by mentioning some new market segments that can be addressed through new business models covered in Part 3 of this book. Although I am mentioning them in this Chapter, they can extend beyond BFSI.

Earlier I mentioned mobile banking in the context of retail banking. The next wave of transformation for corporate customers could come through use of mobile and hand held devices for a wide range of commercial and financial transactions.

With the widespread usage of bar codes and smart phones, mobile computing can also transform global supply chains. Even within a large market segment like trade finance or supply chain financing, opportunities in mobile computing can be quite large.

Indian IT and BPM exporters need to look these opportunities as an entire business ecosystem. They spread across multiple industry segments and different technologies. Each product or each solution can cater to multiple countries. Therefore managers from the industry must view them from a new perspective altogether.

The mobile payment ecosystem comprises of large banks, retail industry, telecom, media and IT companies. In the European continent, it is spread across countries including Central and Eastern Europe. Global banks based in Europe also operate in Middle East and North Africa. Many global IT companies would find it challenging to compete in this crowded and fragmented market segment, especially in Europe.

Since 2008, the City of London has been trying to get a share of the rapidly growing business related to Islamic Finance. I mentioned this briefly in Chapter 2. In 2013, British policymakers and British business leaders have talked of developing London as a European hub for Islamic Finance. India Inc. has a big presence in the Middle East as well as in London. Therefore, Indian IT and BPM exporters have a natural competitive advantage when compared to other global IT service providers.

In the Middle East and North Africa, Islamic banking is growing rapidly. However, addressing this new market segment could involve a change in business model for many global banks based in the US and in Europe. This is because Islamic banking practices are quite different from banking practices common in the US and in UK. Even global IT companies based in the US are new to Islamic banking.

In Chapter 4 I mentioned why trade settlement using the Chinese Renminbi could be a game changer. This is another ecosystem developing across multiple countries. It can offer opportunities related to global supply chains as well as global BFSI.

In Chapter 5, I used the term business ecosystem while referring to the global supply chain of MNCs. The same applies to trade finance and supply chain financing. I also covered the topic of industry verticals. While addressing new opportunities in trade finance and SCF can Indian IT exporters take a cross industry based approach instead of an old BFSI perspective? I will use an example to explain why I am suggesting this approach.

In early 2013, SAP AG executives announced that they were expecting global revenues of $ 2.5 billion from Financial Services providers. In the next few years, they are trying to improve their share of spending by BFSI clients from a current level of 0.5% to 3%. During 2013, SAP announced a cloud-based corporate-to-bank platform called SAP Financial Services Network (FSN). This allows linking ERP systems of MNCs to treasury systems of global banks. This can offer opportunities to offer appropriate solutions or services to MNCs, supply chain partners or large banks.

In Oct 2013, SAP executives announced a SAP FSN deal with Citibank's Treasury and Trade Solutions. They also indicated that they were pursuing FSN related opportunities with many other global banks. SAP is being closely watched from the other side of the Atlantic by many US based IT services companies. Can Indian IT exporters play a big role in this new market segment by being more proactive?

In a global IT company like IBM, managers across the world would first debate on which industry vertical is better equipped to offer a new solution. In the meanwhile, smart Indian IT exporters can go ahead to offer a cross industry solution. I would not like to elaborate further. In Part 3 of this book, readers would understand what I am referring to.

The new market segments mentioned above can offer opportunities for IT products, IT services and IT solutions. However, to address them, Indian IT and BPM exporters need to identify the right partners.

To be effective, they need to change their current business model. What used to work in the US and UK in the past may not be the best way forward! In the next Chapter, I will explain why they need to change course, sooner than later.

CHAPTER 7

Change Course, Sooner Than Later

This is the concluding chapter of Part 2. Indian IT and BPM exporters serve global clients in the US and in Europe. In Part 1 of this book, I explained why they are experiencing a multi-speed global economy. So far in Part 2, I explained the challenges faced by their global clients.

In this Chapter, I will explain why they need to change course, sooner than later. In recent quarters, some of their CEOs have talked about different strategies. These include nonlinear growth, products, platforms, you name it!

Some have mentioned new contract signings; some have talked about acquiring new skill sets through M&A; few have also mentioned about change of geographic focus. However, all of them have indicated that they will continue with a services based business model. I will explain the pros and cons of such strategies by relating them to moving up the value chain.

Let us get started by explaining some barriers or the resistance to change. I will expand topics covered in this Chapter in Part 3 to explain "how" Indian IT and BPM professionals as well as their employers can move up the value chain.

Barriers to Move up the Value Chain

Moving up the value chain would involve change and transformation in every organization. However there could be 4 types of resistance to change among many Indian IT exporters. They are relying on a weak Rupee, inability to change old business models, developing a cost plus mindset and challenges of employee retention.

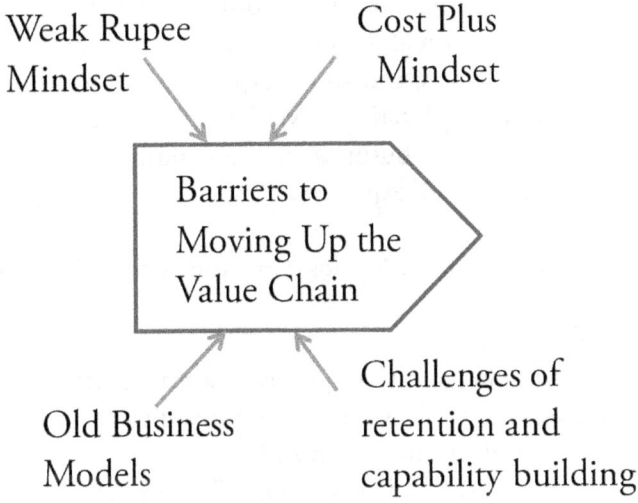

Across this Chapter I will explain each one of them. At an early stage, they can be considered to be a hurdle on the way forward. Very soon, each one can become a big barrier: this is why Indian IT exporters need to change course, sooner than later.

Relying on a Weak Rupee

As I pointed out in Chapter 1, both large and medium sized Indian IT exporters are playing a delicate balancing act. They are pursuing multiple goals simultaneously.

1. Maintaining revenue growth.
2. Maintaining profitability.
3. Building new skill sets and capabilities.

So far, a weak Rupee has come to the rescue of many Indian IT exporters. Many of them are reducing costs by improving utilization. How long can this continue? This is why they need to overcome their weak Rupee mindset. Otherwise, they will be driven into the commodity space where their margins can get eroded every quarter.

Sooner than later, Indian IT exporters need to change their business mix and start managing currency risks. Their business mix depends on many parameters: the technology involved, the type of service rendered, the geography and their share of IT spending by global clients. However, changing the business mix will involve significant investments.

In recent quarters, some Indian IT exporters are facing challenges to manage stock market expectations. Market analysts and even business media have questioned the business mix and business model* of many large and medium Indian IT exporters.

* Please refer to separate box for terms associated with Business Model

Why is this so? They are trying to ascertain whether the company is doing well because of a weak Rupee during this quarter or because of the company's strategy and/or business model.

Currently, most of the Indian IT and BPM exporters depend on US based clients for a significant share of revenues. Developing new markets in Europe or Asia Pacific will require additional investments. While chasing revenues, some of them could risk slipping into the commodity segment of the services business.

As I explained in Chapter 2 and Chapter 3, the market conditions in the US and in Europe are changing. The same business model will not work in both these geographies. Many Indian IT exporters are keen to pursue opportunities in the Asia Pacific or in the Middle East. The best option for them would be to develop a new business model and also tailor this to each geographical market segment over a period of time.

In order to be successful, they need to work on multiple strategies in parallel.
1. They need to change their business mix in terms of services.
2. They need to prioritize between global clients and diversify their geographical mix.
3. They need to get a bigger share of IT spending from each of their major clients.

Of course, all these three are in addition to developing the necessary skill sets! Is this why market analysts and investors are questioning their CEOs during every quarter?

How can Indian IT exporters look beyond a weak Rupee? In the next Section, I will cover this topic.

Managing Currency Volatility

Even though a weak Rupee can help Indian IT exporters in one or two quarters, it can be a challenge going forward. Gains achieved in one quarter may get wiped out in the next quarter. A volatile Rupee also makes it difficult to agree on pricing for long term contracts with global clients.

Typically, global clients would also like to benefit from Rupee depreciation. When multiple IT service providers start chasing a weak Rupee, this can backfire. A wrong strategy could mean a lower profitability for the Indian IT exporter, or a risk of losing a major contract.

A volatile Rupee means that its relative value to USD and EUR could keep changing in every quarter. The impact depends on the business mix of the Indian exporter. This makes it difficult for their CFOs in business planning. CFOs may also find it difficult to set expectations on revenue growth and profitability with their investors.

Going forward, CEOs or CFOs of Indian IT exporters can't unnecessarily blame the Rupee: they could always get caught during the next quarter. A wrong move could result in them getting punished by the stock market, one way or the other.

This is why each Indian IT exporter needs a smart strategy to address currency risks. Their strategy can't be based on a weak Rupee: it needs to be tied to their business mix. They need to meet revenue and profitability targets in spite of currency fluctuations. This is part of their "growing up" and behaving like MNCs anywhere else in the world.

As per RBI, 73.6% of all invoicing by Indian IT exporters was in USD. While negotiating pricing with global clients, Indian IT exporters need to get smarter to achieve currency diversification. For example, they could raise invoices in multiple currencies depending on the project location.

This way, losses due to a rise in the Rupee relative to one currency can be made up by gains relative to another currency. They can also incorporate specific commercial terms like linking rates to exchange rate fluctuations, escalation clause etc.

Typically, Indian IT exporters hedge currency risks by working closely with their banks. A hedging strategy depends on the level of INR as well as the business mix. This is why it is important to get smarter in managing the revenue mix across currencies. Indian IT exporters need to change their business mix and fine tune their hedging strategy. This will require a higher level of business planning, management attention and oversight during every quarter.

Like most MNCs, they need to diversify their costs, revenues and profits from a currency perspective in the long term. Currently, most of them have a major exposure to USD. This is another reason for some of them to venture into the European continent.

Services Based Business Model

For the benefit of readers, I will explain common terms used by Indian IT exporters to describe their service based business model. The table below explains the terms associated: although there may be differences between companies.

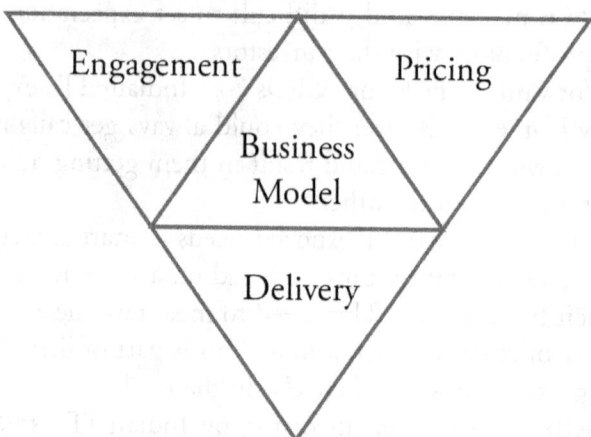

Moving up the value chain will involve changes in each of the 3 areas: engagement, delivery and billing.

Term	What it Means	Old (or Current) Business Model
Engagement	How to approach your global client	CIOs or CIO level organization
Delivery	How services are delivered from the India center	Offshore and Outsourcing model Focus on service delivery metrics
Billing	How clients are billed	Time and Material (T&M based)

The current business model of most Indian IT exporters is based on three typical characteristics.

1. Their relationship with global clients is predominantly at the CIO level.
2. They rely on lower costs at an offshore location and outsourcing contracts extending over several years.
3. The entire effort spent by IT professionals is billed to their global client based on what are called as Time and Material (T&M) contracts.

So far, this business model has worked well in two ways.

1. IT budgets were pooled at the CIO level and the CIO was a major stakeholder in decision making.
2. The cost involved in sales and client relationship was lower, since the primary contacts were at the CIO organization level.

In the next Section, I will explain why their current business model may be losing its effectiveness. Later I will explain the changing role of CIOs.

Pros and Cons of the Current Business Model

In addition to a primary focus on the CIO organization, Indian IT exporters have relied on billing the entire effort spent on a T&M basis. In recent years, global clients are demanding changes to this old model.

They measure the performance of the service provider and also link them to pricing. Many Indian IT exporters now incorporate what are called as service level agreements (SLAs) or key performance indicators (KPIs) in the contract. In Part 3 of this book, I will cover this topic using a simpler term: service delivery metrics.

IT related spending can be classified into three categories*: running the business, improving the business and growing the business. Each category relates to a different type of business impact for the client. The third category is discretionary in nature and can also relate to strategic IT spending. It doesn't come under the purview of outsourcing.

* Please refer to Box: Categories of IT Spending.

For most Indian IT exporters, the primary source of business is from the first two categories of IT spending. They cover services related to running the IT operations; supporting the infrastructure comprising of hardware, software and networking; running and supporting packaged software; supporting and maintaining custom applications.

A significant part of IT spending comes under what is referred to as the application development and maintenance (ADM) business. In newer technologies, IT spending typically happens on a project by project basis. These cover one or more areas: mobile computing, social media, Big Data and/or analytics.

On the one hand, IT budgets are getting squeezed at the CIO level. On the other hand, business units are independently taking decisions on IT spending. Indian IT exporters need to expand their mindshare with the top management team.

If they don't get a bigger share of IT spending, they could be driven into the commodity space. To approach business unit heads directly, they need to change their client relationship model, sooner than later.

The pressure to review an old T&M based pricing model is coming from two directions.

1. Global clients are demanding that billing is related to outcome of the project (results) and not the input (effort spent).
2. Global competition is getting tougher. Even if you aren't willing to offer a different business model, your competitor might offer one.

Clients are pursuing multiple or even conflicting objectives while leveraging IT solutions and IT services. These are cost optimization, improving productivity and growing the business. They are looking at a variable cost model where it is easier to control costs. In Chapter 9, I will cover these topics from a business model perspective.

In the next Section, I will explain the term cost plus mindset.

Categories of IT Spending

Run the Business   Improve the Business

Grow the
Business

Categories of IT Spending

Typically, IT spending by global clients comes under three categories: running the business, improving the business and growing the business. With shrinking IT budgets, Indian IT exporters need to start addressing all the three categories of IT spending.

Decision making by global clients is quite different for each of the 3 categories. Indian IT exporters need to understand this process, in addition to capturing the mindshare of top management. Increasingly, budgets for the first category are shrinking; some businesses are getting commoditized. In the second category, clients expect significant improvements. This category covers areas like social media, mobile computing, Big Data and analytics.

Apart from developing skill sets in newer technologies, Indian IT exporters need to understand the priorities of stake holders from a business perspective. Typically, IT spending by business units is discretionary in nature.

Each business unit can decide on spending on a project by project basis independently. The business impact relative to the costs can be evaluated on a case by case. Business improvements can also involve driving change and transformation.

In the third category of IT spending, CEOs are focusing on driving growth opportunities. Each business unit is trying to grow faster than the rest of the economy and faster than competition. Here, global clients look at IT solutions, not IT services per se.

> To effectively address IT spending in all categories of IT spending, Indian IT exporters need to expand their horizon in two different directions by building the necessary skill set.
> 1. Across multiple services.
> 2. Get into the solution space.

The Cost plus Mindset

I will begin by explaining the origin of this term: it is related to two areas:

1. What some managers in the Indian IT industry refer to as "managing a headcount" authorized by a global client.
2. The widespread use of T&M based pricing, where Indian IT exporters as well as MNC captive units get paid for the entire effort spent, or on the basis of a headcount.

This mindset can apply at various levels.

1. Indian IT professionals serving global clients regardless of whether they are employed by Indian companies or MNCs.
2. Large and medium IT exporters who are too "comfortable" with their old business models based entirely on providing low cost services.
3. India based captive units of MNCs where even senior professionals and managers are happy to continue working as a cost center.

One of the root causes of this mindset is T&M based pricing and/or operating as a cost center. There is nothing wrong in operating as a cost center for your global client as long as you are delivering business value. However, it is important NOT to focus only on the cost advantage from India. This applies to Indian IT exporters and India based captive units of MNCs. Your organization needs to avoid reaching a stage where your client starts assuming that the only way to negotiate is to beat you down on price. Instead of moving up the value chain, your organization would be on a path down the hill.

If pricing is based entirely on the effort spent, project management focus could get diluted. In my long experience including my tenure in IBM, I have observed many situations where this happens. The dilution could happen in many areas: estimation, change control, dependencies and risk management. I am sure readers with project management experience will agree with me, even though some of them don't like the term cost plus mindset.

In T&M based pricing project priorities can also get skewed. This applies to Indian IT service providers as well their project teams. Where is the incentive to optimize costs if all the effort is paid for by the client? Would the project team provide reasonable and accurate estimates or would they simply match the client's expectation? Even if the India team takes ownership of estimates, would the team also own all the risks associated?

Even before discussing the work to be taken up by the India team, managers on either side could get into a "bargaining session" on the estimates. This could also happen in many MNC captive units based in India operating as cost centers. I have observed this tendency in many projects executed by IBM India.

By focusing too much on the funding issue and estimates instead of the final deliverables, you are sending a wrong message to your global client. Is it good to fall into this trap? In case of MNC captive units, this can lead to wrong expectations set up on either side.

When global clients pay based on T&M rates, they need to track budgets, cost estimates and effort estimates at their end. In the current business environment, many of them are not willing to take on these overheads at their end. If they pass on these roles to the IT service provider, they would also like to get value for money through a different billing model.

T&M based pricing forces the client to pay for the risks associated. It also encourages the IT service provider to build in buffers with "room for negotiation". By the time the estimate reaches the end client, it could be inflated, one way or the other.

In T&M based pricing, the client indirectly pays for inefficiencies. Instead of being proactive, project teams can become reactive, waiting for the client to go ahead at various stages. They could ignore some dependencies or risks at an early stage. They may discover them late during the project life cycle. This could lead to delays, wasted effort, waiting time, idle time, you name it!

In IT projects with T&M based pricing, change control is affected directly or indirectly. Firstly, the processes and procedures for change control could be weak. Secondly, change control could involve unnecessary negotiations.

Where is the incentive to enforce change control if all the effort spent by the team in India is paid for by the client? There could be soft pedaling by the team in India while accepting changes. Some estimates for changes may be unrealistic. On the whole, just like estimation accuracy, there could be an erosion of best practices, one way or the other.

Why Cost plus Mindset Can Become a Barrier

Today, leaders from a few large Indian IT exporters "talk" about fixed price projects. However, the fact remains that a majority of projects they currently execute are still performed using a T&M based billing model. Very few projects in newer technologies are executed on a fixed price basis. In fact, the fixed price model is more prevalent in the domestic IT industry when compared to IT exporters.

How does the cost plus mindset act like a barrier for Indian IT exporters to move up the value chain? Why should it be overcome sooner than later? In this Section, I will answer these questions. In Chapter 9, I will relate this to the topic of productivity improvement.

Over a period of time, this mindset can lead to erosion of best practices from a project management perspective. I have observed this happening in IBM India. I have also heard similar experiences from my friends in Indian IT exporters.

Even though the effort estimate includes certain contingencies, the India team may not explicitly communicate them to the global client. If or when there is an effort variance, there can be endless arguments on why this happened. I have observed such tendencies in many projects executed by IBM India. In the services business, should project managers focus on deliverables or spend time and effort trying to control the effort variance?

Risk management is also about sharing responsibilities. In a T&M based pricing model, where is the incentive to assess, monitor and control risks? As a result, the India team could focus only on reporting risks. A tendency could develop where the India team avoids sharing certain responsibilities unless the effort gets paid for. Is this a good sign?

Sharing risks and taking up additional responsibilities are part of moving up the value chain. Where T&M based pricing is the norm, there may be a tendency by the Indian IT service provider to avoid doing this, fearing that such effort may not get funded later by the client.

If all the effort spent by the team in India is paid for, where is the incentive to improve efficiency or productivity from project to project? Where is the incentive to optimize the total cost likely to be incurred by the client? This mindset also applies to India based MNC captive units offering IT services to their parent organization.

The cost plus mind set can affect both sides: expectations of global clients and performance of Indian IT service providers. Eventually, this can become a barrier for many Indian IT exporters to offer alternate pricing models. When pricing is T&M based, even managers could spend a lot of time and effort on internal metrics associated with utilization and bench*. Instead of focusing on project outcomes and project results affecting the business, the entire India team could focus on those internal metrics not related to the client's business.

> * This term is used to refer to employees whose effort is not billed to the client.

A cost plus mindset can also lead to wrong priorities in service delivery. Indian IT professionals could focus all their effort on meeting contract specific SLAs (Service Level Agreements). Of course they are important in IT support services, but they may not be the top priority for the client. Another wrong priority is employee utilization: I need not elaborate on this one!

In ADM services, Indian IT exporters are expected to improve the client's business in different ways. Any global client would also expect their IT service provider offering ADM services to also demonstrate skills related to problem solving. A primary focus on meeting a few SLAs at a lower cost will certainly affect client satisfaction in the long term.

In Chapter 1, I used the term "getting closer to your global clients". In the past, Indian IT exporters have maintained a client relationship at the CIO level.

In the next three sections, I will explain the changing priorities of the top management team in global client organizations. This top management team consists of three CXO level executives: Chief Financial Officers (CFOs), Chief Marketing Officers (CMOs) and CIOs. I will explain their changing priorities and how these affect decision making on IT spending.

Changing priorities of CFOs

In this section, I will mention the changing priorities of CFO in the US and in Europe. This is based on studies published by CFO.com and American Express during 2012 and 2013.

It would be naïve for Indian IT exporters to assume that CFOs typically behave like "bean counters" asking for discounts. They need to capture the mindshare of CFOs especially on decisions related to IT spending and IT budgets. They need to be in sync with their changing priorities and correct any wrong perceptions based on past experiences. Also, relying only on CIOs to put forward their business case can become risky.

In recent years CFOs are facing challenges in maintaining revenue growth and profitability in every quarter. In the 2012 survey, CFOs mentioned three areas where they focused on while extracting better value from their business spending and capital investments.

1. Delivering value to customers, translating into revenues.
2. Delivering value to investors in terms of better profitability.
3. Extracting value from suppliers and vendors.

The primary emphasis is shifting from the third area to the first two areas. It is about getting better value from a business perspective. It is not about beating your suppliers down on prices or squeezing them to offer discounts. What value addition are CFOs looking for? This is about getting more "bang for the buck" from a business perspective. While making decisions related to budgets and capital spending, CFOs could use multiple criteria.

In addition to old criteria of evaluation like return on investments (ROI) or return on capital employed (ROCE), they are also focusing on appropriate metrics related to business impact. The impact could be associated with revenues, profits, expanding market access, launching new products or new services.

The American Express and CFO.com survey for 2013 has reiterated some of the 2012 findings. Economic uncertainty in Euro zone and in the US did force many CFOs to make spending cuts during 2012. During 2013, they are indeed value minded: but they aren't focused on making spending cuts; they are looking at spending differently.

The 2013 survey mentioned that CFOs are focusing on value delivery. This is about delivering value to customers in two ways:
- Extracting value from supply chain partners.
- Deriving greater value from operations and making process improvements.

What does this mean? This is not about slashing expenses or cutting costs per se. Smart CFOs are offering a carrot instead using a "stick" with supply chain partners to extract better value. I gave an example in Chapters 5 and 6. Instead of forcing suppliers to cut costs, CFOs of MNCs are offering supply chain financing. Is this not a smarter way to negotiate?

Accordingly, Indian IT exporters need to offer a better value proposition to CFOs of their global clients. Before CFOs use the stick, why not offer them a "carrot"? This could be offering a cost advantage or cost optimization in some ingenious ways. One can't assume that providing low cost services alone would convince them, going forward.

Importance of CMOs and Business Unit Heads

In recent years, Chief Marketing Officers (CMOs) of large MNCs are playing a bigger role in choosing and deploying technology based solutions. This is happening due to many reasons.
1. The role played by CIOs is changing across organizations in the US and in Europe.
2. CMOs are getting involved in decision making related to IT spending in areas like social media and analytics.

I will cover the first topic in the next Section. In the past, CIOs and the CIO organization provided the "vision" and "strategy" for technology deployment. In recent years, some tech savvy CMOs are independently evaluating new technologies.

For CEOs, increasing sales in the short term is an urgent and an important priority. They are also asking an important question: how can IT grow our business? CMOs as well as business unit heads are looking at how they can leverage IT to achieve both these objectives. For CMOs, improving sales is a short term tactic; growing the business can also be a long term strategy. Many CMOs would find it difficult to strike a balance between the two on their own. The same technology based solution may not apply in both situations. This is where they are relying on the knowledge and expertise of their CIOs.

Recent executive surveys by Gartner, Accenture and several others cover the changing roles played by CMOs and CIOs. One set of findings highlighted a "disconnect", suggesting that CIOs and CMOs are not in sync.

Another set of findings indicate a power shift at the CXO level. In many MNCs offering consumer products and services, the role of CMOs is gaining importance while CIOs are playing a secondary role.

How can Indian IT exporters interpret the findings of these surveys? They need to look at common conclusions and also relate them to their own clients. In many MNCs across the US and in Europe, CMOs are in a hurry to embrace new technologies and deliver business results. On matters like data security, privacy, adoption of mobile devices and use of social media, their priorities are quite different from those of CIOs.

In each major area like social media, cloud computing, analytics and mobile computing multiple stakeholders are involved in decision making. Convergence of multiple technologies also affects decision making on IT spending.

Of course, Indian IT exporters need to understand power shifts associated with each of their global clients. They need to understand the changing priorities and the roles played by CMOs in relation to other members of the top management. They need to get closer to each business unit head and to the CMO organization.

In areas like big data, analytics and social media there will be opportunities for pilot projects to be taken up. Here, CMOs and business unit heads would be involved in choosing such pilot projects. This is why each Indian IT exporter needs to develop new relationships beyond the CIO organization of their global clients.

Is there a power shift away from CIOs?

Experts are divided on this question. Some of them argue that CIOs are losing their influence. Some others insist that they are playing different roles in decision making. Most of them agree that the entire CIO organization can't behave like a cost center. Business unit heads have begun measuring business value delivered in every IT project. Indian

IT exporters need to understand these changing priorities and adapt accordingly.

On the one hand, CIOs are experiencing an erosion of power: the budgets they control have been flat or even reducing in recent years. More business unit heads are taking independent decisions on capital spending and choosing technology based solutions. On the other hand, CIOs are also playing a different role. They are moving towards IT governance, policy making on IT procurement and vendor management. Many CIOs are getting involved in decisions related to cloud computing, data security and privacy.

With technology convergence, the role of the CIO organization is changing. They are also setting policies at an organization level on the use of hand held devices and smartphones. They are playing a different role in managing external IT services providers. Many IT services are also getting "commoditized": they relate to IT infrastructure, packaged software and custom application development and maintenance (ADM).

This is why Indian IT exporters can't remain complacent. They can't follow a Business as Usual (BAU) approach by relying only on the CIO organization of their global client. They can't afford to be putting all their eggs in one basket!

They need to understand the changing role of CIOs and adapt accordingly. For e.g., many CIOs of global clients prepare a business case for cloud computing. They are involved at various stages of choosing and deploying cloud computing based solutions.

I am not suggesting that Indian IT exporters move away from the CIO organization. I am suggesting two specific strategies: getting out of the commodity space of IT services and getting into the cloud computing space of IT spending.

Today, the focus of CIOs is shifting to the output or the outcome of IT spending. They are looking beyond reducing the cost of IT related inputs. They would like to demonstrate the business impact to the top management team. This change of priorities itself can affect many Indian IT exporters one way or the other.

In the next section, I will explain why it is necessary to capture the mindshare of the top management team of global clients. This is also part of moving up the value chain.

Mindshare of Global Clients

Today, most Indian IT exporters would like to increase their share of IT spending in newer technologies. These include social media, smartphones, Big Data and analytics where there are large opportunities spread across multiple business units. However, this can be possible only if they capture the mindshare of business unit heads.

Indian IT exporters need to develop deeper relationships at all levels of management with their global clients. This will enable them to offer the right value proposition. Otherwise, they will be forced to remain in the commodity space of the CIO organization where margins are getting squeezed.

Capturing the mindshare is not only about Indian IT exporters developing skill sets relevant to their client's business. It is also about using the power shifts to their advantage by taking some additional steps. For example:

1. They need to change the mix of services they offer.
2. They need to explore alternate business models.

If their only value proposition is low cost services and restricted to IT related skill sets, they may not have adequate visibility with top management.

Gaining a mindshare is also about delivering business value. Earlier in this book I mentioned some typical questions asked: How can IT help us run our business? How can IT improve our business? How can IT help us grow our business? And so on. In Chapter 5 and Chapter 6, I covered some typical answers sought by MNCs and global banks.

Capturing the mindshare can only happen over a period of time. Senior Indian IT professionals need to first get ready with answers to typical questions mentioned above. They need to answer such questions for major businesses of their global client organization. By demonstrating domain expertise, they can move closer to each business unit. By understanding how decisions are made, they are better prepared. This way, they can improve their visibility with the top management team of their client organization.

Over a period of time, Indian IT exporters can leverage their mindshare to target IT spending at various levels and multiple business units of their client organization. They can address IT budgets no longer controlled by CIOs. This way, they can capture a bigger share of the overall IT spending, even if it remains flat.

Typically, IT spending related to growth markets are strategic in nature. Such projects have better visibility with the top management team. However, even before getting close to them, IT service providers need to first capture the mindshare of CEOs, CMOs and CFOs.

On IT spending related to manufacturing and supply chain, CEOs and CFOs would play a big role. In IT projects related to developing or launching products and services in growth markets, the CMO organization would play a key role.

Any project of a strategic nature will require knowledge of the client's business as well as industry knowledge. In these projects, Indian IT exporters are expected to share risks with their global client. Some of these risks could even relate to the client's business. They also need to accept more responsibilities.

The term moving up the value chain also applies to Indian professionals working in the IT industry. How does a young engineer employed in the IT industry feel? I am sure he or she would feel like a small fish in a big ocean! What does moving up the value chain mean from a people perspective? In the next Section, I will cover this topic.

Employee Retention and Building Capabilities

As per one estimate, the Indian IT industry employed 2,800,000 professionals in 2012. Even with reduced recruitment during 2013, this number is likely to have crossed 3 million in 2014. In this Section, I will cover topics directly affecting them. In terms of hiring, most Indian IT exporters have so far relied on:

1. Hiring a large number of entry level professionals every year and training them on "saleable" skill sets.
2. Project specific lateral hiring of experienced professionals.

Since 2008, the mix of the two types of hiring has been changing every year. In 2013, the mix has changed considerably. CEOs of some Indian IT exporters have talked to business media reporters on how they are improving employee bench utilization through "Just in Time" hiring and reducing the training period.

What does this mean? This means that each Indian IT exporter would cut down or postpone recruitment of entry level professionals. Project specific hiring would go up, while skill development will become more and more project specific.

Indirectly, this means that these Indian IT exporters have begun cutting corners on skill building. Like the cost plus mindset I mentioned earlier, this could create new barriers for them to change their business mix or even try to change their current business model.

It would take them longer to develop capabilities in newer technologies. Some businesses like cloud computing, Big Data and analytics require a different set of capabilities when compared to ADM (Application Development and Maintenance). If they focus on "Just in Time" hiring from a cost perspective, there is a risk of them slipping into the commodity space of IT services, not moving up the value chain!

In terms of retention, Indian IT exporters have relied on:
1. Offering a carrot like an "on site stint" to retain young engineers.
2. Offering promotions and salary increases based on multiple criteria like performance, skill sets, performing project critical roles and client feedback.

In recent years, the first carrot is drying up. Going forward, the second option can be quite limited unless Indian IT exporters also implement the following changes:
1. A change in business mix to offer a variety of new roles both outside and inside India.
2. A change in the business model whereby senior employees can perform different roles and take up additional responsibilities as a part of career progression or a promotion.

If Indian IT exporters follow a Business As Usual (BAU) approach as in the past, they are likely to face one of the following challenges:

1. Talented people or those with deeper skill sets could leave the organization for reasons other than salary. They could be seeking a change in order to move up the value chain from a professional perspective.

2. How long can you retain employees performing project critical roles by offering a "carrot"? What happens if or when they move out of these roles either on their own or due to changes in the project?

3. Senior employees staying behind could develop a "cost plus" mindset or have shallow skill sets that are no longer "saleable". How long can they be "kicked upstairs"?

Based on my long experience in this industry, I feel that these challenges can be addressed if capability building is taken up seriously and if it is also in sync with new business models.

Today several companies in the Indian IT industry employ tens of thousands of Indian engineers. On the one hand, a "cookie cutter" approach to skill building based on rigid processes must be avoided. From a long term perspective, it is also important to avoid an erosion of the existing skill base.

In the past, Indian IT exporters have focused on "saleable" and/or project specific skill sets. Going forward they need to answer typical questions raised by young IT professionals:

• What are the growth opportunities and career path available? This could be a question at the organization level or specific to the business group one belongs to.

• How can I acquire skill sets typically sought after in this industry? This question is also related to internal processes followed for transfers across projects.

• What roles and responsibilities can my employer offer me to fully leverage my capabilities and skill sets?

The above questions are based on my experience in IBM India and inputs from my friends in the industry from large Indian IT exporters.

Of course, Indian IT exporters need to build skill sets in newer technologies such as analytics, mobile computing social media and cloud computing. In addition, they need to build three types of capabilities:

1. Understanding of the clients' business and domain expertise. In Chapter 5 and Chapter 6, I have provided a preview of what global clients expect in this area.
2. Management capabilities at multiple levels to deliver better business value to global clients. These depend on the business mix in terms offer multiple services across different countries and geographies.
3. Management capabilities to address any changes in the business model or a new focus on offering solutions instead of an earlier focus on services delivery.

I will cover this topic again in Chapter 10. Building capabilities and employee retention need to go together. Each of them needs to be in sync with changes in the business mix or a change in the business model.

How to Change Course?

Many CEOs and CFOs in large and medium sized Indian IT exporters talk about increasing "revenue productivity". This implies that revenue contributed by each employee needs to go up. This will require a change of skill sets, a change of business model or both.

One of the areas where large Indian IT exporters need to focus on is to close the gap between their own revenue productivity and that of global IT service providers like IBM. Having worked for IBM India between 1997 and 2011, I am aware of the pattern of growth of IBM's services revenues and the revenue productivity of IBM's services business unit.

However IBM doesn't publish its number of employees by country and business unit. Therefore I will rely on published data from business media reports during 2013. Between the years 2000 and 2012, the share of IBM's revenues from hardware and financing fell from 35% to 14%. This shortfall was made up by growth in software and services revenues. During this period, IBM also expanded its global delivery from India significantly.

Two questions need to be answered by Indian IT exporters in this context:

1. What is the difference between their global delivery model and that of IBM?
2. How can they close the gap in revenue productivity?

In my opinion, 2014 is the right time for them to look at alternate business models while answering the above two questions. I will explain this topic in Part 3 of this book.

Any improvement in revenue productivity will require significant investments. In the short term, it could also affect profitability. Each Indian IT exporter may choose a different trajectory to make necessary changes. This is why each CEO in the industry talks about alternate business models: products, platforms, non-linear pricing, you name it.

Here are a few questions for all large and medium Indian IT exporters. Can you make use of the window of opportunity offered by changes in US visa regulations to change your current business model? Why keep waiting for US policymakers to finalize the fine print associated with immigration reform and visa regulations during 2014? Why not become more proactive and negotiate some changes with some of your major clients based in the US?

In Chapter 3, I used the term "old guard" while referring to the global IT industry. Both in the US and in Europe the US IT industry appears to be divided on some issue or the other. When Indian IT exporters pursue outsourcing contracts coming up for renewal can they disrupt the "old guard"? This is possible only if they are ready to offer alternate business models!

One option is to leverage enterprising SMEs in the Indian IT industry. I am sure that some of them have interesting ideas to disrupt the business model of the incumbent external IT service provider. Why not leverage them in winning new outsourcing contracts?

As per one report, the 4 top Indian IT exporters: TCS, Infosys, Wipro and HCL Technologies had a combined cash chest worth $ 9 billion in mid-2013. Many Indian IT exporters are cash rich and eager to expand their global footprint. Another option they have is to look at options beyond M&A in order to disrupt the "old guard" in the global IT industry.

Here are a few questions to my friends in the Indian IT industry. During 2013, Google and SAP announced that they would set up and/or expand their venture funds by hundreds of millions of dollars. Can they borrow some ideas from Google or SAP to disrupt the old guard? Can they utilize their billion dollar kitty to promote Indian startups?

So far, many cash rich Indian IT exporters have not been successful in the business of software products. Could they convert the churn in the US IT industry into a new window of opportunity? Instead of partnering with a major US based IT company, would they try to acquire a troubled ISV based in the US? In Chapter 3, I explained the challenges faced by ISVs based in the US.

In Chapter 6, I mentioned the rapidly growing market segment of Islamic Finance. This could be another segment where many Indian IT exporters can implement a product or a platform based business model. Large Indian IT companies can build an ecosystem of partners from Indian SMEs, companies in London or in the Middle East. They can leverage this ecosystem to become a solution provider instead of being a traditional IT services provider.

If Indian IT exporters are willing to change their business model, there are many ways how they can quickly move up the value chain. Let us move on to Part 3 of this book where I will cover topics related to business models.

PART 3

HOW TO MOVE UP THE VALUE CHAIN

INTRODUCTION

*I*n *Chapter 7, I explained why Indian IT exporters need to move up the value chain, sooner than later. In the following three Chapters, I will expand how this can be done. I will also cover a wide range of topics related to business models.*

I will try to avoid using terms like business value, business transformation and innovation while presenting my ideas. In my opinion, these terms have become part of the Indian IT industry's jargon and are therefore quite "context sensitive". Readers can associate my ideas and opinions with the appropriate jargon used in their own organization: business value, business transformation, innovation, industry vertical, you name it!

My friends in the Indian IT industry may not agree with some ideas or opinions expressed in Chapter 7 and Part 3. Nevertheless, I would suggest that Indian IT professionals explore them with an open mind.

If you pursue some ideas, you can move up the value chain from a professional perspective. Some ideas can be pursued within your current organization using a new business model. To pursue some ideas, you need to make some important decisions related to your own career. This is because some ideas can be explored only by becoming an entrepreneur!

Recently NASSCOM announced an initiative to launch 10,000 startups in India. I hope that few ideas in Part 3 of my book will encourage change and transformation among large Indian IT exporters. I am happy even if it encourages a few of my friends in the industry to become entrepreneurs themselves or decide to join hands with a successful entrepreneur after reading my book!

CHAPTER 8

Take Advantage of Technology and IT Trends

Typically Indian IT professionals serving global clients focus on technology trends. How can they make a strong business case on technology based solutions? I will provide an answer in this Chapter. I will also explain what affects their client's decision making on adoption of technology based solutions.

In this Chapter, I will explain how Indian IT exporters can move up the value chain by taking advantage of technology and IT outsourcing trends. I will begin by explaining how the consulting business is changing and covering trends related to the global consulting business.

The Consulting Business is changing

During 2013, many Indian IT exporters talked about getting into the consulting business: few of them also acquired a consulting company. Few of them initially set high expectations only to indicate after one or two quarters that they were "going slow".

It is worth watching how an entry into the Consulting business would affect revenues and profitability of Indian IT exporters. Of course, the M&A route can offer them a shortcut: but staying in the consulting business is a different game altogether!

In recent years, the consulting business is changing with three distinct groups. Each of them addresses a different segment of technology integration and IT consulting. When CEOs of Indian IT exporters talk of their consulting business, whom are they competing with?

Strategy firms like Bain & Company, Boston Consulting Group and McKinsey & Company fall under the first group. They have recorded double digit growth rates by expanding into technology consulting. Indian IT exporters don't operate in this market segment.

The second group includes the Big 4: PwC, Deloitte, Ernst & Young and KPMG. The third covers the consulting businesses of global IT services companies such as IBM, Accenture and Cap Gemini. If Indian IT exporters are indeed competing in this segment, they need to offer convincing answers to some typical questions asked by CEOs: How can IT help us improve our business? Transform our business? Grow our business?

In Chapters 2 and 3, I mentioned terms like cost optimization, efficiency, effectiveness, productivity and competitiveness as applicable in the US and in Europe. The answer could involve one of these terms as a value proposition from a business perspective.

To provide these answers, they need to first choose an area of specialization. They must also be able to demonstrate this specialization to prospective clients. The necessary skill sets must be built as early as possible and as effectively as possible. Even if they pursue an M&A route, they need to still achieve synergy between existing IT related businesses and the new consulting business they are acquiring.

In my opinion, Indian IT exporters need to do a lot of ground work. Many of them are still busy chasing outsourcing contracts. As I will explain later, they need to move away from a service delivery mindset towards demonstrating a problem solving approach.

Recent Trends in IT Outsourcing

In Chapter 1, I briefly mentioned IT outsourcing contracts coming up for renewal and/or renegotiation. During 2013, multiple surveys have been conducted on IT outsourcing trends. These include Gartner, KPMG, HfS Research and ISG to name a few. In this Section I will summarize some of these trends at a high level.

Old outsourcing models of the past are changing due to multiple reasons. Apart from cloud computing, cost optimization is a major driver. Another is technology convergence. On the one hand, IT budgets are getting squeezed. Under the cloud computing model, clients and external service providers can mix and match fixed costs and variable costs in many ways. Global clients are striking a balance between these two. They are trying to extract more "bang for the buck" in different ways.

CIOs and Business Unit heads are carving out pieces of hardware, software, applications, IT and networking infrastructure. Some pieces are retained in house; some are outsourced. Applications running on some pieces are migrated to the cloud environment. Business units are also taking back control in different ways. The focus is also shifting towards mobile apps and taking advantage of cloud based pricing for software products.

One set of global clients can go for smaller contracts for a shorter term. This is referred to as multi-sourcing, involving multiple service providers. Another set of global clients may consolidate them and negotiate steep discounts from a new service provider.

Each of the above developments is driving the rebid and renegotiation market. In addition, a volatile Indian Rupee is also encouraging global clients to bargain harder on prices. All these are causing an "industry churn" affecting many external IT services providers.

Indian IT exporters have to make a difficult choice.
1. Offer more (services) for less (price). It means maintaining revenue growth with a lower profitability.
2. Change their business model and also move up the value chain.

Would they continue to pursue the first option or make a sincere attempt to try the second one? In Chapter 9 I will explain how they can compete through new business models.

In the next two sections, I will cover two topics. One is moving away from a service delivery focus to playing the role of a business partner or a solution provider. Another topic is related to the consulting business.

I will explain how senior IT professionals working with Indian IT exporters can play the role of a solution provider. They can assist their global clients on shortlisting, choosing or finalizing technology based solutions. I am not sure if they are currently performing these roles, even if they carry a designation mentioning the term consultant.

Shift from Service Delivery to Problem Solving

Currently, most Indian IT exporters are focused on delivering a service. Their responsibility ends when they provide the deliverables and meet contract specific Service Level Agreements (SLAs).

Of course, SLAs are quite common in IT support services. However, in ADM services where I have a long experience, SLAs are not a big part of the business model especially when pricing is T&M based.

Are global clients satisfied as long as external service providers complete ADM projects on time and within budget? Can providing quality deliverables alone help them capture a bigger mindshare of top management? The expectations of global clients are rising. To satisfy them, the focus needs to shift from service delivery to problem solving.

What is the difference between a problem solving approach and a service delivery mindset? The latter is what you typically expect from a lower level call center employee: he or she answers a query only to "pass the buck" to another stage of service delivery.

Today global clients expect much more. They want a person who can help them solve a business problem while leveraging IT: not someone who can only solve a mundane IT problem. They expect IT professionals to help them complete a complex business transaction.

In Chapter 7, I mentioned the term cost plus mindset and why it can become a barrier to moving up the value chain. A service delivery mindset can also become a barrier for an organization to develop a problem solving approach.

Over a period of time, this can lead to the entire organization focusing on service delivery instead of problem solving. Even senior IT professionals may not develop problem solving capabilities from the perspective of the client's business. Even managers in Indian IT exporters can restrict themselves to the IT deliverables. They may not even appreciate the business problem faced by their client's business.

This could happen due to many reasons. Internal organization metrics and processes may discourage senior employees to get involved with a client's business problem. Instead, they could restrict themselves to meeting SLAs as per the existing contract.

Another reason could be that not enough people understand the client's business, even though they have the necessary skill sets related to technology. In my long experience, I have observed this happening at different levels in the organization, even in IBM India.

Without problem solving capabilities from a business perspective, Indian IT exporters can't be accepted by their clients as IT consultants. If they don't understand the business problem, how can they recommend a technology based solution? Even if they do, will they have credibility?

This could become a barrier for them to succeed in this business even if they take an M&A route to acquire a consulting company.

Acquiring business knowledge and domain expertise will take time, effort and investments. In the meanwhile, how can Indian IT exporters begin to offer IT consulting services? One step would be to get out of the commodity space of services and get a bigger share of IT spending in newer technologies.

The next step is to leverage existing relationships to perform the role of a business partner. For example, they can play an active role while their global clients choose a new technology based solution. However, to gain credibility, they need to develop a problem solving mindset. They must start performing the role of a business partner or a solution provider. Eventually, such relationships can lead to opportunities in IT consulting.

Entering the Business of IT Consulting

Earlier I briefly explained how the consulting business is changing. In this Section, I will cover the pros and cons of Indian IT exporters entering the IT consulting business and using it as a stepping stone to move up the value chain.

To be successful in the consulting business, you need business knowledge. You also need to understand the decision making process in specific technologies. Before being accepted as IT consultant who can offer a solution, Indian IT exporters need to be first accepted as a reliable business partner by the top management team of their client organization.

In recent years, consulting companies have coined the word knowledge economy and knowledge based work. What does it mean? Are Indian IT exporters really performing knowledge based work? I would argue that most of them still perform skill based roles in services delivery. The consulting business is knowledge based, not skill based. I will briefly explain the differences between the two terms.

Typically, knowledge based work is based on relationships, intellectual capital and intellectual property (IP). It leverages prior experience and best practices. Unlike skill based work, it is not billed in terms of labor hours with a primary focus on costs and other inputs.

Skill based roles focus on delivering services with consistency and uniformity. Knowledge based roles go few steps beyond this: by focusing on the outcome while also delivering better business value to decision makers. In Chapter 9, I will cover topics related to creating and monetizing IP to highlight these differences once again.

Knowledge based work also demonstrates thought leadership. Typically, it builds a portfolio of experiences from multiple clients that together add value to the client organization. Two examples of knowledge based work are: offering advice on technology deployment and performing the role of a solution provider.

In the past, some experts have pointed out that the primary focus of Indian IT exporters on services instead of products is a weakness. I would argue that this could turn out to be strength in the IT consulting business. With no vested interests with their own products, they can offer an unbiased opinion to their global clients. If they are accepted as a reliable business partner, they can even offer an independent opinion on technology deployment.

With some clients, Indian IT exporters can capture the mindshare of the top management team by providing new ideas on their own. This proactive approach can be more effective than waiting for other IT consultants and global IT companies to sell their ideas.

Indian IT exporters need to make an independent recommendation on the choice of a new technology. If they keep avoiding this, they will remain behind the shadow of global IT companies. They may not capture the mindshare of their client's top management team. A proactive approach can give them better visibility, better pricing power or both, depending on the global client.

I will mention a few examples later on how this can be done. I am not suggesting that Indian IT exporters avoid partnering with global IT companies. What I am suggesting is that they need to compete as well as cooperate. They need to avoid appearing to have a vested interest or being vendor specific. Their primary focus needs to be protecting the interests of their global client. This is what is expected in the consulting business.

Recommending a specific technology can be one part of playing this new role of a solution provider. By striking the right balance, Indian IT exporters would play the role of a business partner, and not behave like any other service provider.

Business Partner, Solution Provider

When global clients use the term business partner, what do they mean?

1. This is about having a deeper understanding of their business.
2. It is also about sharing risks and responsibilities in a problem solving mode.

A good example is a typical supply chain partner of an MNC: both the MNC organization and the partner have a better visibility on the other side. This is not about order fulfillment but maintaining a continuing relationship. They also collaborate with each other on many occasions. I explained visibility and collaboration in Chapter 5 from the perspective of global supply chains. These terms can also apply to their IT service providers.

Of course, many Indian IT exporters would claim to be performing like business partners with all their global clients. However, they restrict themselves to understanding and solving problems from an IT perspective. They also stick to Terms and Conditions (Ts and Cs) as per their outsourcing contract. They avoid sharing additional risks and responsibilities.

Under such circumstances, few questions need to be answered honestly. To what extent do Indian IT exporters have visibility on their clients' IT budgets and decision making? On how many occasions have they jointly addressed a challenging business situation with global clients? Does the CIO of their client organization refer to them as a business partner? If so, how many other top management executives also accept them as a business partner?

When global clients use the term solution provider, what do they mean? They expect adequate knowledge of the business and the industry. Solution providers are involved in problem definition, evaluating alternate solutions and making a recommendation if or when required. They operate in a problem solving mode at a higher level of management.

Typically, consultants bring to the table a set of best practices and/or a higher level of expertise. They play the role of an honest broker. Even though the client chooses the final solution, the consultant plays an active role in evaluating alternatives.

In the consulting business, Indian IT exporters need to perform the role of a solution provider. This is why credibility is important. Even if they don't have deep industry knowledge to start with, they can leverage their relationships to build credibility.

Of course, many Indian IT exporters will claim to be solution providers. If so, do they offer their clients alternative approaches to solve a problem? Can they define the business problem they are trying to solve in each of the projects they execute? Does the client organization also recognize them as a solution provider? Such questions must be answered honestly.

Earlier in this book, I mentioned 4 questions asked by top management while making IT investments. How can IT run our business? Improve our business? Transform our business? Grow our business? Typically, service providers answer the first question most of the time. Solution providers offer answers to the third and fourth questions. Performing multiple roles like that of a business partner or a solution provider is part of moving up the value chain.

How do technology trends affect the global IT industry in general and Indian IT exporters in particular? In the next few sections, I will answer this question for different areas. Instead of technology per se, I will cover topics from a business perspective.

BYOD and Mobile Apps

In Chapter 3, I introduced BYOD (Bring Your Own Device) in the context of Corporate America. This could disrupt the old business model of many IT service providers in two areas:

- IT support services for the legacy infrastructure
- ADM services where many Indian IT exporters have long term outsourcing contracts.

In the past, employees were provided remote access to corporate applications through desktops or laptops. For CIO organizations, this was standardized with established processes. Now, employees demand access to corporate applications via smartphones. This can offer some new challenges to the CIO organization.

Each corporate customer views BYOD differently, depending on the industry and the organization culture. In some organizations, the workforce is relatively young and tech savvy. This demographic group wants more control and independence. Typically employees dislike restrictions imposed on the usage of internet, mobile phones and social media. In these organizations, a majority of ADM services would focus on mobile apps. However, CIOs need to develop mobile apps for both iOS and Android environments.

From a business perspective, a good combination of BYOD, cloud and mobile apps can achieve productivity gains as well as save costs. Some companies offer employees an option to work from home. In certain roles, it makes sense for employees to access some corporate applications from anywhere at any time. This could help them respond to queries from management as well as queries from customers. Therefore each business unit can have a different approach to implement appropriate mobile apps.

Typically CIOs look beyond mobile apps: they would like to assert themselves. This is probably why there are so many articles in computer magazines on BYOD. Indian IT exporters need to look at all this as a window of opportunity. They need to work with CIOs and the CIO organization to develop innovative mobile apps. While doing so, they can also respond to the growing needs and expectations of business unit heads. If they do a good job, it gives them better visibility with the top management team of their global clients.

Technology Convergence

In Chapter 3, I mentioned that multiple technology trends converging together could disrupt the US IT industry in the next few years. This applies to hardware, software and services businesses. How do they affect large and medium Indian IT exporters? Is it a challenge or an opportunity? In this Section, I will answer this question.

In recent quarters, CEOs of Indian IT exporters have talked about the convergence of newer technologies. Industry jargon like SCAM, SMAC or something similar is used while referring to the convergence of social media, mobile computing, analytics and cloud computing. Many SMEs in India are focusing on mobile apps and platforms for a particular industry taking advantage of such technology convergence.

Technology convergence is already affecting the global IT industry. Each IT vendor needs to offer IT products and services faster, cheaper and with better business value. Independent Software Vendors (ISVs) also need to address support and implementation issues.

If external IT service providers keep focusing on IT operations from a service delivery perspective, they could slip into the commodity space. While they struggle at the back end to manage tough service level agreements (SLAs), someone else with better top management visibility will walk away with a bigger share of the client's IT spending.

In Chapter 7, I mentioned that Indian IT exporters need to expand their mindshare with CEOs, CFOs, CMOs and business unit heads. This is possible if they take advantage of technology convergence instead of focusing only on one area. This applies to mobile computing, cloud computing, social media or analytics.

In the past, Indian IT exporters have partnered with IT product companies and offered appropriate services. They have focused on developing skills in state of the art technologies. Going forward, they have two options.

1. Change their old business model
2. Disrupt the current business model of their competitors, especially IT service providers and ISVs belonging to the "old guard"

Of course, while backing the "right" IT companies or ISVs, Indian IT exporters also need to move up the value chain. If they are smart, they can leverage technology convergence to spread their footprint across their client organization. With the proliferation of mobile and hand held devices, the variety of mobile apps is exploding. The ADM (Application Development and Maintenance) services business can continue to expand.

However, the business of developing and deploying mobile apps for corporate users can be quite different compared to the old model of ADM and support services for desktop applications. Apart from a different skill set, external IT services providers need to manage a different set of expectations from a new set of stakeholders.

Would Indian IT exporters continue to rally behind the CIO organization? Would they take advantage of technology convergence to get closer to business unit heads? This is not about playing politics: it is about understanding multiple stakeholders in the top management team and delivering better business value.

Smart CIOs are taking advantage of technology convergence to assert themselves with other business unit heads. They are consolidating IT infrastructure across business units and across locations. They are proactively getting involved in choosing or deploying cloud computing solutions. In some MNCs and global banks, CIOs are also getting involved in defining policies and processes related to BYOD (or mobile apps), data security and privacy.

Given the variety of hardware, software and versions associated, CIOs are also pursuing automation opportunities. In some industries like BFSI, CIOs need to address data security considerations, protect corporate data, prevent the occurrence of any fraud and also avoid misuse. This is where appropriate IT solutions can strike the right balance.

The economics of cloud computing is quite complex. Given that cloud computing initiatives are taken at the organization level, one can expect CFOs to play an important role in decision making. For example, they would evaluate the business case and make sure that they can extract better value for money from IT investments.

At the same time, Business units are independently taking decisions related to ADM services. For example, they are looking at how mobile apps can improve employee productivity. In some MNCs and global banks, business unit heads are even independently choosing technology based solutions for their business. Such power shifts can affect the current business model of many US based IT companies and global service providers.

Indian IT exporters have been quite successful in reacting to a disruption in the global IT industry since the 1990s. Can they leverage technology convergence during this decade and also cause this disruption by being more proactive? This is the time to offer "smart solutions" to customers by being more proactive on convergence of technologies. This is the right time for them to become aggressive in disrupting an outdated business model of their global competitors. This is another part of moving up the value chain.

In earlier chapters I covered topics related to Big Data, Analytics and Business Insight from a client's perspective. In the next two sections, I will consolidate them from the perspective of Indian IT exporters.

Why Analytics can be a Game Changer

In Chapter 3, I mentioned that in a recent report McKinsey covered what it called "game changers" for the US economy. Big Data and analytics were one of them. In this section, I will explain why this could be a game changer for many Indian IT exporters.

Increasingly, global businesses need to make data driven decisions. This new business of Big Data and Analytics is data-driven; it is not based on the software development life cycle. It is also quite different from business intelligence (BI) where the focus has been on data mining and requirements are more defined. In this new business, the focus is on data-driven decision making while the data itself may be unstructured.

For many Indian IT exporters, what used to work well in addressing opportunities related to ADM or BI may not suit this new business opportunity. So far, they have been offering two types of IT services by operating at the CIO level in their global client organization.

1. Services related to IT infrastructure and IT operations.
2. Services related to application development and maintenance (ADM).

Providing business insight through analytics will require a new skill set. It would also involve working with Chief Marketing Officers (CMOs) and Business unit heads.

Skill building in analytics would require additional investments. IT professionals who are used to working on software development and testing will require a significant amount of reskilling before they can do a good job on analytics.

In some situations, postgraduates in mathematics, statistics and management may be more suitable than an existing team of engineers. Recruiting them and developing the necessary skill set will require big investments by many Indian IT exporters.

The business model that worked for traditional ADM services may not be very effective for analytics. Here, it is difficult to estimate the effort involved upfront. Providing business insight is more about offering a solution, not providing services. Even with the right skill set, it could be a big leap forward.

First of all, it requires a problem solving mindset. The Indian IT exporter needs to play the role of a solution provider. As I explained earlier this is quite different from the current focus on services delivery.

Secondly, analytics is associated with a business problem. This is different from providing ADM services to the CIO organization. In ADM, it is possible to identify an IT project with a well-defined requirement in terms of skill sets. To be effective in analytics, one has to understand the client's business and also have visibility with business unit heads.

Thirdly, many global clients are looking at analytics not because they have a problem waiting for a solution. The business unit may not even know where the problem lies! To be effective, the project team needs to have adequate knowledge of the customer's business apart from skills related to crunching data.

Many projects are considered as business critical either because of the data associated or because they would involve working closely with business unit managers. This is why an old business model that worked with CIOs in the past may not be effective to address new opportunities related to analytics.

Moving from ADM to analytics could require a major investment and a sustained effort over a period of time. Some projects involve use of analytical models and analytical techniques. Sometimes, the outcome of an elaborate analysis may not provide enough insight in the first attempt itself. The global client would be convinced only after a few pilot projects. How many Indian IT exporters are ready for this long journey?

Getting into the Business of Big Data

Earlier, I explained why getting into this business even with existing clients will require big investments in skill building by Indian IT exporters. In this Section, I will explain few possible options available.

Apart from knowledge of the client's business, the team based in India working on analytics must demonstrate a problem solving mindset to become fully productive.

One option could be to collaborate with existing global clients to identify a good opportunity. Once they have the necessary skill sets, they can identify a problem and work on a pilot project. This could be more effective than trying to "sell your skills".

Why is it important to look at the business problem and skill set together? If the Indian IT exporter is primarily focused on service delivery and lacks problem solving capabilities, the global client may find it difficult to get the work done by the team. This is why choosing a pilot project in close consultation with the global client can help.

As mentioned in Chapter 4, many MNCs and global banks based in the US and in Europe are setting up captive units specializing on business analytics. Can Indian IT exporters address opportunities in analytics through these captive units?

To achieve this, they need to understand decision making by captive units. While engaging an external service provider for skills related to analytics, the CIO organization of the global client is likely to play a limited role.

In some cases, business unit heads may decide on their own, with little or no involvement by their CIO. This is why Indian IT exporters need to relook at their current engagement model. They need to develop relationships with the appropriate business unit.

In the recent past, providing business insight through analytics has gained importance among many Indian BPM exporters. Some of them use the term Knowledge Process Outsourcing (KPO) to address these opportunities.

Many startups and smaller IT companies in India have the necessary skill sets in Big Data and analytics. Indian IT exporters can address such opportunities through partners. They can also piggy back on global IT companies already active in this market place.

Big Data and analytics are evolving into an entire business ecosystem of external service providers and software companies. In Chapter 5, I mentioned that SAP AG is building its own ecosystem related to cloud computing and Big Data.

Earlier in this book I mentioned that 4 large Indian IT exporters are holding cash reserves worth US$ 9 billion. Some IT consultants have recommended an M&A route for them to acquire a foreign company either based in the US or in Europe.

Indian IT exporters can't assume that they can become part of the ecosystem of Big Data and analytics through M&A. They need to proactively develop a solution strategy and even change their current business model. Can they look at the combination of cloud computing, databases and/or analytics as an entire business ecosystem?

By doing so, they can make strategic investments on Big Data and Analytics. On the one hand, they can use analytics as a stepping stone to expand their footprint across their client organization. On the other hand, this can also offer them an opportunity to compete more effectively in the cloud computing space.

Whether they take an M&A route or otherwise, their investments need to be in sync with their strategy and business model. Otherwise, they would not be able to challenge US based software vendors and global IT service providers.

They need to look beyond a services and outsourcing based business model. They need to think big while working with existing global clients. One option could be to develop a proof of concept (POC), a new service offering or even a new product.

With existing clients, they can leverage analytics to improve their mindshare with top management. Through a POC, it may be easier to gain better visibility with CEOs and Business Unit heads.

Cloud computing leverages internet technologies and promises to offer a wide range of service options. It also promises to convert fixed costs into variable costs. The question is: can cloud computing be a stepping stone for Indian IT and BPM exporters to move up the value chain? In the next few sections, I will answer this question.

The Cloud Computing Marketplace

This market comprises of different segments:
- Infrastructure as a Service (IaaS)
- Software as a Service (SaaS)
- Platform as a Service (PaaS)

Some Indian BPM exporters also refer to a fourth segment: Business Process as a Service (BPaaS). Currently most Indian IT exporters primarily offer professional services, not "off the shelf" solutions related to cloud computing.

Industry experts like Gartner group and IDC periodically publish reports on these market segments. In my opinion, it is more important for Indian IT exporters to look at how they can leverage cloud computing to change the mix of their services portfolio. For example:

1. Getting out of the commodity space like infrastructure or any other services segment that is getting too crowded or less profitable.
2. Moving beyond managing SLAs towards getting a bigger share of the client's IT spending on cloud computing.
3. Getting into sophisticated services requiring multiple skill sets.

The US has been an early adopter of cloud computing. The competitive landscape is already getting crowded. You have companies like Amazon, Microsoft, Google and IBM: each has its own "vision" and/or "ecosystem" of partners. You also have companies like Salesforce.com challenging SAP and Oracle through pricing.

If you take a closer look you find that each heavy weight is trying to grab a bigger share of Corporate IT spending. More than technology, this competition is all about brand image, marketing and economics (or pricing). It will be interesting to watch how each of them would perform inside as well as outside the US.

On the one hand, you have "off the shelf" solutions for cloud infrastructure where a vendor says "swipe your credit card and go ahead". On the other hand, software pricing in a cloud environment is quite complex. Customers have high expectations on cost savings. The criteria of decision making also varies by industry and geography.

In Europe, apart from the economics and politics of cloud computing, geography also matters! As I explained in Chapter 2, European clients also look at data security, privacy and taxation issues.

How can each major US based company position or even customize its solution to satisfy European clients?

This is why Indian IT exporters need to make an independent assessment looking at their own business model. Indian IT exporters of all sizes are not only competing with one another but also with global companies. Each one of them needs to specialize as well as be selective. Being just another service provider competing on a skill set may not be effective.

How can Indian IT exporters get a bigger share of IT spending by their clients on cloud computing solutions?

1. They need to be in the right market segment. The market segments for cloud computing solutions and services are already crowded.
2. They need to engage with their global clients early, even before a cloud computing solution is chosen.
3. They need to understand and adapt to the "economics and politics" in their client organization. In any global client organization, decision making on choosing and deploying cloud computing solutions will involve multiple stakeholders.
4. They need to fast track the adoption of cloud computing based on the above.

Later I will explain each of these topics. It is important for Indian IT exporters to leverage cloud computing to achieve multiple objectives:

- Change their mix of services portfolio
- Get out of the commodity space of IT services where there are too many players or where they are likely to be less profitable
- Move beyond a back end focus on SLAs towards offering real business value.
- Getting into sophisticated services requiring multiple skill sets.

In short, they need to revisit their value proposition, as a part of moving up the value chain. As I explained earlier, Indian IT exporters typically rely on CIOs of their client organization. They could get caught in the crossfire of political struggles at the CXO level during or after the selection of a cloud computing model. If they are ready to make the right investments, they can get a bigger share of this fast growing market. They can also improve their revenue productivity and pricing power over a period of time.

As I explained in Chapter 5, MNCs and their supply chain partners are trying to leverage cloud computing. Many of them use packages from SAP, Oracle and Salesforce.com. In the past, Indian IT exporters have focused on support and implementation services for these packages. However, some of these services are also getting commoditized. To be successful, they need to take their partnership model to a new level.

While doing so, they can also address downstream opportunities in global manufacturing and supply chains. However, they need to answer some important questions. How would a new partnership model be different from an older one? In what areas would they specialize in? If they are working on a partnership with SAP, would it cover cloud computing, analytics or both these areas? What is the nature of investments they are willing to make? Are they offering their own solution or remaining in the services space? The answers will determine whether they are indeed moving up the value chain and if so, how.

Economics and Politics of Cloud Computing

In this Section I will explain topics related to the cost case of cloud computing. I will also explain the changing role of CIOs and the CIO organization in the context of cloud computing. This is what I mean by the terms economics and politics! In Chapter 9, I will cover topics related to alternate pricing models and productivity. They are quite relevant for cloud computing.

While choosing a solution in cloud computing, the economics is far more important than technology. If Indian IT exporters can develop a strong business case, they can capture a bigger share of this market. Most Indian IT professionals understand the technology of cloud computing. If they are able to present their solutions or services from a business perspective, they can convince multiple stakeholders involved in decision making.

I will briefly explain the economics of cloud computing. Certain types of IT services can be priced based on a "Pay per Usage" billing model. Computing power and infrastructure can be priced incrementally in what is referred to as a "Pay As You Go" (PAYG) model. This is like a rental service instead of an upfront payment.

The role of CIOs and their priorities are changing across the world. In some organizations, they are losing their influence while in some other organizations, they are playing different roles. This change is more relevant in decision making related to cloud computing solutions.

Given that cloud computing affects multiple businesses CFOs will get involved. For each global client, CIOs would play different roles in examining the cost case and assessing risks. This is why Indian IT exporters need to get in early; get involved at all stages of decision making and also avoid getting caught in any political cross fire!

Each business unit head will be looking beyond cost optimization on improvements from a business perspective. CEOs would be looking at the overall impact and how their business can be transformed through cloud computing. All these imply that client expectations are high and that there will be multiple stakeholders.

Even if the global client ends up choosing an "off the shelf" cloud computing solution by "swiping a credit card", this requires groundwork and preparation. The business case has to match high expectations of clients. In the current economic scenario across the US and Europe, can this offer a window of opportunity for Indian IT exporters? This will depend on what choices they make during 2014.

In Jan 2014, HCL and CSC announced a partnership. Business media reports in the US and in India mentioned how two former rivals are getting together in the already crowded cloud computing marketplace. In this context, a few questions need to be answered:

1. Would Indian IT exporters continue to rally behind the CIOs of their client organization or would they move closer to business unit heads, CMOs and CFOs?

2. Would they remain a service provider working under the shadow of a global company? What partnership model would they pursue going forward?

If Indian IT exporters can develop a strong business case on their own, they can serve their global clients better. While doing so, they can leverage their strengths in three areas.

1. In addressing technology issues.
2. In addressing the economics of cloud computing.
3. In positioning cloud computing based solutions from a business perspective.

Developing a business case for cloud computing will require a different skill set. Apart from understanding technology related issues, knowledge of the client's business and business processes are also very important.

As I explained in Chapter 2, business executives in Europe have a different perspective on cloud computing solutions when compared to their counterparts in the US. Accordingly, the business case for the same global client can be different in Europe from what is applicable in the US. This requirement for customization of the business case can offer additional opportunities for Indian IT exporters.

Typically in a global client organization, stakeholders evaluate solutions based on multiple criteria apart from costs. They look at performance and integration issues; data security and privacy concerns. This is where Indian IT exporters need to understand the decision making process and organization politics.

If they enter the scene after a solution has already been chosen, they could slip into the commodity space where margins are lower. There is also a risk of them getting caught in the political crossfire between different stakeholders while managing tough SLAs!

An early engagement with their global client can provide them an advantage in subsequent services related to migration and cloud integration. They can also understand organization politics and position themselves accordingly.

An early entry can help them understand different priorities of CIOs, business units and the top management team of their global clients. This way, they would be able to fast track the adoption of cloud computing.

While presenting a business case, they need to address the priorities of each stakeholder. They need to make a comprehensive assessment. By presenting a strong and realistic business case, they can capture the mindshare of the entire top management team.

A business case will involve making a workload assessment and addressing important areas related to migrating (or moving) into a new cloud environment from an existing one. While migrating, there could be a disruption to the business; this may impact customers directly or indirectly. There could also be integration issues between the cloud environment and the legacy environment.

Interfaces need to be developed and tested between applications together with the business processes. All of these can be part of the preparatory work to be done. Of course, this would require a significant investment in terms of time and effort.

Earlier, I mentioned the nature of competition in this market. In the past, Indian IT exporters have adopted a skill based approach to new technologies. Of course, there is a shortage of skills related to cloud computing. To be successful, they need to specialize in those areas where they can add value to their partner as well as to their global client.

For example, in cloud specific testing, they can demonstrate cost savings as well as reduce the cycle time involved. If they are smart enough, they can even position themselves in the solution space of cloud computing, or being vendor neutral.

Of course, Indian IT exporters can identify and develop partnerships with global vendors. At the same time, they can't operate behind the shadow of a global vendor. They can't afford to get caught in the crossfire of economics and politics.

The market for cloud computing services is quite complex. I will explain possible strategies that Indian IT exporters can explore to capture a bigger share of the professional services market segment.

Possible Strategies

If Indian IT exporters can make appropriate changes to their current business model, they can pursue different strategies.

1. They can proactively present a business case.
2. They can also offer an alternate solution for cloud computing.
3. They can fast track adoption of cloud computing solutions and thereby deliver business value.

However, each strategy will require the appropriate skill sets and also involve investments. This is why for every Indian IT exporter, skill building needs to be in sync with the business model being pursued for cloud computing.

One long term strategy is to perform the role of a systems integrator instead of being yet another service provider. The system integration market segment is also referred to as cloud brokerage services.

I am not sure how many Indian IT exporters have the necessary capabilities to call themselves as cloud systems integrators. Even if they do, I am not sure if their clients are ready to accept them in such roles immediately.

This requires a higher level of partnership with software vendors and cloud service providers. To address this market Indian IT exporters need to expand their mindshare and develop relationships at the top management level. It will require a different engagement model. While performing this role, one needs to wear multiple hats: those of a business partner, a solution provider or even a consultant. An Indian IT or BPM exporter can't remain yet another service provider.

As a first step, they need to develop deeper relationships with existing clients. If they can leverage their existing relationships and play multiple roles, they can get a bigger share of client spending on cloud computing. If they play a secondary role, their opinions may not be taken seriously by the top management of their global clients.

Depending on their skill sets and customer relationship, they could still perform different roles. Before global clients choose a cloud computing solution, they can provide advisory services related to cloud computing. This involves performing an assessment and analysis of workloads and applications. Later, they can get involved at different stages of choosing, testing and implementing cloud computing based solutions.

They need to understand business requirements, assess the workloads and prepare a detailed plan together with their partners. While pushing a particular technology, they must address costs as well as risks associated. The business case can involve a tradeoff between costs, risks and client's concerns. However, all of these will require appropriate skill sets.

Currently, medium and large Indian IT exporters are active in the Application Development and Maintenance (ADM) market segment. Some of them are involved in migration of applications to a cloud environment.

Given the multiple scenarios of integration, they can look at becoming big players in the market segment for cloud integration services. The scenarios are: application to application (A2A) integration, business to business (B2B) integration, Cloud to Premises integration or even integrating a private cloud and a public cloud.

By fast tracking the adoption of cloud computing, IT service providers can get a bigger share of the client's IT spending on cloud computing. This will require a combination of technology skills and knowledge of the client's business. For example, they can demonstrate the benefits of cloud computing to business unit heads as well as CIOs by reducing time to market and delivering productivity improvements.

In Chapter 9, I will cover a wide range of topics related to pricing models, delivery metrics and productivity. If Indian IT exporters can incorporate them into their business model, they can offer an attractive business case in the area of cloud computing to their existing clients. Eventually, they can leverage this experience to address bigger opportunities and get into the solution space of cloud computing.

CHAPTER 9

Try New Business Models

In this chapter, I will leverage my industry experience to explain a wide range of topics related to the business model of Indian IT exporters.

- How can they quickly move up the value chain?
- What challenges could they face in doing so?
- What alternate business models can they explore?
- How can large Indian IT exporters successfully compete with global companies?
- How can mid-sized Indian IT exporters also get into the big league and compete with global players in the next few years?

Besides answering such questions, I will also cover few topics relevant to MNC captive units operating in the global IT services industry.

Move Up the Value Chain, Sooner, Not Later

Currently, most Indian IT exporters are associated primarily with the CIO organization, not business units. Many of them are busy pursuing outsourcing contracts coming up for renewal or renegotiation. Of course, there will be a short term focus on maintaining revenues and profitability. At the same time, they need to overcome any resistance to change.

This is not the time for Indian IT exporters to remain complacent in terms of global competitiveness. They need to move quickly in multiple areas: avoid a cost plus mindset, build the necessary capabilities and also target IT spending across their client organization.

In 2014, the economies in the US and Europe are showing signs of growth picking up. IT budgets will eventually go up. If Indian IT exporters don't increase their mindshare with CEOs, CFOs, CMOs and Business Unit heads, they could lose out on new opportunities.

Another focus area is to develop alternate pricing models. In recent years, global clients are demanding that pricing be linked to the output, outcomes and project results. Some Indian IT exporters have talked about outcome based pricing and outcome based contracts. Later I will explain the pros and cons of this model.

I will briefly explain why this can be tricky and challenging in the short term. Later I will also explain how Indian IT exporters can transition from an old T&M based pricing model towards these models in a smooth and effective manner.

When global clients refer to terms like outcomes or results, they often associate them with their own business. However, in many IT projects, external service providers have limited control over risks and uncertainty associated with their client's business.

Indian IT exporters need to first exercise control over the project outcome before trying to relate pricing with a business outcome. This is probably why many senior executives in the industry are cautious while offering an outcome based pricing option.

Let us get started. I will begin by introducing the broad requirements of a new business model for the IT services business. I will explain this in simple words so that they can be understood even by techies! I hope that my ideas will lead to meaningful discussions or debate. Young Indian IT professionals can relate them to a business model already used in their own organization.

New Business Models

Any new business model needs to be quite different in one or more of three areas. The figure and table below summarize these changes.

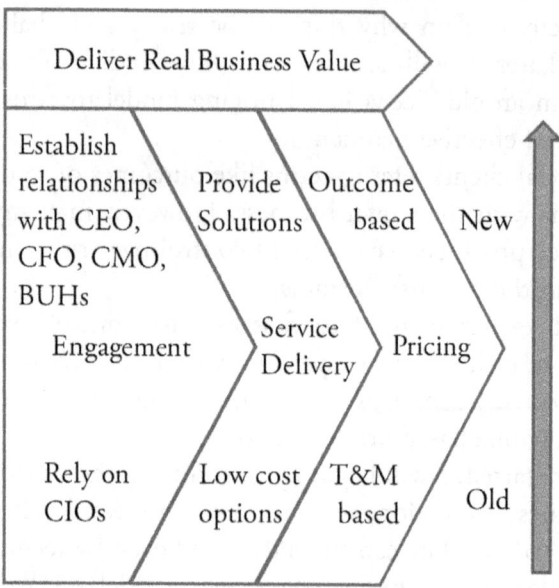

Business Model and Value Chain

Changes Required in a new business model	What the new model could involve or offer	How these changes relate to moving up the value chain
How Indian IT exporters address opportunities	Develop relationships at the CXO level and with Business unit heads	Address opportunities at multiple levels of IT spending beyond the budget controlled by CIOs
How they manage delivery of services from India	Provide solution to a business problem beyond low cost service delivery	Deliver real business value; manage project outcomes, share risks, accept additional responsibilities
How the global client pays the Indian IT exporter	Move away from T&M based billing to offer other alternatives	Relate price to project outcomes, share rewards, adopt non-linear models for higher revenue productivity

The first step reflects a change in the customer relationship model. From a focus at the CIO level, this extends other CXOs* and business unit heads. The term engagement is used by the IT services industry to refer to this area.

> * CXOs refer to top management executives. CEO: Chief Executive Officer; CFO: Chief Financial Officer; CIO: Chief Information Officer and CMO: Chief Marketing Officer.

The second step reflects a change in focus from low cost services delivery to offering better business value. The focus needs to shift towards providing solutions to the client: I explained this difference in Chapter 8.

The third step reflects changes in the billing model and commercial terms associated with the contract. If they are more attractive to the client the service provider can get a bigger share of the client's IT spending. Later I will explain alternate pricing options.

In the table above, I have explained the changes required. Of course, making changes in each of these three areas simultaneously could be challenging. The impact of some changes may not be felt in the short term. Each Indian IT exporter needs to have a clear road map to make progress in each of the three areas during every quarter.

Necessary management capabilities have to be developed. Suitable partners have to be identified. Large Indian IT exporters need to build their own ecosystem of partners, just like their global competitors. If incremental changes are made quick succession, Indian IT exporters can quickly transition to their new business model in the next few quarters. The impact can be felt in their balance sheets and also experienced by their major clients.

This is why multiple objectives need to be pursued in every quarter.
1. Maintaining both revenue growth and better profitability while pursuing new business.
2. Prioritizing the changes in the current business model instead of postponing them.
3. Improving revenue productivity in every quarter, even if improvements are small.
4. Acquiring better pricing power with major clients.
5. Building the necessary skill sets across an ecosystem of partners.

I will cover each of these topics later. This approach can apply to any Indian IT exporter: not necessarily large companies.

One of the focus areas for many Indian IT exporters during 2014 are contracts coming up for rebid and renegotiation. How can large and medium sized Indian IT exporters compete with global companies? How can they get into the big league? I will cover this topic first.

Competing and Winning New Business

In recent quarters, large and medium Indian IT exporters have begun reporting new business wins related to outsourcing contracts coming up for renewal and/or renegotiation. Of course, they would compete on price and skill sets. In this section, I will cover some other competitive strategies they could adopt.

Many large Indian IT exporters have a mature global delivery model and are also cash rich. As I pointed out in Chapter 7, they need to close the gap between their revenue productivity and that of global service providers like IBM. How can they identify weaknesses of the incumbent service provider and get prepared to disrupt the "old guard"?

Each global service provider such as IBM is facing some challenges in the US and in Europe. One strategy is to look behind the smoke screen created by business media reports, understand these challenges and offer a more attractive business model. This is the best way for Indian IT exporters to move up the value chain. I will offer a few hints.

Since mid-2011, IBM's hardware revenues have fallen for 9 successive quarters ending Dec 2013. In Sep 2013, IBM sold off its CRM BPO business to Synnex. In Jan 2014, IBM sold off its x86 server business to Lenovo. IBM also announced spending $ 1.2 billion during 2014 to set up 15 new data centers. Business media reports speculated during Feb 2014 on whether IBM would hive off two more of its businesses: its Software Defined Networking (SDN) business and its semiconductor business, specifically the chip division.

Large Indian IT exporters need to ask some pertinent questions:

1. Is IBM conducting a "garage sale" to reorganize its business portfolio? How do these developments affect its revenue productivity in the services business?

2. How do these developments enable IBM to move up the value chain in the cloud computing market place?

Some readers might wonder why I am using term "garage sale" in the context of IBM. IBM's announcements must be viewed in the broader context. During Jan and Feb 2014 Google, Intel, Microsoft, Samsung, Cisco and Lenovo all made some major announcements. During 2014 could there be a major realignment in the global IT industry? Indian IT exporters need to watch out and change course accordingly.

In the past, global service providers like IBM have focused on large deals with a wide range of services: IT operations, IT support, Application Development and Maintenance (ADM), BPM, etc. However, delivery of multiple services would typically involve multiple contracts.

In recent years, some global clients are looking at a multi-vendor strategy to drive down costs and drive up specialization in terms of skill sets. This is why Indian IT exporters of all sizes can go after one or more contracts coming up for rebid or renegotiation.

Indian IT exporters need to build relationships based on prior qualification. If they identify vulnerable accounts, they can establish executive level contacts at the appropriate level. Capturing the mindshare must begin long before contracts are due to come up for a rebid.

For many global clients, the priorities of CIOs and CFOs are changing. Decision making on new contracts is most likely to involve multiple stakeholders. They would look beyond cost reduction by using multiple criteria to evaluate service providers.

Most large Indian IT exporters follow a centralized decision making based in India. In recent quarters, few of them have cut down the number of senior IT professionals located at customer site to optimize costs. This has its own pros and cons.

How would they build client relationships at the CXO level with a hydra shaped organization structure with tentacles spread across the world? They need to adopt a right engagement model especially while pursuing each major contract. Given that each global client could be different, they need to avoid a "one size fits all" approach.

Few Indian IT exporters have talked about an industry vertical based organization. While competing with global giants, they need to establish contact with the top management team of their global clients. To be effective, they need to put together a team with the right profile of people. More than the organization structure, what matters is the skill sets in this team!

Their engagement model has to match the size, mix of services and complexity of the contract. Concerned managers and executives have to be empowered to take decisions. In Chapter 6, I mentioned few opportunities across industry segments. This is where medium sized Indian IT exporters may be better placed than their larger compatriots.

How can Indian IT exporters upset the incumbent IT service provider? In the next Section, I will point towards few targets based on my experience. My friends from Indian IT exporters need to figure out how to go after each target. These targets are also relevant for medium sized IT exporters who are eager to get into the big league.

Identify Vulnerable Areas

One obvious target is to look for symptoms of what I referred to as the cost plus mindset in Chapter 7. In older contracts already in operation for several years, this mindset could have developed in the project team of an incumbent IT services provider. This mindset can also manifest at various levels of the service provider's organization.

Another target area is project management. In some contracts, there could be gaps from the service provider's perspective. In other contracts, the overhead could be quite high or the management chain quite long. The global client may not be getting enough value in terms of project management. As a result, the client may still not be satisfied.

Accordingly, Indian IT exporters need to develop a strong value proposition. They must be able to demonstrate specific areas of improvement. This is not about offering a better skill set at a lower rate. They need to look at the total cost of services delivery.

There can be many reasons why a global client is not satisfied with the incumbent IT service provider. There could be a mismatch between expectations and project outcomes. The underlying reasons could relate to the billing model or the delivery metrics. Some global clients may not be satisfied with the productivity of service delivery. Others may not be satisfied with processes and practices of the incumbent service provider.

Accordingly, areas of improvement can be identified. The new contracts can include better delivery metrics, new billing models, sharing of risks and responsibilities, improved productivity, you name it! These could be achieved through automation, usage of tools, intellectual property etc. I will cover each of these topics later.

In the past, CEOs of Indian IT exporters have focused on improving their own revenue productivity. It is time they focus on productivity from the perspective of services delivery. Based on my experience, I can confidently say that this requires a change of mind set!

In recent quarters, global clients and consulting organizations have mentioned terms like re-shoring, near shoring and insourcing. Each Indian IT exporter needs to understand the rationale behind such terms. Each global client could be redistributing jobs across the world for different reasons.

Many Indian IT exporters talk about growing their business from newer technologies. Each global client has a different priority for these projects. For some clients, the need for speed can be more important than lower costs. If so, the value proposition and the business model needs to change accordingly. Skill sets alone can't drive growth in the business.

Some clients would like to reduce the cycle time*. If so, can the use of agile methodologies reduce the effort or crunch the schedule? Indian IT exporters need to explore various options and adapt accordingly.

* Cycle time in IT projects is defined as the time taken from start to finish. Typically, the start and end points are defined in the project life cycle based on the software methodology and milestones associated with the client's decision making cycle.

Older outsourcing contracts followed a top down approach where decisions were made by the CIO organization. The management chain could involve multiple layers:

1. In the CIO organization of the global client.
2. The account team of the IT service provider based in the US or in Europe.
3. The management layer in the offshore delivery center.

A new contract need not be structured as it used to be in the past. Typically, old T&M based contracts were based on a headcount where sharing of skilled resources was difficult. In the new contract, multiple services could come under one umbrella.

By avoiding water tight compartments between project teams, Indian IT exporters can offer better synergy to clients. Cost savings could be achieved through economy of scale as well as specialization. This strategy is applicable to companies of all sizes.

In earlier contracts, the CIO organization of the global client was part of the management chain between respective business units and the India delivery team. In some incumbent global IT service providers with an India based delivery center (like IBM), this chain could be long due to other reasons.

How can this management overhead be reduced? This is where Indian IT exporters need to explore various options and strike a balance. Where possible, they can offer a flatter organization structure. They can supplement this with the right model of project governance, global delivery and thereby reduce the total cost. If they can do a good job, they can even disrupt their competitors from the "old guard"!

Indian IT exporters need to examine each role performed across the management chain in the new contract. They need to improve its effectiveness from a business value perspective. Later I will explain topics related to project management and project governance.

The above discussion also applies to medium sized Indian IT exporters. They need to understand why their global clients are seeking a rebid or a renegotiation. Accordingly, they can offer a better value proposition and get into the big league. In the next Section, I will cover topics related to pricing models.

Alternate Pricing Models

Before discussing a new pricing model, Indian IT exporters need to understand the changing priorities of global clients. They could dislike old T&M based billing models due to one or more of the following reasons:
1. They are open ended.
2. It forces them to make commitments upfront.
3. It requires additional management oversight.

Typically, global clients have a new set of priorities.
1. Optimize total costs (focus on cost savings).
2. Get more "bang for the buck" (focus on productivity).
3. Achieve the right type of project governance (reduce management overhead).
4. Convert fixed costs into variable costs through usage based pricing

Accordingly, Indian IT exporters need to offer a pricing model avoiding the pitfalls of an old T&M based model and also matches with stake holders' new priorities.

In this Section, I will describe a few billing models gaining importance in recent years. I will also introduce the topic of outcome based pricing. This discussion is not specific to cloud computing: outcome based pricing can be applied in many services. They could be ADM, IT Operations, BPM, analytics, you name it!

As IT budgets get squeezed, CFOs as well as CIOs are adopting what they call "asset light" strategies: this means avoiding fixed costs. They are trying to make IT related costs more predictable and more controllable. This means pricing is based on usage and variable costs. It is not based on a fixed headcount as per the old T&M model. These help them to optimize costs and make better use of the available IT budget at various levels.

One of the pricing models gaining popularity among CIOs and Business Unit heads is what is referred to as "Pay As You Go" model (PAYG) for IT services. Here, services components are added or modified to change the scope of work to match with changes in IT budgets. Another model is referred to as pay for usage pricing.

These two models can be applied together through complex contracts addressing a wide range of services. They can be offered regardless of whether a cloud computing model is applicable or not.

Interestingly, most Indians are already familiar with such pricing models, since they are offered by telecom and media companies in India. In this Section I will describe these models in the context of IT services.

Here, customers choose a suite of services they intend to make use of. As far as possible, they pay the service provider only for services they actually use. If or when required, they can modify the suite of services and the pricing using one or more packages offered by the service provider. This model is also prevalent in the BPM industry in the form of transaction based pricing. Can this be applied to IT services?

What I am referring to is an "IT version" of this model, meant for corporate users. This has already been adopted in many large outsourcing contracts for IT support services. With cloud computing gaining acceptance, this could be the most preferred pricing model by global clients going forward.

In Application Development and Maintenance (ADM) contracts, a PAYG model is becoming popular for a wide range of services. Global clients would make changes periodically based on their business criticality, IT budget and seasonal patterns. Service providers need to accommodate changes in the components of service based on funding, usage by business units and appropriate delivery metrics (typically SLAs).

Earlier, pricing for support services was based on a headcount depending on the number, complexity and criticality of applications. A PAYG model offers more flexibility. It could be based on delivery metrics and SLAs (service level agreements).

Earlier, development and ongoing enhancements were authorized by the CIO organization of global clients on a headcount basis. Here, CIOs as well as business unit heads are demanding more flexibility because IT spending has become more discretionary.

In IBM, I have worked in a large ADM contract where several features of a PAYG option in the contract were successfully implemented over a period of time. Based on my experience, I would therefore recommend that Indian IT exporters need to start offering a "pay for use" billing model and/or a PAYG option instead of a headcount based model.

This will help their clients reduce fixed costs and increase the component of variable costs. In order to successfully deliver such projects, Indian IT exporters need to engage with their global clients in the planning and budgeting process. They also need to set up appropriate practices in project management and project governance.

PAYG is also gaining acceptance in the cloud computing environment. It can be applied in a shared services delivery model already being used by many Indian BPM exporters. This is why PAYG could be the "way to go" for many Indian IT and BPM exporters.

In any services business, customer satisfaction is all about setting and managing expectations. A PAYG option can be made more attractive if the IT service provider can assure that the outcome of an IT project will meet a certain level of expectations. This is why the term "outcome based pricing" is gaining importance with global clients.

In this Section, I will introduce this topic. Indian IT service providers need to first understand the context of this term "outcome". Accordingly, they can develop a smart and sustainable business model that matches with their client's priorities.

Many global clients are not satisfied with the outcome of IT projects in recent years. This is why IT service providers need to first control the outcome from a deliverable perspective. They need to put in place a process to measure and control the project outcome. The next step would be to offer outcome based pricing. Jumping to offer an outcome based pricing instead of the current T&M based model could be risky.

An outcome based pricing model must have three major ingredients.
1. Set expectations on the project outcome before the client and service provider finalize the price.
2. Manage the project delivery where the project outcome can be measured and controlled from both sides: the client as well as the service provider.
3. Incorporate rewards and penalties linked to the project outcome in the final price to be paid.

Later I will cover topics related to each of these three ingredients. I will explain how Indian IT exporters can manage project outcomes. I will also explain how they can share the risks and responsibilities associated.

In recent quarters, India's BPO industry has rebranded itself into BPM (Business Process Management). Of course, Indian BPM exporters have got rid of the "O" word. Many CEOs have talked about strategies they refer to as nonlinear growth, products, platforms, you name it! In the next Section, I will relate these terms to moving up the value chain.

Non Linear Growth, Platform based BPO

In my opinion, it is important to understand terms like "nonlinear" and "platform" strategies in terms of its impact on revenue productivity and/or pricing power. Usually, these terms refer to new business models.

In a nonlinear pricing model, clients are not charged for the effort (on the input side) but the outcome or results (on the output side). This allows Indian IT exporters to improve revenue productivity and also acquire pricing power. They can grow their revenues faster than the rate of growth in terms of number of employees.

In Chapter 8, I mentioned the term Platform as a Service (PaaS) and topics related to pricing. The term nonlinear pricing can also be used in a cloud computing environment. Here, the IT service provider will bundle together several components of hardware, software and/or intellectual property (IP).

The term platform based BPO is used in the BPM industry. Typically, the term platform involves one or more of the following:

1. It involves packaging or bundling of hardware, software and services.
2. The platform offers a business process or an IT solution incorporating IP.
3. There is some customization and optimization done to provide a better performance at a lower cost to the client.

A reusable platform allows Indian IT and BPM exporters to offer attractive pricing options like payment per transaction to their clients. They can achieve higher revenue productivity through bundling or packaging. By leveraging both nonlinear pricing and platform strategy the IT service provider can improve revenue productivity and also acquire pricing power over a period of time. They can also build a revenue stream over a longer period of time.

Nonlinear growth can also be based entirely on IP. Such an IP based strategy can help Indian IT exporters improve their revenue productivity significantly over a period of time. In the next Section, I will cover topics related to creating and monetizing IP.

Role of Intellectual Property (IP)

Industry experts tend to compare the revenue productivity of Indian IT exporters and global software or services companies. The latter tend to have higher revenue productivity because a major part of their revenues includes an IP component.

Most Indian IT exporters rely on a business model based on services and outsourcing. However, most of their competitors based in the US offer IT products and/or leverage their IP. This is why industry consultants recommend an IP based strategy.

In Chapter 8, I explained why Indian IT exporters need to enter the IT consulting business. Consulting companies command better pricing power because of many reasons. One of them is related to creating and monetizing intellectual capital as well as intellectual property (IP). The former term is commonly used in the services business; the latter is more prevalent in the product business. The difference lies in how knowledge is packaged, reused and monetized.

Over the years, consulting companies leverage their industry experience to create Intellectual Capital based on best practices, processes, tools and techniques. They package this into IP and also leverage IP on client projects by charging a hefty fee. They not only monetize their IP but also use IP to improve their pricing power.

Any IP based strategy has its own pros and cons from a legal perspective. The global IT industry has witnessed some interesting disputes as well as deals related to patents and IPs. In recent years, there have been many lawsuits filed across patent holders, businesses, the software industry and customers. There are also some interesting deals.

Google and Oracle are fighting over copyright issues related to Java. In Jan and Feb 2014, Google finalized two deals: one with Samsung and another with Cisco. These deals cover major patent cross licensing agreements. In Jan 2014, Google sold off its handset business to Lenovo. However, Google also mentioned that it still retains the ownership of a "majority" of Motorola's patent portfolio. In Feb 2014, Google also won an important lawsuit worth $ 1 billion on behalf of its users. Indian IT exporters need to understand the significance of these developments. How do they affect patents in the rapidly expanding Android ecosystem?

During 2013, few Indian IT exporters made M&A deals. Some CEOs proudly spoke about how many patents were held by the companies they recently acquired in the US or in Europe. I am asking two simple questions: Can this translate into better revenue productivity in 2014? Can this also provide them pricing power? If so, can this happen without a major change in their current business model and/or their organization structure?

Most Indian IT exporters are in the services business. They need to first get smarter while addressing the commercial and legal aspects associated with IP. They need to understand how to share costs, benefits and ownership of IP with global clients. Each of these is more important than acquiring a company holding some interesting patents.

Creating an IP or acquiring a patent has to tie up with an IP based business model. A Feb 2014 report by KPMG and Nasscom also highlighted this fact. Indian IT exporters have a long way to go in creating, managing and monetizing IP.

Often, creating and monetizing IP are discussed in the context of IT product companies. Based on my experience in IBM India, creating and monetizing IP in the services business is a different paradigm altogether. I will explain why this is so by highlighting the pros and cons of creating IPs in the IT services business.

This applies to Indian IT exporters as well as captive units of global IT service providers. Creating an IP or a patent by itself can't imply that an Indian IT exporter is moving up the value chain unless it is monetized and is also part of the business model.

Creating IP will require making proactive investments: many Indian IT exporters have avoided this in the past. They have not only stuck to a T&M based billing model but also use a "cost recovery" model for IP. These can further weaken their ability to negotiate with their global clients on terms and conditions related to IP.

When global clients pay for the entire effort spent they usually demand the right to any IP that gets created. This is why many Indian IT exporters have faced restrictions in the past in the creation and usage of IP. In many cases, they are unable to reuse the IP created in one project for a similar project with another client.

By following a cost recovery model, the Indian IT exporter could forfeit an opportunity to monetize IP for subsequent projects. Even if the IP is jointly created the client can settle by paying a one-time fee, effectively "buying the IP" for a small sum.

How can Indian IT exporters break this deadlock?
1. They must move away from a T&M based billing model and also negotiate better terms with clients on matters related to IP.
2. They need to make big investments to create IP, especially on newer technologies.
3. They need to integrate the process of creating and monetizing IP through an appropriate business model.
4. They need to create an environment internally where employees realize the value of creating IP and actively participate in this process.

Until each of these steps is taken, moving up the value chain through an IP based route in the services business will remain elusive for many Indian IT exporters.

Today, managers in many India based captive units of MNCs talk about creating IP. I would like to ask a few questions to those working on IT services projects. Do their employees take this seriously? How many of their senior IT professionals have created IPs from projects executed for global clients in recent years?

No doubt, Indian IT professionals have achieved a lot in the IT services business. But Indian IT exporters have a long way to go in developing the mindset to create IP in the services business. There is still some confusion among many senior IT professionals in India on how filing patents can help them individually or how these patents can also translate into revenues.

This confusion exists whether they are employed by Indian IT exporters or by India based captive units of global IT service providers. Many of them don't understand the difference between patents related to software products and patents in the services business. They also face several barriers at multiple levels. Why is this so?

Most Indian IT professionals working in IT services are focused on service delivery. Would they spend more time and effort creating an IP? If their managers don't have a clear strategy to monetize this IP, how can they convince employees to spend time and effort to create IP in the first place? This is the first type of barrier.

Let us assume that some experienced employees are capable of creating IP. Before taking this up, they would ask a few questions. Can IP created in my project be reused in another project? If so how? Without understanding this, in what form would they create IP? This lack of clarity is the second type of barrier.

Let us assume that some employees did create IP in one project. In a cost recovery model, how do they benefit in the short term as well as long term? Do the internal evaluation system, rewards and recognition encourage further creation of IPs? This lack of a reward mechanism could discourage many of them to create subsequent IPs.

Many of the questions I have raised above are based on my experience in the services business of IBM India in one of IBM's largest ADM accounts. I would not like to elaborate further in this book.

I would conclude this discussion on a key message for Indian IT exporters. Most global clients are aware of IP in the IT services business.

If you can integrate IP with a business model and also present this to your client, you can certainly move up the value chain!

Earlier I introduced outcome based pricing. In the next Section, I will expand this topic.

Learn to Manage Outcomes, not SLAs

I will begin by explaining some terms used in the IT services business. One term is referred to as service level agreements (SLAs). Another is referred to as Key Performance Indicators (KPIs). When someone uses this jargon, it is important to understand the context.

The term SLA is typically associated with metrics used in services contracts. SLAs refer to service level thresholds required to be met by the service provider. KPIs measure the performance of external service providers from a business perspective. KPIs can also be used to measure the performance of the IT organization end to end by business unit heads.

While the term SLA is used from a contract perspective, KPIs are used from a management perspective. While CIOs have been focusing on SLAs in the past, many business units now measure KPIs. Some KPIs are also mapped or correlated with outcomes from a business perspective. For the benefit of readers, I will use a simpler term: delivery metrics to explain how Indian IT exporters can manage service outcomes or project outcomes. Readers who are familiar with SLAs and KPIs can associate them with the appropriate metrics in their own organization or in the contract they are familiar with.

When clients talk about outcomes, what metrics are they referring to? This is the question to be first answered by all Indian IT exporters. By understanding the term outcome and also managing the outcome, they can meet the expectations of global clients.

The payment model may not matter as long as the client is confident that their service provider, the Indian IT exporter in this case is delivering business value. The table below summarizes the stages involved.

Stages involved	How to Progress towards Outcome based pricing
Measure and Monitor Delivery Metrics	Report delivery metrics to your global client; Demonstrate improvements periodically
Incorporate delivery metrics into existing services contracts	Start offering delivery metrics as SLAs; meet these SLAs and also raise the bar periodically
Incorporate metrics into risk and reward based pricing	Link few delivery metrics or SLAs to payment terms; offer some form of outcome based pricing

The first step is to start measuring and monitoring services delivery while continuing with existing contracts. Even if the pricing model is T&M based, this can be done.

Typically, Indian IT exporters use delivery metrics for internal reporting and as part of their quality management processes. These metrics include effort variance, schedule variance, cost variance, defect data, risk data and other delivery metrics.

One set of metrics can be used internally by the Indian IT exporter to measure, monitor and control the project outcomes. Another set of metrics related to project outcome can be periodically reported to the global client.

Some of my friends from Indian IT exporters may ask: why should we stick our neck out to report internal metrics to global clients? After all, internal metrics need not be the same as SLAs applicable in a T&M based contract.

My answer is that such reporting helps capture the mindshare of stakeholders. Indian IT exporters can demonstrate improvements from one project to another or from one quarter to another. The services business is all about setting and managing expectations. Why not use delivery metrics to set the right expectations and also meet them? This can avoid a tough negotiation down the line.

The next stage is to incorporate few delivery metrics into the existing contract. In major projects, global clients try to strike a balance between effort, schedule and costs. The client may be willing to pay for the effort only if this balance is maintained. In such situations, some delivery metrics can be incorporated into the contract as appropriate SLAs.

In the call center industry, typical metrics reported in the past were on the input side. For example: average handle time, abandonment rate, average speed of response, total time to answer etc. The focus is shifting towards metrics related to customer experience and customer satisfaction. Some BPM service providers offer appropriate SLAs. The next step is to link pricing with business outcomes instead of transaction volumes.

In IT projects involving ADM, certain limits can be set for effort variance and schedule variance. A penalty clause can be incorporated in the event of Indian IT exporters not meeting such thresholds. This would give the necessary confidence to CIOs and business unit heads to continue with existing T&M based pricing models.

Capturing the mindshare of business unit heads can be done though the third step: offering risk and reward based pricing. In IBM I have worked on project governance where some projects carried a penalty clause based on delivery metrics. Some delivery metrics were outcome based. I will leverage my experience to explain this topic.

In many key projects, a global client may withhold a payment or levy a penalty if a delivery deadline is not met. Extending this model, it is also possible for Indian IT exporters to incorporate rewards for good performance. Business Unit heads might agree to this if they are confident that this will not end up in a cost escalation on either side.

For example, an Indian IT exporter can negotiate with a global client for an extra payment as a reward or as a bonus. This could be applicable for an early delivery or a large negative variance in costs.

An early project completion can offer direct business benefits by reducing the time to market or result in cost savings. This bonus payment could be a fixed fee for cost savings between X and Y. Beyond a certain threshold, the reward can be a percentage of cost savings.

A proactive approach to risk and reward based pricing could be a good way to gain the mindshare of a global client. By doing so, Indian IT exporters can convince their global client that they are a reliable business partner. In the next Section, I will explain how they can leverage their project management expertise.

Manage Projects based on Outcomes

In the last decade, many Indian IT exporters have acquired certification related to Quality at an organization level. Senior IT professionals across large and medium companies have acquired certification in Project Management. Can Indian IT exporters effectively leverage skills related to project management in their business model?

When business unit heads deal with external service providers directly, they expect a higher level of project management skills and capabilities. PMs need to perform certain roles that were earlier performed by their client's CIO organization.

The difference lies in many areas.
1. Controlling costs.
2. Sharing risks and responsibilities.
3. Project planning and governance.

PMs in India need to play a bigger role in each of these areas.

In the past, project managers (PMs) in India have focused on project deliverables and meeting SLAs. They have consistently delivered complex projects on time, within budget. Have they really focused on project outcome from a business perspective? This is a question to be answered honestly and sincerely by most Indian IT exporters.

I am not trying to undermine the current role played by project managers (PMs) in the IT industry. I am pointing out the constraints they face due to the business model. In the past, most Indian IT exporters have accepted a limited role of project management when the pricing model is T&M based.

Here, PMs tend to focus on the input side of services delivery: they may not share risks with their global clients and accept more responsibilities. Going forward, this needs to change. PMs also need to focus on demonstrating productivity improvements in service delivery. In the next Section, I will cover the topic of productivity.

Can PMs control the costs even if the pricing is T&M based? I mentioned two areas in Chapter 7 while discussing the cost plus mindset: estimation and change control. In addition, PMs need to manage project dependencies, share risks and accept more responsibilities.

By controlling costs, PMs can gain the mindshare and improve visibility with business unit heads. This is also a good way for Indian IT exporters to overcome the cost plus mindset I explained in Chapter 7. This will help them in the next step: focusing on project outcomes.

Managing and controlling the project outcome is different from completing a project on time as per estimated effort. In the past, PMs with Indian IT exporters have focused on the latter. The former is much more than managing the costs associated with IT.

As I mentioned earlier, business unit heads have different requirements and expectations on PM roles. Of course they would like PMs to control the project cost. They would also look at project outcomes. In short, PMs need to demonstrate the project's impact on the business directly or indirectly.

Earlier, Indian IT exporters interacted with one major stakeholder: the CIO or someone from the CIO organization. Going forward, their PMs need to also work with CMOs and business unit heads. Accordingly, PMs need to understand the stakeholders involved and the decision making process.

Business units could control budgets while CIOs can perform vendor management and project governance functions. Respective business unit heads may choose which projects are to be taken up and when. Accordingly, PMs need to interact with multiple stakeholders.

Another focus area is do-ability. When the CIO organization is involved, the pros and cons of the solution and project delivery are also evaluated at the customer end. When Indian IT exporters are directly interacting with business units, they need to address this area almost entirely on their own.

Some business unit heads can have unrealistic or unreasonable expectations. PMs need to set and manage these expectations. They need to evaluate the pros and cons from a technology perspective as well as a project delivery perspective.

Each business unit head of global clients has a different requirement of project management. Project management is also about successful execution in spite of the risks associated. Some business unit heads could measure this in terms of a project scorecard. Their expectations could be quite different from that of CIOs.

Earlier, PMs were focusing on a narrow set of delivery metrics while dealing with CIOs. Today global clients demand that PMs manage and control metrics related to the project outcome and even metrics specific to their business like costs per transaction.

Accordingly, PMs need to develop a system of project governance: this can be a new paradigm for some of them. This will involve sharing risks and responsibilities with business unit heads.

In the past, PMs of Indian IT exporters have managed projects typically billed on a T&M basis. They have also interacted primarily with the CIO organization. Going forward, they need to offer other pricing models and also interact with business unit heads. This will require a new set of skills related to risk management.

Earlier I mentioned the term do-ability. This is about addressing project dependencies and the associated risks. Some of them could be technology related dependencies associated with the solution. Some others could be related to delivery issues specific to the project. PMs need to evaluate the pros and cons associated and effectively manage risks.

Instead of merely tracking and reporting risks, PMs need to play a bigger role. They need to share risks and responsibilities with the CIO organization of the global client and the business unit funding the project. By doing so, they can manage the outcome and also improve results. This is a different paradigm altogether.

Going forward, the skill sets required for PM roles to be performed by Indian IT exporters could be quite different from what was applicable in earlier projects. They need to develop deeper relationships in their global client organizations.

They need to participate in project planning with business unit heads and CIOs. They need to jointly control project costs so that budgets are not overspent. Each of these will require a higher level of maturity in project management from Indian IT exporters.

Accordingly, PMs need to demonstrate a higher level of expertise and competence. They need to get smarter in negotiating contracts and commercial terms. This is also a part of moving up the value chain. Being smart in contracts will depend on one or both of the following:

1. How effectively PMs can manage a contract and also make a profit. For e.g., risk and reward based pricing* I mentioned earlier.
2. How PMs from one company can force their counterparts from a competitor to accept a tougher contract and "bear the burden".

* PMs can accumulate penalties and rewards by appropriate terms and conditions in the contract. These are referred to as performance credits. They are adjusted against project

payments. Here, penalties and incentives are carried forward from one project to another for a major client. This way, managing them becomes easier over a period of time.

In the past, not many PMs in India have got this opportunity simply because Indian IT exporters relied on T&M based pricing. I am confident that smart PMs in India can quickly learn the "tricks of the trade". However, this will also require changes by Indian IT exporters on how they measure and reward the performance of their PMs and delivery teams.

Focus on Productivity Improvement

Having covered topics related to project management, I will explain productivity improvement in services delivery. For several years, I worked on this area in one of IBM's largest ADM accounts. I am also an industrial engineer by qualification.

I will avoid discussing definitions of terms like efficiency, effectiveness and productivity. Instead, I will explain why productivity improvement can be a part of the business model and also a strategy to move up the value chain.

First of all, Indian IT professionals need to understand productivity in the right context. This term must not be confused with revenue productivity from their employer's perspective. What I am referring to is productivity in services delivery from a client perspective.

Productivity is related to both output and input: it is not about cost optimization. Any improvement in productivity must be directly or indirectly be associated with the client's business. Each client can view productivity improvement differently.

For some, it means delivering more "bang for the buck" in terms of IT services. For others, it relates to faster execution, reduced cycle time or reduced time to market from a business perspective. Accordingly, appropriate metrics need to be used to demonstrate improvements.

In IT support services, one example is a better turnaround for problem resolution. In BPM services it could be the number of customer queries or transactions successfully completed in a given period of time.

In application development it could mean delivering more end user functionality with the same effort. Productivity metrics can also relate to performance improvements with a direct business impact: such as the time taken to complete a business transaction.

In IT projects, reducing the cycle time can translate into productivity improvements. This is quite relevant in new technologies where the top management of clients would be looking at metrics like "time to market" or "time to go live".

To measure as well as demonstrate productivity improvements, Indian IT exporters need to leverage their skills in three areas: technology, project management and understanding of the client's business.

It doesn't matter how productivity is improved: it could be based on automation of manual effort; process improvements or even based on intellectual property (IP). The end result must translate into better business value delivered to global clients.

Many Indian IT exporters have an automation strategy. This term can refer to use of tools, techniques and process improvements associated with IT services delivery. This strategy can be fine-tuned to improve services delivery and thereby demonstrate business value.

A good automation strategy needs to focus on the business impact from a client's perspective. Even a reduction in effort can translate into reduction in cycle time. The focus needs to shift away from cost optimization to cycle time improvements. This may be difficult to demonstrate in a traditional T&M based pricing: this is why a change in the business model may be necessary in many cases.

Many Indian IT exporters have built an impressive repository of home grown automation tools across the software development life cycle. In the past, they have recovered the cost associated. Instead of a cost recovery, can they charge their customer a usage fee for the tools, as if it is another software product? This strategy can not only improve productivity but also enable them move up the value chain.

This is why Indian IT exporters need to think big. If they continue to adopt a cost recovery model, I would consider this as a symptom of their "cost plus mindset". I would not elaborate further: I hope readers get the message!

I will mention a few "big ideas" for productivity improvement.

1. Indian IT exporters can develop a sound automation strategy based on creating and monetizing Intellectual Property (IP). Earlier, I covered topics related to IP.

2. They can demonstrate productivity improvements through delivery metrics and also incorporating productivity related SLAs into the contract.

3. They can improve IT services delivery by what experts refer to as predictive analytics. For example, IT service providers can proactively analyze IT operations data, predict what could go wrong and also prevent a major crisis from happening.

Such ideas not only help Indian IT exporters to become globally competitive but also get into the big league. These ideas can be applied in companies of any size for any global client.

I will conclude by covering topics related to India based captive units of global IT service providers, MNCs and global banks. The associated industry churn also affects Indian IT and BPM exporters of all sizes.

India based Captive Units

In Chapters 4, 5 and 6 I mentioned topics related to captive units of MNCs and global banks. In this Section, I will explain the industry churn they could be experiencing during 2014 and beyond.

Based on data from NASSCOM, India based captive units of Fortune 500 companies together have more than 500,000 employees. The term moving up the value chain also applies to each employee in India based captive units of global IT service providers, MNCs and global banks. They include engineers, banking, finance, IT and BPM professionals.

Firstly, Indian professionals working with such captive units need to acquire necessary skill sets. Otherwise, they can lose out: some of them could even get laid off!

Secondly each captive unit based in India needs to move up the value chain by offering high end services. This could be in areas like analytics, Engineering and R&D services. By doing so, the India center will have better visibility with the top management of their parent company. With unemployment and economic uncertainty in the US and in Europe, one can't assume that work will continue to flow to India based captive units.

This is why each senior professional or manager employed in India based captive units need to demonstrate business value to their parent organization. In addition to acquiring the necessary skill sets, they need to perform multiple roles and accept more responsibilities.

Each India based captive unit needs to demonstrate better business value to its parent organization. In the past, many of them have operated as a cost center. They have followed a "parent child" relationship. Going forward, they need to start performing like any other business unit located elsewhere in the world.

Today, global clients don't talk of insourcing and outsourcing in isolation. Some experts use the term "hybrid offshoring model" where companies try to get the best of both worlds: captive units and external service providers.

Going forward, work could be moved near shore or taken back from external service providers based on cost, skill set or business criticality. This represents an industry churn: it can affect Indian IT and BPM exporters directly or indirectly.

From the perspective of an industry body like NASSCOM, building advanced skill sets will certainly encourage MNCs to look at India more seriously. However, this may not prevent an industry churn.

External service providers in India can't rely only on providing low cost services. What prevents an MNC, a global bank or even a global IT service provider to move the work being done in India to another low cost location elsewhere in the world?

This is why Indian IT service providers need to change their business model. They must develop a retention plan for their key employees. Otherwise, what prevents their key people to be poached by MNCs setting up captive units in India?

The ideal solution would be where both India based captive units and Indian IT service providers make the best use of their skill sets. Both of them need to move up the value chain with an appropriate business model. This way, the industry as a whole will benefit.

In the next Section, I will explain the implications of industry churn from the perspective of Indian IT and BPM exporters. How does this affect their model of global services delivery?

Industry Churn Related to Global Delivery

This is not the time for Indian IT and BPM exporters to remain complacent. They need to understand the decision making process and the priorities of their global client. Each MNC or each global bank will adopt a different approach to distribute work between external service providers and captive units. Such decisions can go through multiple steps. Each global client can use a different set of criteria to redistribute work.

Step one could be insourcing: taking back work from external service providers. Step two could be adopting a shared services delivery model. Step three could be setting up a captive center. Indian IT and BPM exporters need to identify the stage of decision making and accordingly work on how they would respond to the industry churn. Fortunately, the 2014 elections, business sentiment and investment climate in India offers them a window of opportunity. I don't expect MNCs or global banks to set up captive units in India in a hurry.

If or when MNCs take back work from external service providers to be performed by captive units, they would use multiple criteria in decision making. Apart from leveraging necessary skill sets, MNCs could look at process improvements. While implementing a shared services model, they could look at achieving economy of scale and retaining control.

Eventually, global clients will redistribute work: this will certainly affect external service providers. Some work could be moved near shore based on cost, skill set or business criticality. Some work can get redistributed across MNC captive units.

Already, some MNCs refer to a multi-sourcing model. Here, work is distributed to multiple external service providers. In some MNCs, a core team of management could follow a complex model of governance to supervise and oversee work performed by external service providers as well as captive units.

For some Indian IT and BPM exporters, this industry churn can imply a loss of business in the short term. For others, it could be an opportunity to move away from the commodity space of IT services and provide high end services. Either way, they need to maintain client relationships and pursue alternate business models.

They can make use of this industry churn as a window of opportunity to move towards new models of global services delivery. If they follow a

Business As Usual (BAU) approach with an old business model, can they expect their global clients to continue offering them business?

In recent quarters, almost every CEO in medium and large Indian IT exporters have mentioned that they are building skill sets in analytics. Like software development in the past, can analytics be a new engine of growth? I am not so optimistic! Acquiring new skill sets alone can't help them to expand into high end services. They need to also develop an appropriate business model. Otherwise, they could face challenges in retaining skilled professionals, or retaining their global clients or both.

I have a simple question. Why should MNCs engage external services providers in the area of analytics? If skill sets are available in India, what prevents them from setting up a captive unit to leverage these skills? The same applies to any other type of high end services.

Similarly, one can't assume that MNCs would outsource engineering or R&D services to external service providers in India as long as the latter have the right skill set. After all, engineering and R&D are business critical functions. What prevents MNCs to set up their own captive unit?

As mentioned earlier in this Book, business units are taking control over IT budgets. In many industries, Chief Marketing Officers (CMOs) are leveraging technology to drive growth opportunities. This is the right time for Indian IT and BPM exporters to present their capabilities in high end services to the top management of their global clients. They need to look at moving out of the commodity space of services.

Once they build visibility and mindshare, they need to behave as trusted and reliable business partners. Even if their global client is setting up a captive unit in India for specific skill sets, they need to get a reasonable share of business in the remaining skill sets. Some of them could move into the consulting business by transforming themselves into solution providers instead of service providers.

A Nov 2013 report in The Times of India mentioned that 4 major global IT service providers employed 288,000 people across India. They are IBM, Accenture, Cap Gemini and CSC. The industry churn I explained above also affects each one of them, directly or indirectly. I hope my friends and ex-colleagues in the Indian IT industry get this message!

CHAPTER 10

The Way Forward

We have reached the last Chapter of this book. Currently, the Indian IT industry employs nearly 3 million people. How can each one of them move up the value chain from a professional perspective? In this Chapter, I will answer this question by covering some additional topics relevant to all Indian IT professionals.

Implications for Indian Policy makers

In the past, the Indian IT and BPM industry has grown and progressed *in spite of* constraints faced by the Indian economy and *sometimes* because of a weak Rupee! Given the size and maturity of the industry, a favorable policy environment will go a long way in facilitating companies of all sizes to move up the value chain.

In the past, Indian IT exporters have been viewed as a cash cow by the Indian stock market. For Indian policy makers, this industry has been a big job creator. Sometimes, even politicians from two states have gone out of their way to attract and retain large Indian IT exporters. Going forward, could this change? Let me explain why.

In the next few years, the industry may not generate as many jobs as it used to generate in the past. Even if it does, the skill sets required would be quite different. Already, major IT exporters have cut down hiring of young engineers: they are likely to hire more experienced people. On the one hand, the IT and BPM industry must avoid setting a wrong expectation with policymakers on employment. On the other hand, business leaders must pursue policy changes by offering a "big picture" in terms of the overall impact the industry could have on the Indian economy.

India Inc. needs to pitch in on attracting more FDI for the IT and BPM industry. In the current global economic environment, many MNCs and global banks could be keen to set up their own captive units in India. This could offer two types of benefits to the Indian economy:
1. The Indian IT and BPM industry can move up the value chain.
2. India as a country can attract foreign investments through FDI.

If more MNCs set up captive units in India, this can help in different ways. It will attract more FDI and help the government control currency volatility, one way or the other. It will create jobs, both for young as well as experienced Indian professionals. Of course, it will also put pressure on Indian IT and BPM exporters to move up the value chain. Each of these can be a positive development from an industry perspective.

Going forward, a volatile Rupee can be a bigger problem for all Indian exporters, even those outside the IT and BPM industry. Apart from elections in India, there could be surprises from the US or from Europe. This is another reason for Indian policymakers to act: the Rupee also needs to gain better credibility with foreign investors!

As I explained in Chapter 7, the industry can't afford to take a short term approach on skill development and capability building. If Indian IT exporters cut corners on skill development, they could end up competing for a shrinking pool of skills.

So far, skill development has been one of the focus areas for the industry body NASSCOM. This needs to be taken up more seriously and at multiple levels: including educational institutions, universities and policy making on higher education.

Optimal and Better Utilization of Skill Sets

In my opinion, the term "utilization" in the Indian IT industry is one of the most misunderstood jargons. In this book, I would not like to comment on another misunderstood jargon: bench. In my long experience, I have observed that whenever top management discusses utilization metrics during any meeting or gathering, there is a noticeable reaction in the faces of employees as well as managers!

What do I mean by optimal and better utilization of skill sets across the industry? In this Chapter I will explain this in different contexts.

1. Opportunities for Indian professionals to move across "artificial borders" created by the IT and BPM industry in the past.
2. Enabling senior IT professionals to deliver real business value to global clients.
3. Senior professionals with industry experience operating in the domestic (Indian) market.
4. Women professionals employed by IT and BPM exporters.

Currently the Indian IT and BPM industry operates under artificial borders created within the organization or by the industry due to various reasons. These borders are quite distinct and include one or more of the following "silos":

- The domestic Indian market and exports (IT and BPM) within large organizations across India. These include MNCs with India based captive units.
- The BPO or BPM industry segment and the IT services segment.
- IT Support services on the one side and ADM services on the other side.
- Business groups or "industry verticals" within large organizations.

Like the Berlin Wall, I am sure readers in the Indian IT industry can relate the above to one or more "borders" within their own organization. It is time for such artificial barriers to be broken down or dismantled. Otherwise, the industry can't move up the value chain.

So far, major Indian IT and BPM exporters have a limited presence in the domestic market. They operate water tight business units across exports and the domestic market within India. I am not referring to reasons like location or government policies related to STPs. I am referring to the mindset of managers, internal policies and bureaucracy. These make it almost impossible for internal transfers to take place.

This is why the industry needs to take a holistic approach. This also applies to captive units of MNCs and global banks in India. Many employees serving global clients have little contact with their own colleagues operating the domestic (Indian) market.

The industry needs to leverage skills across multiple segments and also offer a better career path to Indian professionals. Employees need to be encouraged to perform roles across exports and the domestic market through appropriate incentives. This could improve the organization capability in terms of project management and industry knowledge.

Another artificial border is between the BPO or BPM industry segment on the one side and the IT services segment on the other. Today many experienced employees in the Indian BPM industry have business knowledge or even industry knowledge. Some of them also have better customer relationship skills that can be useful in IT support services. Can business groups offering IT services utilize them more effectively? As I will explain later, it can also be offered as a career option to many women employees.

All Indian IT exporters talk of high end services. With digital transformation happening across the world, I am sure one can look at several options. It is time to look beyond old service lines like BPO, BPM, IT support services or ADM and offer a package of services or even a complete solution. I am sure CMOs and business unit heads would be interested to deploy cross functional teams with multiple skill sets. This could be one way of delivering better business value in many existing contracts!

Of course, cross training and transfers between business groups may require a major change in internal policies and HR practices. It is still worth trying! This is where the industry as well as managers will need to look "beyond borders", identify opportunities and pursue them.

Today many large Indian IT exporters are stuck with an IT services organization structure of the past. On the one side you have IT infrastructure services and software support. On the other side, you have services like ADM and Packaged Application Support. Often the two operate as independent silos. In cloud computing solutions, all these skill sets are relevant. This is another area where managers can create teams with multiple skill sets. If they are successful, moving up the value chain in cloud computing can be much easier!

Earlier in this book I mentioned the need to look beyond industry verticals. Based on my long experience, I have observed that HR policies, organization politics and compensation often discourage movement of senior people across industry verticals in many large organizations. As I will explain later, building management capabilities are more important than retaining skill sets of the past. This is another area where serious "reforms" may be required.

In captive units of MNCs as well as Indian IT companies, T&M based billing is quite common. In order to cut down costs, many of them have begun deploying less experienced IT professionals in recent quarters. Senior IT professionals are being moved to different roles. Some of them could eventually face a tough choice: perform roles and responsibilities that may not match their skill set.

This is where capability building comes in. The industry needs to focus on building broad management capabilities among senior IT professionals. This way, they can play a bigger role in the organization and also move up the value chain from a professional perspective. One area is project management, as I explained in Chapter 9. I will cover the topic of capability building later in this Chapter.

The Indian IT and BPM industry also needs to optimally utilize the talent of women professionals. Some companies in India follow a quota based approach to improve the representation of women; few others fast track promotions for key women employees. Instead (or in addition), they could offer women employees a package of skill development and options for a better work life balance. I am sure these will be appreciated by women employees across the IT and BPM industry.

The Indian BPM industry currently employs a large number of women. A well-structured program based on skill development can prepare them for a wide range of roles as the entire industry moves up the value chain.

Many women employees move out of the IT industry or take a break for a few years. If or when they would like to resume, they face challenges in finding the right position. Many companies don't provide them adequate support and assistance to develop skills in newer technologies. As a result, many women employees still find it difficult to work on projects in newer technologies in spite of getting support from their employers!

Women employees taking a break need to develop the necessary skill sets for new roles as early as possible and as effectively as possible. This is why I am recommending a skill based strategy: not a quota based strategy. I am sure this is a better option to increase the participation of women employees in the Indian IT industry. I am sure both women and men reading this book will agree with me!

Employee Services, Work Life Balance and Technology

In recent years, the Indian IT industry has extended a wide range of employee services. For example, most Indian IT and BPM exporters offer employee security and transportation services to their employees. These expenses are also part of the cost case of projects. I will discuss the pros and cons from a business perspective as well as an employee perspective.

In the last few years, I have observed that Indian IT exporters as well as captive units of MNCs routinely ask their employees to work for at least a few hours during US day time. Earlier, this was common among employees in the BPM industry. On the one hand, working during the US day time can improve communication with global clients. On the other hand, it also affects the work life balance of many employees.

The industry has responded to this by extending security and transportation services to employees on a selective basis. Some companies even offer a gym, sports and recreation facilities. These compensate employees both directly and indirectly for late working or extended hours of working. I have heard from my friends in the industry on how these "carrots" improve work life balance. However, during 2013, some companies have begun scaling down transportation services to employees from a cost optimization perspective.

How are Indian IT and BPM exporters leveraging technology to improve work life balance? In my opinion, this has been lacking either due to a focus on cost optimization or because of sticking to an old business model and operating model of the past.

In many companies, a large part of the project team still relies on desktop computers. In these companies managers don't encourage use of laptops as per company policy or as a part of cost optimization. They even prohibit project team members to perform project related tasks while they are on vacation or are working from home.

This is where industry executives need to apply some common sense. On the one hand, they are implementing sophisticated solutions to their global clients. On the other hand, can they impose restrictions on their own employees to leverage technology? They need to leverage technology and improve both employee morale and productivity in service delivery.

Is it worth spending more on transportation and security while forcing your employees to be physically present in the office during US day time? Instead, why not spend the same money to leverage technology based options and also offer a better work life balance?

In my opinion, it is not fair to have double standards: one for your client and the other for your employees. Of course, some global clients have security restrictions due to reasons of business criticality or confidentiality. I am also sure that a reasonable solution can be worked out to strike a balance.

This is another area for the entire Indian IT and BPM industry to introspect on how they would like to "move up the value chain". The total cost involved on IT infrastructure and employee services like transportation and security need to be viewed from an employee perspective. Offering better working conditions and work life balance is also important.

I am sure that all of these not only encourage more women to join the industry but also be appreciated by their family members! In addition to technology, managers need to look at changing their business mix and adopting an appropriate operating model for global delivery.

Earlier I mentioned about Indian IT exporters getting out of the commodity space of IT services. Likewise, moving up the value chain also means offering job enrichment and a better work life balance from an employee perspective. I am sure my friends in the industry would understand the "common sense" I am referring to.

Where do I Specialize In?

This question is often in the minds of most young Indian IT professionals. Each one of them needs to choose an area of specialization early in the career. One can't afford to be a "jack of all trades". At the same, one must have a certain depth of knowledge to grow from a professional perspective. However, many young Indian IT professionals also need to make some tough choices based on the business plans of their employers.

In order to move up the value chain, Indian IT professionals need to develop skill sets in three different streams. I will briefly explain their importance.
1. Technology covering a broader set of skills.
2. Business and domain specific areas.
3. Project management and customer relationship.

In the past, Indian IT professionals have focused on technology skills. They have also focused on skills across the software development life cycle. Going forward, it is important for them to come out of their "shell" or "pigeon hole" in terms of technology focus. By choosing a mix of skills in the three areas mentioned above, they can also pursue a chosen area of specialization.

Of course it is important to develop deeper skills in technology: this can enable IT professionals to also perform roles related to IT consulting. For this, they need to specialize in a particular technology to such a level that they can offer a solution to their global clients. If their skills are shallow, their opinions will not be considered seriously.

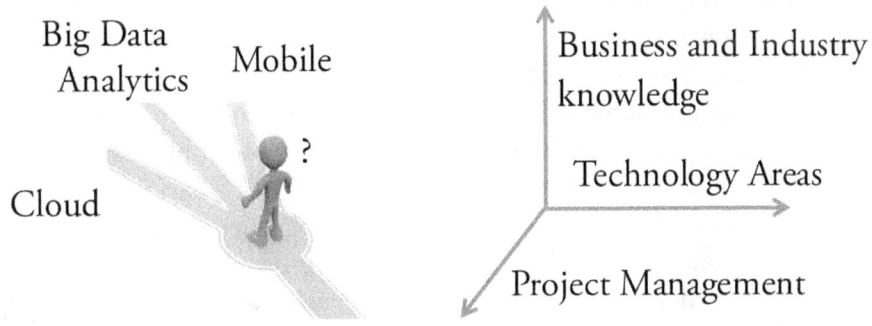

Leveraging technology with multiple skill sets

How can Indian IT exporters enable their employees to develop skill sets in all the three areas mentioned above? In the following paragraphs, I will offer some ideas based on my own experience and based on topics I have covered in this book.

Many Indian IT exporters are trying to specialize in newer technologies: social media, mobile computing, Big Data and analytics, cloud computing, you name it! However, they need to offer a career plan for technology specialization. Otherwise, preferences of experienced employees will not be in sync with business needs. This could lead to employee dissatisfaction and even attrition.

In order to move up the value chain, this industry needs managers with a combination of skill sets in project management, customer relationship and knowledge of the client's business. How long can companies rely on managers who are good in "managing a matrix organization" or an "industry vertical" based organization structure? I am sure my friends in the industry reading this know what I am referring to. I would not like to elaborate further!

In the past, a T&M based billing model has caused some discrepancies in the skill set of senior IT professionals and managers in this industry. In my long experience, I have found many gaps in project management and customer relationship.

In many projects, a significant number of senior IT professionals play a secondary role in both these areas. Utilization based organization metrics and project rotation policies discourage many of them to focus on gaining adequate knowledge of the client's business.

In my long experience, I have found that many senior professionals in this industry manage to climb the organization ladder in spite of gaps in two important skill sets: project management and customer (or client) relationship. This is because T&M billing, an inadequate focus on delivering business value and utilization based organization metrics make it easier to get promoted as long as they are "managing a large team".

I am not trying to undermine the importance of people management skills. What I am pointing out is the fact in a T&M based model of the past, it has been easier for some managers to be "kicked upstairs". They can get promoted even if their track record in project management is not the best or if they haven't performed key roles in customer relationship. Unless this changes, the industry can't quickly move up the value chain.

In the past, senior IT professionals in India have given more importance to moving up the organization ladder, not specializing in a specific industry. Many of them don't actively pursue specialization in a client's business or in a specific industry. Even if they do, they perform such roles on site and leave the company if or when they return to India. This needs to change from the perspective of the organization and the individual employee.

In the next Section, I will explain why developing capabilities in project management need to be in sync with developing alternate business models.

Capability Building vs. Skill Development

How is capability building different from developing skill sets? In the past, Indian IT exporters have focused on the latter. Not much emphasis has been given to build capabilities at multiple levels of the organization.

This includes team leaders, technical leaders, project managers and senior managers.

This is because of many reasons: reliance on a T&M based billing model, very high growth rates, a cost plus mind set you name it! Going forward, this must change: otherwise, moving up the value chain will not be easy.

As I explained in Chapter 9, there are many opportunities for senior employees to perform key roles in managing the customer relationship and managing projects while delivering business value. For this to happen, project manager roles need to be in sync with the business model. For example, does it make sense to have many certified project managers if the service provider is continuing with the old business model of T&M based billing?

Alternate business models need to be in sync with capability building. If senior IT professionals have to perform new roles and take on additional responsibilities, they need to have the necessary skill sets. Otherwise, they will not be effective.

In recent quarters, some medium and large Indian IT exporters experienced attrition at senior levels. Many changed their compensation packages during 2013. Some others revised their policies for promotion and progression. This is why capability development becomes important: it must be taken up proactively and not after losing key people.

Capability building also needs to be in sync with internal metrics and business practices. Policies for promotion and assignment need to be in sync with a newer set of metrics. For example, many large Indian IT exporters still focus on metrics like employee utilization and revenue productivity while evaluating the performance of managers. It is only in recent years that customer feedback and project delivery are being given more importance.

As I explained in earlier chapters, Indian IT exporters need to build relationships beyond the CIO organization. Along with managing and controlling project outcomes, senior IT professionals and project managers need to periodically present project results and outcomes to their clients. One of the areas where capability building is ignored is project governance and tailoring the management system to suit the global client.

Global clients, especially MNCs and global banks have mature management systems. However, given their size, there will always be differences between business units and between priorities at the CXO level.

Senior IT professionals need to understand the management system of their client. In the past, they could have been capable enough to relate project management practices to the CIO organization of their global client. Going forward, they need to deal with business unit heads and even other CXO level executives. This will require a much higher level of knowledge about their client's business.

As I explained in Chapter 9, business unit heads can have a different view or a different set of expectations from project managers. Accordingly, they need to set up appropriate processes and practices in project governance. If they don't have the necessary capabilities and the maturity, they will not be able to perform effectively.

Soft Skills and a Global Mindset

In the past, most Indian IT professionals have performed the role of a "techie". As the industry moves up the value chain, each of them needs to develop additional skill sets. Along with these, he or she needs to improve on soft skills and also develop a global mindset. In this Section, I will explain why this is important.

As Indian IT and BPM exporters adopt new business models, negotiation skills become very important. This could be a new paradigm for many senior professionals simply because this is not about negotiating price. It is about managing and controlling project outcomes and getting paid for results, not necessarily for the effort spent.

Negotiation skills become very important for team leaders and project managers in areas like change control. Again, this could be quite different from negotiating effort estimates using the old T&M based billing model.

Another area is setting and managing customer expectations. This requires a certain discipline and the right mind set apart from communication skills. I don't expect every IT professional to be good at negotiating with customers: sometimes this could even back fire. What is important is to articulate and understand expectations from both sides.

In the past, most Indian IT exporters executed projects for clients based in the US. Going forward, they would be serving more clients in Europe and elsewhere in the world. This is why Indian IT professionals need to develop a global mindset and a global outlook.

In Chapter 2, I explained why Europe can offer a window of opportunity for Indian IT and BPM exporters. In the past, they have been focusing on UK and a few countries where English is the primary language for business. Indian IT professionals are very quick in learning programming languages. I am sure they would be quick to learn French, German and a few other European languages!

A global mindset also means looking beyond what is typically considered an "Indian perspective" on where work gets done. On many occasions, even senior Indian IT professionals use terms like offshore and onsite while communicating with their clients from a narrow perspective. Going forward, an offshore center need not be based in India. As I mentioned earlier, the industry also views IT exports and the domestic Indian market as two water tight compartments.

Earlier in this book, I used the term multi-speed global economy. Increasingly, global clients are becoming country neutral. They are also leveraging global services delivery in different ways. Accordingly, the Indian IT industry needs to help them become globally competitive. It doesn't matter where the work gets done and in what currency you get paid!

Position Yourself Correctly

In this Section, I will narrate an interesting experience I had almost 20 years back to provide some tips for Indian techies. As a part of my US based role in Tata Unisys Limited between 1994 and 1996, I worked with partners and customers on large proposals.

In one of the meetings held near Washington DC, a techie presented a complicated solution as a part of a proposal. Many of us felt that the solution was "over engineered" with bells and whistles. After a patient hearing, a senior project executive (also a managing partner) asked the team a simple question: "The customer is prepared to pay the price of a Chevy. Why are we offering a Cadillac solution?" This question is about the mismatch between the solution, customer expectations and the budget.

Many readers in India are aware of GM's global brands. Chevy (or Chevrolet) is a low end model and Cadillac is a high end model. In the current economic environment, it is common for global clients to demand a better value proposition. This means, they expect a Cadillac solution, but are prepared to pay the price of a Chevy. How can Indian IT professionals strike a balance?

In every IT project and every IT solution they need to focus on three areas:

1. Set and manage customer expectations.
2. Analyze the pros and cons in terms of do-ability.
3. Deliver business value.

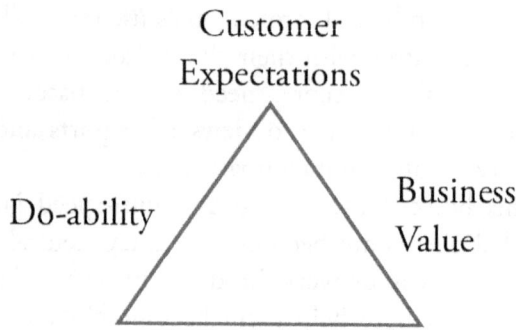

Before offering radical ideas and suggestions, techies need to match them with customer expectations as well as the budget. They need to evaluate the pros and cons of whether the solution they are promising can be delivered. This is what is referred to as Do-ability. At the end, the solution must also offer real business value. By addressing each of the three areas, they can be more effective and more successful in serving their global clients.

In the past, Indian IT professionals have focused on offering "value for money" at any cost. Sometimes they offer too much functionality; not necessarily better business value. Going forward, they need to focus on setting and managing expectations. They need to avoid a delay or a situation where they are unable to deliver business value commensurate with client expectations. This is not a one-time activity but a continuous process of striking a balance.

Some global clients have unreasonable expectations; the schedule may be unrealistic or the do-ability itself being questionable. It is better to raise an alarm at an early stage itself. Delaying this will only make it more difficult for everybody to change course later.

In the IT services business, it is better to promise less and deliver more. This way, you are more confident that the customer or client will be satisfied. However, in the current competitive environment, you can't afford to be conservative. It can lead to a loss of business to your organization. Therefore, it is important to set reasonable expectations at every level. At each stage, it is better if expectations are also realistic and doable. If you deliver more business value compared to initial expectations, you can always take the credit!

I hope that the example and the three areas mentioned above provide the right message. In the next Section, I will relate the terms innovation and business value.

Innovation in the Services Business

In earlier chapters I avoided using the term innovation for two reasons.

1. This term has become part of the industry jargon; it is also "context sensitive"!
2. In the IT services business, innovation can be related to delivering business value. This is quite different from creating new products.

I will end this Chapter by briefly explaining one example on relating innovation to business value in the services business. I hope that this will also explain innovation in the context of topics covered earlier on moving up the value chain.

Often, people associate the term productivity with offering "more bang for the buck". I explained this in earlier chapters. One way to innovate in the services business could be to "deliver more business value for the buck". This is quite different from the focus on a low cost advantage of the past.

There is one key difference: the business value must relate directly to the customer as well as to the customer's business; not the service provider. It would be even better if business value can refer to the end user making use of the solution or service. If business value only relates to the service provider, which customer or client would call this innovation?

In the past, Indian IT and BPM exporters have focused on their cost advantage. The business value they offer through this approach is quite limited. As I have explained in earlier chapters, global clients no longer relate innovation only to cost savings.

When global clients refer to business value, what do they mean? This could be: increased efficiency, improved productivity, new business models, creating new products or new services faster and cheaper, the list goes on. In the services business, you must relate business value to one or more of these areas before you claim to be offering an innovative solution.

Another key difference is about measurement. While implementing a new technology based solution, how can you justify that solution A is more innovative than solution B without appropriate metrics? Like benchmarking, innovation metrics give credibility to service providers in any industry. Such metrics can also be used to enhance the brand value of service providers. This also applies to Indian IT and BPM exporters.

Without a metric, how can they demonstrate that they are delivering any business value whatsoever to their clients? They can begin using one of the client's own metrics. If they can measure the impact of a solution or a service to their client's business, they can also start talking about innovation with business unit heads.

In Chapter 9, I mentioned about delivery metrics. It would make sense for Indian IT exporters to also incorporate appropriate metrics related to business value. Once they start collecting the right metrics, they can also relate them to innovation. They can also demonstrate innovation to their clients in a credible manner. I will explain one example in banking.

Take mobile banking where a bank could offer multiple options to their customer. The difference between an innovative solution and any other ordinary solution can be measured in terms of parameters related to the banking business and value from a customer perspective.

For example, an innovative solution is one that offers better banking services to the customer at a lower cost per transaction. It could also be a solution that enables the bank to improve its revenues per customer over a period of time. Using such metrics, one can measure various parameters and also demonstrate innovation.

I am sure most of the banks use internal metrics to measure business value. For example, value to the customer can be in terms of better facilities and convenience. It can be measured in terms of the time taken to complete a banking transaction. It can be based on customer feedback using a score. The "buck" can be measured in terms of the cost per transaction. I hope readers understood what I meant by "bang for the buck" in the context of innovation. In these days of social media, one can give many examples of appropriate parameters or metrics.

A banking customer or client will be convinced that your banking solution is innovative if you can make use of such metrics in your business case. It would be even better if your solution also has a measurable impact on the bank's business in terms of revenues, profitability or customer satisfaction.

APPENDIX

List of References by Chapter and Section

Chapter 1 Introduction and Overview

Indian IT Exports are Slowing Down

TCS, Wipro, Infosys, HCL Tech need to keep pace with IT's once-in-a-lifetime transition, By Siddarth A Pai, Economic Times, 21 Apr, 2013

Real salaries of software engineers lowest in 15 years: Credit Suisse, By: Varun Sinha, NDTV, November 25, 2013

Interpreting Business Media Reports

IT margins headed inexorably downwards, may fall below 20%: Analysts, Indu Nandakumar & Akanksha Prasad, ET Bureau, 19 Feb, 2013

TCS, HCL Tech show how growth is taking precedence over high margins as Infosys & Wipro lag (article quoting ET Intelligence Report), By Ranjit Shinde, ET Bureau, 25 Oct, 2013

What can Readers expect in this book?

India's $100-billion low-cost IT business model 'maxed out', must invest in proprietary software: Constellation Research, ET Bureau Jan 22, 2013

Industry Insight

Indian IT firms double market share in 6 years, Times of India, Economic Times, 26 Mar, 2013

What's Next for India's Outsourcing Industry? By Stephanie Overby, CIO. com, January 07, 2014 (Excerpts of interview with Som Mittal, former President of NASSCOM)

Understand Industry Churn

Global IT firms hunt for properties in Indian cities to expand business, By Sobia Khan & Akanksha Prasad, ET Bureau, 4 Dec, 2013

Top global IT firms have more staff in India than home nations, Shilpa Phadnis & Sujit John, Times News Network (The Times of India) Nov 6, 2013

How India's IT Outsourcing Leaders Can Stay on Top, By Stephanie Overby (article quoting interviews with industry experts), CIO.com, May 20, 2013

Multi-Speed Global Economy

New study says $ 2 trillion corporate cash hoard not Obama's fault, By Stephen Gandel, Fortune, June 6, 2012

Chapter 2: Take a Fresh Look at Multi-Speed Europe

Mixed Signals from Europe

Indian IT outsourcers like TCS, Infosys, Cognizant want a Bigger Byte out of Europe, By Reuters, 9 Oct, 2013

What led to a Multi-Speed Europe?

Europe's manufacturers caught in a vice, By Chris Bryant in Frankfurt and Richard Milne in Oslo, Financial Times, May 26, 2013

Understanding Multi-Speed Europe

Germany: the miraculous machine, By Ralph Atkins, Financial Times, April 19, 2012

Profiting from Pain: Europe's Crisis Is Germany's Blessing, By Stefan Schultz, Spiegel International, 01/10/2012

'We Need To Learn from Germany': How the German Economy Became a Model, By Thomas Schulz in New York, Spiegel International, 03/21/2012

Example: European Automakers

Divided Europe: Car Industry Winners and Losers Drift Apart, By Dietmar Hawranek, Spiegel International, February 13, 2013

Eastern boom belies western gloom for car makers in Europe, Michael Winfrey and Martin Santa Bratislava, Reuters, Oct. 16, 2012

South Koreans speed ahead in sluggish Europe, Financial Times (and CNBC.com), 31 Oct 2013

Autos: In Germany, the Company Car Is a Porsche, By Dorothee Tschampa, BusinessWeek, January 10, 2013

Can Belt Tightening work?

Volkswagen: Das auto giant, By Alex Taylor III, Fortune, July 10, 2012

Why GM and Ford Face a Tough Uphill Battle in Europe, Micheline Maynard, Forbes, 5/02/2013

Impact on European BFSI

Banks slapped with $2.3 billion fine for rate manipulation, CNBC, 4 Dec 2013

EU investment banks: trending down, Financial Times Analysis (Lex), April 21, 2013

Investment Banks Resist Shrinking on Europe Debt Crisis, Bloomberg, 22 Aug 2012

Impact on UK and City of London

The paradox at the heart of Britain's EU posturing, By Janan Ganesh, Financial Times, October 28, 2013

Analysis: UK trade may struggle to stand still after EU exit, By Tom Miles, (Reuters), May 16, 2013

Britain is hurtling along the road to a European exit, By Philip Stephens, Financial Times, May 16, 2013

IT Spending and IT Outsourcing in Europe

Outsourcing Contracts Leave IT Leaders Feeling 'Stuck in the Past', By Derek du Preez, Computerworld UK and CIO.com (articles covering survey by Alsbridge), July 03, 2013

TCS, Infosys, Wipro & HCL Tech build $8 billion cash chest, By PTI, 21 Apr, 2013

Is there a divergence across the Atlantic?

NSA Snooping Triggers Cloud Strategy Reviews: WSJ CIO Network Poll, By Evelyn M. Rusli and Michael Hickins, Wall Street Journal CIO Report, February 4, 2014

EU Launches Attack on Corporate Tax Avoidance, By Tom Fairless, Wall Street Journal, Nov. 25, 2013

Corporate Tricks: EU Faces Tough Battle to Close Tax Loopholes, By Christoph Pauly and Christoph Schult, Spiegel International, May 21, 2013

EU accuses US of improperly trawling citizens' online data, By James Fontanella-Khan in Brussels, Financial Times, November 25, 2013

IBM Uses Dutch Tax Haven to Boost Profits as Sales Slide, By Alex Barinka and Jesse Drucker, BusinessWeek, Feb 4, 2014

Cloud Computing in Europe

NSA's Prism Could Cost IT Service Market $180 Billion, By Clint Boulton, Wall Street Journal, August 16, 2013

Analysis (Reuters): European cloud computing firms see silver lining in PRISM scandal, By Leila Abboud and Paul Sandle, Jun 17, 2013

Internet: Data Centers Spring Up in Santa's Backyard, By Ashlee Vance, BusinessWeek, January 30, 2014

Payments Ecosystem in Europe

Indian technology firms: Looking for India's Zuckerberg, The Economist, Mar 16th 2013

Chapter 3: Get Used to the New Normal in the US

Challenges Faced by the US Economy (Box)

IMF cuts US growth outlook, warns on budget paralysis, By AFP, 8 Oct, 2013

Push for minimum wage hike led by localities, Democrats, By Mike DeBonis and Reid Wilson, Washington Post, Nov 30, 2013

Separate the Signal from Noise

States Moving Beyond U.S. Minimum Wage as Congress Stalls, By William Selway & Jim Efstathiou Jr., Bloomberg, Nov 12, 2013

The battle over the US budget is the wrong fight, By Lawrence Summers, Financial Times, October 13, 2013

Changing Demographics

Why young people are saying 'no' to the workforce, By Steve Hargreaves (CNNMoney), October 22, 2013

Rural US shrinks as young flee for the cities, By Norma Cohen, Financial Times, June 4, 2013

'Rural America' Slow To Recover, By Norma Cohen, Demography Correspondent, Financial Times, November 11, 2013

America's Moving: Hello Texas, Bye-Bye Wyoming, By Ira Sager and Evan Applegate, BusinessWeek, January 28, 2013

Understand a Multi-Speed US Economy

Job Gap Widens in Uneven Recovery, By Ben Casselman, Wall Street Journal, Nov. 11, 2013

More U.S. Profits Parked Abroad, Saving on Taxes, By Scott Thurm and Kate Linebaugh, Wall Street Journal, March 10, 2013

The Economy: The Uneven Politics of the Patchwork Recovery, By Eric Chemi, BusinessWeek and Bloomberg, September 24, 2013

Only the wealthy feel economic recovery, By Stephen Gandel, Fortune, July 1, 2013

Forecasts: The U.S. Economic Recovery: Long, Slow, but Still Going, By Rich Miller and Steve Matthews, BusinessWeek, June 13, 2013

Wages stink at America's most common jobs, By Tami Luhby (article quoting data from Bureau of Labor Statistics), CNNMoney, April 1, 2013

Young Americans ditch the car, By Steve Hargreaves, CNNMoney, September 17, 2012

Technology in the US Retail Industry

Technology: A Holiday Surprise: Amazon Growth Slows, By Brad Stone, BusinessWeek January 30, 2014

Retailers Open Technology Labs in Silicon Valley, Hire Top Talent, Create Mobile Apps, Anne D'Innocenzio, The Associated Press, Nov. 15, 2013

More Than Half of Americans Own a Smartphone. Now What? By Matt Hamblen, Computerworld, June 05, 2013

Impact on the US IT Industry

Microsoft Learns to Love Apple's iOS and Google's Android, By Dina Bass, BusinessWeek, July 25, 2013

Android's momentum eats into Apple's bragging rights, By Richard Waters Financial Times, August 14, 2013

Data Gathering by US Intelligence

NSA's Approach to Spying Questioned, By Siobhan Gorman, Wall Street Journal, Dec. 19, 2013

The cloud goes global: Amazon, Google, Rackspace, Microsoft, Savvis all expand international footprints, By Brandon Butler, Network World, May 29, 2013

Look Beyond US Political Debates

U.S. Competitiveness: U.S. Manufacturers Lose Ground at Home, By Matthew Philips, BusinessWeek, January 11, 2013

Boeing Looks Around, and a State Worries, By Kirk Johnson, New York Times, December 10, 2013

Software Firms Find Tax Advantages, By Steven D Jones, Wall Street Journal, January 28, 2013

Immigration Reform vs. Outsourcing

After Infosys visa row, other IT companies under US scanner, By Jochelle Mendonca, ET Bureau, 4 Nov, 2013

Infosys' Record Fine Targets Outsourcing Abuses, By Kartikay Mehrotra & Sarah Frier, BusinessWeek, Oct 30, 2013

US Public Sector and Health Care

U.S. Cities Grapple With Finances, By Jeannette Neumann, Wall Street Journal, Oct 27, 2013

Uncle Sam's first CIO (Interview with Vivek Kundra), Fortune Magazine, July 13, 2011

Chapter 4: Clients Operate in a Multi-Speed Global Economy

Currency Volatility

Weak rupee poses a big pricing problem for Indian IT firms, By: N Shivapriya, ET Bureau, 24 Sep, 2013

New models of Global Delivery

CIOs May Evolve as Leaders of Global Corporate Services, Shvetank Shah and Matthew Charlet (article quoting survey by Corporate Executive Board), Wall Street Journal CIO Blog, June 20, 2012

CFOs Benefit from Shared-Services Shakeup, David Axson, Accenture, CFO.com May 13, 2013

Chapter 5: Industry Trends—Global Supply Chains

Industry Shift: Global Automakers

Dongfeng, Renault Receive China Approval for $1.3 Billion Car-Making Venture, By David Pearson, Wall Street Journal, Dec. 5, 2013

Peugeot Reviews GM Pact to Possibly Pave Way for Dongfeng, By Mathieu Rosemain, Bloomberg News, October 23, 2013

GM to Open Singapore Headquarters to Back Emerging-Market Thrust, By Bloomberg News, Nov 13, 2013

Spain's car industry at heart of nascent recovery, By Tobias Buck in Valencia, Financial Times, November 3, 2013

Can Car Sharing Services be a game changer?

GigaOM: Car-Sharing Services Take Paris by Storm, By Katie Fehrenbacher, BusinessWeek, June 28, 2013

Car Sharing Grows With Fewer Strings Attached, By Sally McGrane, New York Times, June 25, 2013

Transport: Freed from the wheel, By Robert Wright, Financial Times, October 6, 2013

Big European Players Embrace the Car-Sharing Trend, By Beth Gardiner, New York Times, November 19, 2013

Car sharing zips into a new era, By Henry Foy, Financial Times, November 5, 2013

Retail Industry and Consumer Goods

How Cloud Computing Changes the Game for Retail Industry CIOs, By Jack Sepple and Michael Schmaltz, Wall Street Journal, October 8, 2013

Global Growth and Competitiveness

Autos: Why Germany's Used-Car Salesmen Are Busier, By Dorothee Tschampa, BusinessWeek, June 27, 2013

BMW pursues Daimler in making car-sharing operations profitable, (Bloomberg and BusinessWeek) January 26, 2013

Big demand for Ford EcoSport, Honda Amaze, Renault Duster: One-car wonder story for MNCs? Malini Goyal, ET Bureau Dec 1, 2013

Selling cars, having fun: How Toyota stays No. 1, By Alex Taylor III, Fortune, November 14, 2013

VW Is Already The World's Leading Automaker, Forbes, 4/18/2013

Interview with Volkswagen CEO: 'European Auto Crisis is an Endurance Test', Spiegel International, February 13, 2013

Supply Chain Resilience and Agility

Supply Chain Disruption a Major Threat to Business, Steve Culp (Accenture), Forbes, 2/15/2013

What Makes a Company Resilient? Julian Birkinshaw, BusinessWeek, October 16, 2012

Leveraging Technology in Supply Chain Solutions

SAP and Swift: vying for connectivity? By Duygu Tavan, The Banker, 02 September, 2013

Which Industry Vertical?

The Art of Reinvention: SAP Puts Its Weight Behind a Better, Faster And Stronger Cloud Computing Strategy (article includes interview with SAP Executives), Reuven Cohen, Forbes, 5/09/2013

SAP Takes It All to the Cloud, By Quentin Hardy, New York Times (includes interview with Mr. Vishal Sikka), May 7, 2013

Engineering and R&D Services (Box)

Low-cost, high-tech talent lures European companies to set up R&D centres in India, ET Bureau, 2 May, 2013

Chapter 6: Industry Trends—Global BFSI

Understanding Industry Churn

Technology take-off threatens bank foundations by Helen Avery, Euromoney, Sept 2012

Is banking on the right track or about to go off the rails? By Chris Skinner, The Banker, 02 January, 2013

Regulatory Overhaul

Mohamed A. El-Erian: Remarks to the 12th Annual International Seminar on Policy Challenges for the Financial Sector, Washington, D.C., PIMCO Viewpoints, June (7), 2012

Understand Industry Reports and Surveys

The state of investment banking today: Morgan Stanley's definitive guide, By Sarah Butcher, http://sg.finance.yahoo.com/ Apr 11, 2013

Banks' adjustment to IT threat barely begun (article quoting industry reports), By John Authers, Financial Times, January 27, 2013

Shifts in Investment Banking

Costs: Leaner and meaner, The Economist, May 11th 2013

Investment banking: Dream turns to nightmare, The Economist, Sep 15th 2012

Shifts in Retail Banking

The future of mobile money, By Duygu Tavan, The Banker, 01 May, 2013

Assembling the digital payments supply chain, By Daniel Barnes, The Banker, 01 May, 2013

Mobile Payments Ecosystem

Card transaction fees to be capped under EU proposal, By Alex Barker in Brussels, Finacial Times, July 16, 2013

Payments & Cards, The New Ecosystem for Mobile: Technology Alliances for M-Payments and M-Banking, By Eyad Hasan, http://www.banktech.com/ March 21, 2013

Industry Shift: Mix of Banking Businesses

Balkanised banking: The great unravelling, The Economist, Apr 20th 2013

Asian Trade Finance

Transaction banking: Once-neglected segment is now banking's belle of the ball, By Daniel Schäfer in London, Financial Times, October 29, 2012

RMB Now Second Most Used Currency in Trade Finance, by CFO Innovation Asia, 03 December 2013

Supply Chain Financing (SCF)

Banks look to follow supply chain financing trend, By Duygu Tavan, The Banker, 02 July, 2012

Corporates shape a new global transaction banking landscape, By Duygu Tavan, The Banker, 01 November, 2012

Holistic Supply Chain Finance, Adrian Rigby, Global Head of Receivables Finance and Supply Chain, HSBC website, 05 October 2012

Job Redistribution in Global BFSI

Financial Giants Are Moving Jobs Off Wall Street, By Nelson D. Schwartz, New York Times, July 1, 2012

Risk Management, Big Data and Analytics (Box)

The age of analytics: what banks have to gain, By John Beck (article includes interviews with bank executives), The Banker, 01 November, 2012

SAP Eyes $10 Billion Sales Boost From Banking Software, By Cornelius Rahn, Bloomberg, May 8, 2013

Chapter 7: Change Course, Sooner Than Later

Categories of IT Spending

7 Lessons of the Offshoring Pioneers (article covering surveys by KPMG and HfS Research), By Stephanie Overby, CIO.com, April 19, 2013

IT Increases Application Outsourcing Despite Disappointing Strategic Value, By Stephanie Overby (article covering surveys by KPMG and HfS Research), CIO.com, July 12, 2013

Changing priorities of CFOs

More Department Leaders Make Their Own IT Decisions, Taylor Provost, CFO.com, May 07, 2013

IT Services Spending Power Shifts Away From IT Leaders, By Stephanie Overby (article on survey by Forrester Research), CIO.com, March 01, 2013

Importance of CMOs and Business Unit Heads

Houston, we have a Disconnect: CIOs and CMOs on Separate Missions, By Helen Beckett, businessvalueexchange.com October 4th, 2013

The Dangerous Tension between CMOs and CIOs, by Glen Hartman, Harvard Business Review, August 29, 2013

Digital Marketing Battlefield Map: CMO Vs. CIO And Gartner Vs. Forrester, Forbes, 7/10/2013

Gartner Says CIOs and CMOs Must Learn to Collaborate on Digital Marketing, By Kenneth Corbin, CIO.com, October 18, 2013

Is there a power shift away from CIOs?

Are CIOs Destined to Work for the CMO? By Paul Rubens, CIO.com, October 07, 2013

CIOs Scale Back Outsourcing, Favor the Cloud, David Nichols (Ernst & Young), Wall Street Journal, May 11, 2012

Companies & Industries: The Role of the CIO: Evolving or Evaporating? By Ira Sager, BusinessWeek, June 20, 2013

Employee Retention and Building Capabilities

Non-IIT and second-tier engineering colleges looking for ways to beat placement blues, By Devina Sengupta & Sreeradha D Basu, ET Bureau, 6 Aug, 2013

Why the current slowdown may be the worst ever for job-seekers, By Malini Goyal, ET Bureau, 11 Aug, 2013

Time for a Change?

IT top four-TCS, Infosys, Wipro and HCL Technologies build Rs. 56,000 crore cash chest, By PTI, 28 Oct, 2013

SAP launches $650 million fund, highlights corporate venture growth, By Sarah McBride, (Reuters) Oct 2, 2013

Chapter 8: Take Advantage of Technology and IT Trends

The Consulting Business is changing

Management consulting: To the brainy, the spoils, The Economist, May 11th 2013

Where the Growth Is in Management Consulting, By Ira Sager, BusinessWeek, June 13, 2013

The strategy consultants in search of a strategy, By John Gapper, Financial Times, August 28, 2013

BYOD and Mobile Apps

BYOD Lawsuits Loom as Work Gets Personal, By Tom Kaneshige, CIO.com, April 22, 2013

Why Analytics can be a Paradigm Shift

The Need for Speed with Big Data, By Nick Millman, BusinessWeek, August 06, 2013

Getting into the Business of Big Data

Data companies a poaching ground for big IT, By Akanksha Prasad & Swathi Akella, ET Bureau, Aug 8, 2013

From Selling Information to Selling Insight, Thomas H. Davenport, Wall Street Journal, July 10, 2013

The Cloud Computing Marketplace

Amazon Web Services Competitors Get Bad News From Gartner, CIO.com, September 04, 2013

Amazon Web Services has no reason to worry about IBM, By David Linthicum, InfoWorld, November 12, 2013

Economics and Politics of Cloud Computing

Why IT's Economics Revolution Is More Than OpEx and CapEx, By Bernard Golden, CIO.com, October 02, 2013

This is Likely How You Will Buy Cloud Resources Moving Forward, By Brandon Butler Network World (CIO.com), September 10, 2013

Possible Strategies

Cloud price war is bad news for technology industry's old guard, By Richard Waters in San Francisco, Financial Times, December 4, 2013

Is Integration-as-a-Service the IT Model of the Future? (article includes interview with industry experts) By Stephanie Overby, CIO.com September 13, 2012

India can still become hub for global cloud computing, By Jochelle Mendonca & Akansha Prasad, ET Bureau, 21 Aug, 2013

Chapter 9: Try New Business Models

New Business Models

How to Close Your Next IT Outsourcing Deal: Handshake vs. Contract, By Stephanie Overby (article including interviews with industry experts), CIO. com, May 03, 2013

Identify Vulnerable Areas

Benefits of outsourcing come under scrutiny (article quotes Ovum and interviews with Indian executives), By Paul Taylor, Financial Times, October 15, 2013

Alternate Pricing Models

IT firms may face dent in profit as industry transitions to outcome-based pricing model, By Indu Nandakumar, ET Bureau, 24 Jun, 2013

4 New IT Outsourcing Pricing Models Gain Popularity, By Stephanie Overby, CIO.com April 13, 2012

Non Linear Growth, Platform based BPO

Samsung, Google Sign Patent License Deal, By Min-Jeong Lee and Jonathan Cheng, Wall Street Journal, Jan. 27, 2014

Growth of platform BPO: Indian BPO firms re-invent business model, Rahul Sachitanand, ET Bureau Jun 21, 2012

Role of Intellectual Property (IP)

Intellectual Property: A Cheaper Way to Defuse Patent Claims: Kill the Patent, By Susan Decker, BusinessWeek October 24, 2013

Patent wars unite US left and right, By Stephanie Kirchgaessner in Washington, Financial Times, October 17, 2013

US plans to crack down on patent 'trolls', By Aaron Stanley in Washington, Financial Times, October 20, 2013

Apple, Google, Microsoft and Samsung plead for a patent-troll-free Europe, by David Meyer, GigaOM, Sep. 26, 2013

Industry Churn Related to Global Delivery

IT firms like TCS, Infosys & Wipro losing work as MNCs' captive centres are back into fashion, Akanksha Prasad & Lison Joseph, ET Bureau Jan 31, 2013

www.ingramcontent.com/pod-product-compliance
Lightning Source LLC
Chambersburg PA
CBHW071416050326
40689CB00010B/1867